5+2
3-28-08

See you in a Hundred years

See you in a Hundred Years

FOUR SEASONS IN FORGOTTEN AMERICA

Logan Ward

BENBELLA BOOKS, INC.
Dallas, Texas

BENBELLA

BenBella Books, Inc.
6440 N. Central Expressway, Suite 617
Dallas, TX 75206
www.benbellabooks.com
Send feedback to feedback@benbellabooks.com

Printed in the United States of America
10 9 8 7 6 5 4 3 2

Library of Congress Cataloging-in-Publication Data

Ward, Logan.
  See you in a hundred years : four seasons in forgotten America / Logan Ward.
    p. cm.
  ISBN 1-933771-15-1
  1. Country life—Shenandoah River Valley (Va. and W. Va.) 2. Farm life—Shenandoah River Valley (Va. and W. Va.) 3. Country life—Virginia—Charlottesville Region. 4. Farm life—Virginia—Charlottesville Region. 5. Ward, Logan—Homes and haunts—Shenandoah River Valley (Va. and W. Va.) 6. Ward, Logan—Family. 7. Shenandoah River Valley (Va. and W. Va.)—Social life and customs. 8. Charlottesville Region (Va.)—Biography. 9. Shenandoah River Valley (Va. and W. Va.)—Biography. 10. New York (N.Y.)—Biography. I. Title.
  F232.S5W27 2006
  975.5'9—dc22
                                    2006101293

Proofreading by Jennifer Thomason
Cover design by Allison Bard
Text design and composition by Laura Watkins
Printed by Bang Printing

Distributed by Independent Publishers Group
To order call (800) 888-4741
www.ipgbook.com

For special sales contact Yara Abuata at yara@benbellabooks.com

For Heather

Table of Contents

Prologue

The past is our definition. We may strive, with good reason, to escape it, or to escape what is bad in it, but we will escape it only by adding something better to it.
— WENDELL BERRY

The twentieth century began on a Tuesday.
— IAN FRAZIER

I am standing behind a rundown farmhouse in Virginia's Shenandoah Valley. The yard is rank with weeds. A massive gray barn looms above. Something catches my eye, a jerky movement near the henhouse. A snake dangles from the rafters. It stretches its body over to an old window missing its panes. Doubling itself between the muntins, the serpent rests its head on its bulging body, soaking up the day's final sunlight. Mesmerized, I ease up the garden path for a closer look, shadows creeping like gnomes between the plants. The snake stares dead at me, tongue silently probing. It's a real beast, as thick around as my forearm and probably six feet long, brown-black—though in the dying light it's hard to tell—with faint diamond markings. Behind me, a crunching sound. I swing around to find Luther trundling up. "Da-da," he says in his raspy voice, arms outstretched. I scoop him up and hustle back toward the house, suddenly aware of those tender feet stepping through the high grass.

Of all the dangers we will soon face during our trip back in time, including gashing a shin with a wild axe swing, searing flesh on the woodstove, and getting kicked by our draft horse—due to arrive in three weeks—none worries me more than a snakebite. There are two breeds of poisonous snake found here in the Valley—the rattlesnake and the copperhead. Both are pit vipers, and both carry venom lethal to children under three. Last week, our son turned two.

As we struggle to meet our project's start date, I am racked by doubts. I lie awake at night, tortured by visions of Luther toddling across a serpent coiled beneath a stack of rotting fenceposts—the lightning-fast strike, the innocent shrieks, the chance we won't even know it was a snake given Luther's limited vocabulary. And when the leg swells and blackens, there we'll be, miles from town with no phone, one of us—me probably, Heather staying behind to hold him—sprinting the half mile to the nearest house for help, praying I'll find someone home, and if not, running another half mile to the next.

I enter the kitchen and strap Luther into his high chair against kicks and screams of protest. Earlier in the day, Heather said that I was smothering her, that she'd go crazy if she didn't get a break from our frenzied preparations. Tight-lipped and petulant, she sped away in the station wagon to a yoga class, leaving me here to stew, distracted by the many unfinished tasks—fitting stovepipe, hammering together an outhouse, planting the beans and corn that will sustain us for the year—while also dealing with Luther. *Why the hell won't he stop screaming?*

When I return to the henhouse, the shadows are deeper. The snake is gone.

CЗВD

"Wait here," I say the next morning, leaving Luther and Heather at the picnic table and marching up to the henhouse gripping a hoe. Three steps into the tall grass, I freeze. A different, smaller snake warms its scales in the sun.

"Here's one," I say, eyes fixed on the snake. From the coloring and the shape of the head, I'm sure it's neither rattler nor copperhead, but that fact does nothing to calm my trembling hands. "I'm going to try to catch it."

"What for?" Heather asks.

"To get it away from the henhouse. Snakes eat eggs." In a few weeks, after our chickens have moved in and we're cut off from supermarkets, we can't allow a thief in their midst.

Sizing up the serpent, I try to remember if I've ever handled a live snake and faintly recall a school field trip, a candy-striped garter, and a funk that took forever to wash off my palms. *Okay*, I think. *Pin the head, and grab the neck, just like Marlin Perkins used to do.* But when I extend the hoe, the snake jerks back and whips its body into a coil, tail quivering, head bobbing away from the blade. I dance around like a stooge, unable to gain the advantage.

"Just kill it," Heather spits.

You don't kill non-poisonous snakes, I think. But I feel cornered and edgy, embarrassed by my impotence. A rage wells up inside me. I raise the hoe above my head and bring it down with a fleshy thud on the coiled body. I hack again, leaving the snake confused, hissing, mouth agape, and bloody. *Hack! Hack!* Soon the head hangs by a sinew and the body lies torn into several lengths. My arms are shaking. They sting from the blows. The anger leaves me like an exhalation, replaced immediately by shame.

ಃಞಂ

Over the next few weeks, as we grind ourselves down preparing to begin our experiment—bickering, fretting, racing to and from town on the single-lane farm roads—the snakes haunt us. I find a snakeskin hanging like a giant condom from a limb outside Luther's second-story window and another poking out of the backyard downspout. I shoo snakes out of the barnyard and the grass encircling the house. A small brown patterned snake that could be a copperhead zigzags across the driveway. I hear a scream and rush to find Heather pointing at a fat rat snake sunbathing on the back step. "Why won't they leave us alone?" she says, having almost stepped on it. I go around the house jamming strips of T-shirt in knotholes in the floor after learning that in winter snakes slither up from crawl spaces for warmth. One day the old-timer who used to manage this farm delivers a warning. "I killed a rattler behind the barn a couple years back," he says. "When it gets dry, watch out! That's when they come down from the mountains hunting water."

PART ONE

Green

CHAPTER ONE

Goodbye, New York

*I*n the City, you don't stargaze. You don't dig through wildflower field guides for the name of that brilliant trumpet burst of blue you saw on your morning walk. You don't hunt for animal tracks in the snow or pause in that same frozen forest, eyes closed, listening for the chirp of a foraging nuthatch. You forget such a creature as a snake even exists. It's as if New York is encased in a big plastic bubble, where humans sit atop the food chain armed with credit cards and Zagat guides. Native wildlife? Cockroaches, pigeons, rats. Disease transmitters. Boat payments for exterminators. Our story begins in the bubble.

The year is 2000, the dawn of a new millennium. The Y2K scare is barely behind us. Economic good times lie ahead, with unemployment at an all-time low, the U.S. government boasting record surpluses, and the NASDAQ composite index raising a lusty cheer by topping 5,000. The stock market is making everyone rich—at least on paper. Living in the wealthiest city in the wealthiest nation at the wealthiest moment in history, Heather and I should be happy. We aren't.

Which is why I find myself in the back of a cab one day, lurching down Park Avenue, all bottled up with excitement over the news I carry.

Out the window I see cows standing amid the tulips on the median strip, with Mies's Seagram Building jutting up behind. They're fiberglass cows. One wears the broad stripes of some third-world flag. Another, the geometric lines of a Mondrian painting. My cabbie tilts his head toward the rearview mirror to catch my eye and says in a clipped Bombayan singsong, "I keep wondering what is the meaning of all these cows."

"It's art," I yell through the plastic safety shield.

"In my country, cows are for eating," he says, and it dawns on me that since cows are holy in India, he must be Pakistani.

Leaning up so I don't have to shout, I say, "Sometimes I wonder if people in this city even know where their hamburgers come from. Last Sunday I was at the Brooklyn Zoo pushing my one-year-old in a stroller, and this girl—she must have been twelve—looks right at a cow in the farm-animal pen and can't say what it is."

"A real cow?"

"A real cow. It was just a baby, but it was clearly a cow. Anyway, the girl's mother is getting frustrated. She keeps saying, 'Come *on*, you *know* what that is.' Meanwhile, my little boy's screaming 'moooo, moooo.' I couldn't believe it." I sink into the seat thinking *not my kid, never* and feel a rush of joy knowing just how true that is. Then I lean forward again. "I didn't stick around to see if she recognized the goat."

"In my country," he says, "goat is a favorite meat."

Just then another taxi swerves into our lane. "Hey!" my driver yells, slamming the brakes and banging the horn with the heel of his hand. The lurching and jerking stirs up the butterflies in my stomach.

At the intersection, we ease through a gauntlet of pedestrians, who stray into the street like ballplayers trying to steal a base. The ones hustling by on the sidewalks stare at their feet, mumbling and gesturing with their hands. Smokers huddle around the pillars of another corporate tower looking pathetic, all the glamour gone from their habit.

They all look terminal, the smokers and the non-smokers. The young, the old. The dapper and the bedraggled. All desperate, frenzied, bound for the grave, but too distracted to notice amid the crush of flesh passing through this landscape of concrete, glass, and steel. Until recently, I was one of them. Now I am leaving.

"My kid's going to know what a cow is," I declare, feeling compelled to share my news. "My wife and I are moving to a farm."

"You are a farmer?" he says, glancing doubtfully in the mirror.

"No. But I'm going to learn. I bet people still farm in your country. Regular people, I mean. To put food on the table." And then, getting more worked up, thinking about this man and his decision to leave his home country, "Don't you ever get sick of things here? Sick of the traffic, of living behind locked-and-latched doors, sick of the assholes? Jesus, you drive a cab. Your day must be one long parade of assholes."

The driver swerves to the curb and stops. He stares at me in the mirror. About to protest, I see Bryant Park and realize we have arrived. I pay, grab the receipt, and charge into the street before the changing light hurtles traffic at me.

I enter a marble lobby against the afternoon exit flow and ride the elevator alone to the seventeenth floor, where I step into the offices of *National Geographic Adventure* magazine. It is a new magazine, a how-to offshoot of the venerable gold-rimmed flagship. Adventure—the pastime, the attitude—is hot. Stories about the frost-bit heroics of Ernest Shackleton and tragedy atop Mt. Everest leap off bookstore shelves. Patagonia is no longer just a place; it is a fashion statement. When I first met with the editor during the hush-hush days of the magazine's infancy, the name was still a secret. "I bet you can guess it," he said with a sly grin. "It's a word you see everywhere these days."

Sure enough, I pegged it.

Growing up, I devoured adventure stories—*Robinson Crusoe, The Arabian Nights, My Side of the Mountain*, about a Manhattan boy who runs away to the Catskills to live in a hollow tree. I hunted Indian arrowheads, panned for gold with my father, stood by as Dad blasted copperheads with scatter shot from his .38 caliber pistol. The idea of escaping the confines of society in the wilds of nature appealed to a shy boy with a big imagination, even if society was a sleepy South Carolina mill town. When I graduated college, I boarded a plane for Kenya with a folder full of topo maps—bush schools circled in red—and directions to the home of two American teachers. I found a teaching job and stayed for a year, collecting rain water in a barrel, cooking over kerosene, and writing aerograms home by candlelight. When I returned to the States, I moved to Manhattan and worked as an editor for a start-up digest called *The Southern Farmer's Almanac* (I was a southerner, though I knew nothing about editing or farming). In what little free time I had, I struggled to publish freelance articles. Finally, a decade later, *Adventure* is sending me to places like Uganda and Ecuador.

Now, I sit in the magazine's conference room with a different adventure in mind, trying to find the words to explain my plans to the young editor across the table.

"James," I say, "did you know that two-thirds of the people in this country can't see the Milky Way?"

"No. . . ."

"Don't you find that depressing?"

"Yeah, I guess so," he says, frowning, "but what's this meeting all about? You've got me curious as hell."

I hesitate, peering around at the magazine covers tacked to the wall. Beautiful people in colorful outdoor gear pose in front of glaciers and waterfalls and half-moon bays. "I can't write the *NGA Guide* anymore."

Nodding his head, James leans back in his chair. "I know it's a lot of pain-in-the-ass research."

"It's not that." More nervous than I had expected, I pause. "I'm . . . taking myself out of the twenty-first century."

"What the hell does *that* mean?"

"It means I'm burned out. Heather and I are killing ourselves to keep up. We want to try something different—you know, while we're still young." I explain our plan—to live the life of dirt farmers from the era of our great-grandparents. We have a lot of details to work out, of course, but the basic premise is this: If it didn't exist in 1900, we will do without.

"And that means," I say, "we're not going to have e-mail, phone, computer, credit cards, utility bills, or car insurance."

"That's awesome!" James says. "Sounds like a real adventure."

Heather's supervisor, Meryl, a public-interest attorney raised in Queens, has a different take on the idea when, a week later, Heather breaks the news that she is quitting her job. "You," Meryl says, "are fucking crazy."

Maybe we are. Like everyone we know in New York, we work too much. Job stress follows us home at night, stalks us on weekends.

Heather's work at a justice-reform think tank and mine hustling free-lance magazine assignments keeps each of us either chained to PCs or traveling. Within the past two years, Heather has flown to every conti-nent but Australia and Antarctica to interview cops and meet with gov-ernment officials. When she was seven months pregnant, she gave a talk in Ireland, flew back to New York and left the same day for Argentina and an entirely different hemisphere. We figured that if she happened to give birth prematurely, it was a coin toss whether we'd have a summer or winter baby.

As it turned out, Luther was born more or less on time in Manhattan, in a hospital towering over the East River. By the tender age of four months, he was already in the care of a nanny, leaving us feeling guilty for having to hire her and also guilty about how little we could afford to pay her. (We felt guiltier still upon learning from another mother that our nanny was locking Luther in his stroller so she could gab at the park. We fired her and put Luther in daycare.)

We spend too much money on housing and not enough time out-doors. We order dinner from a revolving drawerful of ethnic take-out menus and rent disappointing movies from a corner shop where the owner hides behind bulletproof glass. There's something missing from our lives—from our relationship—and yet we're too busy to confront the problem. At least that's our excuse. So the two of us plod through our days hardly talking. And at night we collapse into bed, kept awake by the sound of squeaking bedsprings in the apartment above but too exhausted for any bed-squeaking ourselves.

It isn't a physical exhaustion. The beneficiaries of a multi-genera-tional pursuit of the American dream, we have traded the farm and fac-tory work of our small southern hometowns for education and urban living. Instead of a tractor accident or a limb lost in some mercilessly churning assembly line machine, we suffer the stress-related ills of our times: anxiety, depression, e-mail addiction, debt.

My tipping point came the day my beige plastic Dell tower—the tool of my trade—whined to a halt. The screen went black. With mounting panic, I punched the keys and poked the on/off button on the front. Nothing. Fingers followed the dusty power cord from wall socket to box. Plugged tight. My mind reeled at the thought of all that accumulated data trapped inside the wiry guts of a machine that I so little understood: pages of research, interview transcripts, an almost-finished article due three days earlier, book ideas, addresses, e-mail correspondence with friends and editors, family photos, business records, tax records. That computer was everything to me. And like a fool, I had not bothered to back it up.

Once I recovered from my initial panic, I thought back to my grandfather, a country doctor and cattle farmer. He was born in 1886, before all this so-called time-saving technology—cell phones that tie people to their jobs 24/7 and computers that keep them answering e-mails past midnight. Could someone whose tools were hand-shaped from iron, steel, and wood ever grasp the ethereal nature of lithium-ion-powered digital devices? This was my dad's dad—a mere generation stands between us—and yet he came of age in a world completely different from the one I know.

It dawned on me that no one yet knows the long-term side effects of Modern Life. Can we really adapt to all this brain-scorching change—the technological advances, the teeming cities, the breakneck pace of daily life, the disappearance of the human hand from the things we buy and the food we eat? Maybe my ambivalence about technology (and dread over my failed computer) was not something to be ashamed of. It was as if something in me shouted, *Hold on a minute! You've been staring at the computer screen too long. When was the last time you dug in the dirt or tromped around a field, not to mention had anything at all to do with producing the food you eat?* Maybe our disconnect with the natural world causes a sort of vertigo, and if so, maybe that explained my recent unhappiness. Or maybe I was just pissed off things weren't going my way. Whatever the reason, on that day I dreamed of escape.

And yet I dutifully called a Dell technician. With a wife and child, and a career to pursue, what choice did I have?

A few weeks later, I had a moment of clarity that in a flash changed everything. I was reading a newspaper story about an upcoming PBS show that pitted an English family against the rigors of 1900-era London life. Thinking back to my computer crisis and the question still ringing in my mind—*what choice did I have?*—I realized I had found my answer! Not the reality show itself, but rather its core concept—adopting the technology of the past. If I were so desperate for a change, why not trav-el backward in time as a way of starting over?

The year 1900 immediately felt right. I wanted to ditch certain tech-nologies, but I did not want to be a pioneer, having to build a log cabin or dig a well by hand. The year 1900—almost within memory's reach— would serve well. A bit of research bore out my intuition. In 1900, rural dwellers still outnumbered urban dwellers. In 1900, agriculture was still the predominant occupation, thanks to millions of small-plot American farmers who raised most of what they ate for breakfast, lunch, and din-ner. In 1900, the motorized car—alternately called the viamote, mocle, mobe, or goalone—was still a novelty. In rural America, there were no televisions, telephones, or, of course, personal computers. People still wrote letters by hand. And this was crucial: In 1900, you could buy toi-let paper.

I nervously told Heather my idea one Saturday as we juggled our fussy baby in a cramped Brooklyn pub. She smiled, and I remembered why I fell in love with her.

CRED

Four months later, we are heading south, crashing from pothole to pot-hole on the Brooklyn-Queens Expressway, the Manhattan skyline jig-gling in the rearview mirror of our beat-up Taurus station wagon. Heather rides shot gun. Luther squirms in back. Every other inch of space is stuffed with possessions. A moving van will bring the rest. My gaze drops from the World Trade Center Towers in the mirror to the mountains of gym totes and teddy-bear-filled Hefty bags threatening to avalanche Luther's car seat. The plastic clamshell luggage carrier that I bought the day before at a Sears auto store off Flatbush Avenue rattles the roof rack, and I muscle for a slot in the fast-moving traffic.

We're amped up and all singing together.

"*Old McDonald had a farm. E-I-E-I-O. And on his farm he had a . . .*"

"A REAL COW," I yell.

E-I-E-I-O.

Three days later, we are exploring Virginia, home of Thomas Jefferson, who wrote that "cultivators of the earth are the most virtuous and independent citizens." Though Heather and I are not farming yet, I haven't felt so independent in years.

West of Richmond, released from the Interstate, we whiz past farmhouses, mobile homes, and rundown full-service filling stations, the kinds of places that sell live crickets and pickled eggs in big, brine-filled jars.

"Look, Luther," I say, tapping my window toward animals grazing in a pasture. But he's more interested in the goldfish-shaped crackers in his fist. Soon we're turning off the state highway, easing the station wagon into a gravel parking lot beside a small house with a deck and a treeless yard. Flush with the profit we made from selling our Brooklyn apartment, we've arrived for our first real-estate appointment.

Jerry Byrd is tall with neatly clipped black hair and a black goatee, and he wears a golf shirt and tasseled loafers. The scent of cologne shadows him around the office. His wife, Ashley, appears dressed for a cocktail party, strange given the dusty roadside location. Jewelry spills from her wrists, neck, and ears; her hair stands in a meringue of stiff curls. In addition to real estate, the pair sells insurance and rents metal storage units, which stand on a piece of flat ground scooped out of the hillside out back. They're a pair of red-dirt entrepreneurs.

It's October, and I have packed long sleeves and wool sweaters. But it has turned hot—eighty-five degrees—and for days now I've worn the only summer shirt in my suitcase. It smells—and not of cologne. The contrast between these country slickers and us city yokels is as stark as the contrast between their shiny new Ford Explorer parked in the gravel lot and our Taurus, filled full of junk and dusted with cracker crumbs.

"I've got a couple properties in mind that are perfect for y'all," Jerry says as we crunch back out to the cars. Heather and I glance knowingly at one another. We haven't told him about our project. As far as he is concerned, we are a couple of disillusioned urbanites searching for greener pastures. Dollar signs probably danced in his head when I first phoned and introduced myself as a New Yorker shopping for country property.

We drive about ten miles on successively smaller and more remote country roads. Jerry is behind the wheel, while I take notes. Heather and Luther sit in back. Without exception, Jerry waves at every car and truck that passes, greeting some by lifting his index finger off the steering wheel and others by peeling all four fingers off the wheel in sequential order.

My curiosity eventually gets the best of me. "Do you know everybody around here?" I say.

"No," says Jerry, eyes never leaving the road. "Maybe about 50 percent of the time I know them. In my business, you can't afford *not* to wave at everybody. You'll see somebody at church on Sunday, and they'll say, 'I *saw* you the other day, Jerry, and you didn't wave.'" His father, he says, waves at horses.

I think back on my childhood, when everyone in my town waved to strangers, and wonder if they still do. The terrain, too, reminds me of the pine-covered piedmont of my youth—the red dirt, the kudzu, the thicket-choked new-growth forests. Childhood memories of weekend outings with my brother and father come rushing back, hot days spent digging for smoky quartz crystals, tracing moss-covered tombstones in forgotten, deep-woods cemeteries, and scouring newly plowed fields for Indian artifacts. I picture my father, stooping over the dirt and calling out to us, "Boys, I've got a sweat-er!" We would bound over the furrows to watch him uncover with slow, dramatic scrapings of soil—"sweating it out," he called it—a half-buried arrowhead, our eyes bugging with the hope that it was whole.

"You ever find any Indian artifacts around here?" I ask Jerry. "I bet those fields are full of old bird points and pottery shards."

"Sure," he says. "Around here you find stuff left by the Fukarwi Indians."

"Really?" I brighten, as if he is scratching away at a sweat-er. "How do you spell that?" I hold my pen poised above my pocket-sized reporter's notepad.

"Don't ask me," Jerry says. "All I know is they were nomadic. Roamed all around."

"Really? I've never heard of the Fukarwi."

"Yeah. Story goes that the chief would stand on a hill peering out at the horizon"—Jerry raises his hand importantly to his brow, slowly pivoting his neck—"and he would yell 'Where the FUCK ARE WE?'"

Jerry guffaws and slaps his knee with his free hand. At least three cars slip by without a wave.

The first place Jerry shows us, a fifty-five-acre farm in the middle of nowhere, is a real dump—shattered windows, plaster ceilings littering the floors, the land a barfight of brambles, vines, and low trees. As far as we're concerned, the only thing it has going for it is that it is in the middle of nowhere. The next place is equally disappointing, only for the opposite reason. Its eighty-odd acres contain an immaculate old farmhouse and a handful of the prettiest outbuildings you can imagine, all lovingly kept and only recently vacated. But the home's insides look too new and the farm, situated only a couple miles outside of town, abuts a four-lane divided highway.

And that's how it goes as we crisscross the state, aiming for the blank gaps between red and blue highway lines on our road map. Though we say goodbye to Jerry, we find other land brokers in other one-light towns. Like those Jerry showed us, the farmhouses we see are either too run down or too modernized. Our prospects dim. Sick of motel rooms and powdered-donut breakfasts, we begin to wonder if the right place exists at all. It's a tall order, buying a property today that is suitable for life 100 years ago. Small farms are a rare breed these days. And old farmhouses have updated kitchens and bathrooms, satellite dishes, electric well pumps, and other modern accoutrements. Thanks to freezers and the convenience of grocery stores, even farmers have abandoned their root cellars.

Then we find a farm named Elim, and things begin to look up. Located south of Charlottesville, near the broad, black James River, Elim is an attractive place—from a distance. A cedar-lined drive meanders over a rolling pasture to a hilltop, where a two-story frame house sits, its front porch grinning from side to side. In back are weathered outbuildings, the weedy remains of a kitchen garden, and some sort of fruit tree humming with bees. The pasture slopes to a creek, with a thick stand of trees springing up on the other side.

The owners, explains the real-estate agent, a middle-aged woman named Barbara, are a family of nine from Richmond, Seventh Day Adventists who bought the place in anticipation of the apocalypse that their Bible said would coincide with the arrival of the new millennium. The name comes from Exodus 15, verse 27: "And they came to Elim, where there were twelve wells of water, and threescore and ten palm trees: and they encamped by the waters." With the modern world going to hell, Elim was their oasis—until Y2K passed without incident and farm life lost its charm. Now they're looking for a buyer. When we hear this, Heather and I smile at one another. We, too, are seeking a patch of green earth for sanctuary and survival.

The closer we get, however, the more flaws scream out at us. Most jarring is the shit. It's everywhere—chicken droppings littering the yard, peacock poop dotting the front porch like wads of chewing gum on a subway platform, and a pile of not-so-fresh scat (dog? cat? toddler?) greeting us from the shaggy carpet of one of the bedrooms. The house is a wreck. We step around heaps of clothes, dodge toys cascading from closets. So much for the fresh-baked-cookie approach to hooking potential buyers. The place smells like a dirty kennel.

In the family room, the agent points to a black iron behemoth, the size of a compact car, sprouting ductwork that stretches through the house like aluminum tentacles. "The owner has a metal-fabrication shop," says Barbara, doing her best to remain cheery. "He made this stove himself." While the fuel the stove burns is 1900-compatible, the look and scale are post-World War II. I've been imagining us huddled around a quaint Franklin stove. This monstrosity looks more like a Franken-stove.

Clouding our judgment is the pressure to land a farm. Even if we sign a contract tomorrow, we're still at least a month away from closing— from being able to rip out electrical wiring and plumbing pipes, dig an outhouse hole, and make the myriad other period adjustments we'll have to make. We've got to start by spring, with a garden in the ground. The clock is ticking.

Despite our niggling concerns, we focus on the bright side of Elim— the remote location, mix of pasture and woods, stream that irrigates the property, functional outbuildings, fruit trees, and affordable price. A buggy ride away sits a country store that sells not only food staples and garden seeds but hardware. Seven miles in the other direction, down a quiet sandy road, is a feed-and-seed store, a real boon we never expected to find.

Elim even has a root cellar, or so we're told. Built by the God-fearing smithy, it's out back, entered through a chest-high black metal door that looks like a submarine's conning tower rising up through the dirt. But on this day the cellar—or whatever's beyond that black door—is locked, and Barbara does not have a key. We've got to see it, we say, without explaining why but knowing that without a cellar, a family in 1900 would likely starve. A proper cellar is a must.

While she tries to locate a key, we drive to the feed-and-seed. Heather stays in the car with Luther, who naps in his seat. I pop in for a look.

"Can I help you?" says a tan, fit man, fifty-ish, stepping from behind some shelving. He looks country in an aristocratic Virginia way, wearing a faded polo shirt beneath a buttoned work shirt.

"Yes," I say. "My wife and I are considering buying a farm down the road. I wanted to look around your shop."

A pleasant but skeptical look lingers on the man's face. "What kind of farming you planning on doing?"

I pause, not wanting to launch into the whole 1900 song-and-dance. "We're going to try our hand at making a living off the land."

"Is that so?" he says.

I don't have anything to add, and neither does he, so I poke around, handling objects that mean nothing to me and then knowingly returning them to their places. Checking out this store seems important, but I'm not quite sure why.

"Where's the nearest livestock auction?" I say, finally. "Somewhere to buy a milk cow."

"You sure you want a milk cow?" the man says, raising an eyebrow.

"Why wouldn't we?" I say, trying not to sound defensive. Truly curious to hear his answer, I almost reach for my notebook.

"Well," he says, "you've got to milk a cow twice a day, seven days a week, Thanksgiving and Christmas included. Pigs, chickens, horses, you can take a day off, and it won't matter much to them, but with a milk cow, it's twice a day, every day of the year."

I breathe a sigh of relief. *Of course you have to milk a cow twice a day,* I think, thankful he has not sprung some unknown fact about milk cows on me that might hinder our plans. Now that we have uprooted our lives, I worry daily about unearthing some modern-day can't-do-without that will fatally undermine our project's authenticity. Back in New York, as Heather and I first batted around our radical plan for escaping modern life—*could we really? do we dare?*—we gave ourselves one week to name a single reason why it would fail. We couldn't come up with one—

12

or at least one we didn't think we could overcome. A week later, we had a buyer for our apartment.

What this well-meaning stranger does not know is that no matter where we end up, without a car we'll be sticking very close to home for a year, Thanksgiving and Christmas included. That twice-a-day business is something we're counting on.

"Oh, we're prepared for that," I say.

With skepticism still painted across his face, he asks, "Where are you from?"

"South Carolina," I say. "Originally. My wife is from Alabama."

"As long as you're not from up North," he shoots back. "That's the only thing I can't stand. Yankees moving in, raising the price of land and taxes along with it."

Great.

"Actually," I say, "we spent time in New York. Ten years to be exact." It sounds like we were incarcerated.

He smiles and shakes his head. "That's it, huh? Get rich in New York and move south, where your money's worth something?"

"No, that's not it." But he just looks at me, bemused, as if to say, *Yeah, I've run across your kind plenty—city folks who decide they want to be farmers. Well, it won't last. It's a romantic fantasy. Just wait.*

Back at Elim, after phoning the owner, Barbara has found a key to the cellar's padlock. I slide a bolt and open a heavy iron door with a peephole in the center. I descend a series of iron rungs into a cramped bunker—formerly a concrete cistern.

"How does it look?" Heather says, hopefully, poking her head in through the hatch.

"Come see for yourself," I reply.

She creeps down the rungs and turns to take it all in. "Oh, my God."

The space—roughly six-feet-wide by ten-feet-long—is dark and dank and not even cool, thanks to the sun-sucking entry tower. Lining the walls on thin shelves are plastic bottles of lamp oil, car batteries, and swollen, oozing gallon cans of peaches and tomatoes. The floor and walls crawl with crickets and granddaddy longlegs. The stench of spoiled food and battery acid nearly turns my stomach.

"This is no root cellar," I say. "It's a bomb shelter." And I shudder at the thought of a family of nine bunched shoulder to shoulder in this hellhole, waiting for the end of the world.

∾

The concrete deathtrap is a deal-breaker, leaving us even more worried we might never find the right farm for our experiment. Shortly after we walk away from Elim, however, we discover a true oasis over the Blue Ridge mountains in the Shenandoah Valley community of Swoope. One glimpse of the real estate flier showing the 1885 brick farmhouse fronted by a sweet little porch with scrollsaw pickets and our fate is sealed.

And, yes, there is a root cellar. Redolent of seasons past, the cool, brick-walled space hunkers beneath the house, waiting patiently for potatoes to once again fill its bins and jars of preserves to line the rough-hewn oak shelving. The rusty water heater and nest of black PVC pipes in the corner don't bother us. They are temporary, like the cobwebs spreading between the pine log joists. Over the next few months, we will remove them, along with all the other layers that have settled in the twentieth century's wake.

CHAPTER TWO

Old Year's Eve

*B*elle arrives on a bright June Sunday, one week before we plan to pull the plug on the twenty-first century. In seven days, our Taurus wagon, with its missing hubcap and 174,000 miles, will be gone. In its place will be Belle, a 2,000-pound Percheron—a draft breed descended from the Norman war-horses of William the Conqueror—towing an antique wooden wagon. The only thing I know about horses is that you never stand behind them, but then that becomes clear as soon as Marshall Cofer, Belle's owner, leads her out of his long tan trailer. *My God*, I think. *She's no quarter horse.* Only a fool or a blind man would loiter within striking distance of those meaty haunches.

I bought the wagon the week before in West Virginia, where it had gathered dust in a barn for years. The man who had taken out the classified ad seemed surprised to find someone who actually wanted it, and who was willing to give him $1,100 cash and haul it away. The problem is, I have no idea how to connect the buggy to the animal now fertilizing my front lawn, an embarrassing truth to admit to a country horse trader in the middle of a deal. After months spent firing outhouse-construction queries into cyberspace, test-milking goats, and peppering the staff at the county farm co-op with questions that elicit either bemused grins or frowns of impatience, I should be comfortable admitting my ignorance. But I haven't told Marshall about 1900, and I don't want to now for fear of ridicule—or worse, a lecture. Something in me whispers, *No, you can do this yourself.*

Perhaps sensing my uneasiness, Marshall, who chomps an unlit cigar, says, "You want me to hitch her up?"

"As long as you're here, you might as well," I say, relieved he has given me an out.

At the barn, Marshall slings the harness over Belle's broad back.

"You pay attention, too," he tells Heather. "He's gonna forget something."

After buckling and cinching straps from Belle's eyeballs to her tail, he backs her into the wagon shafts and buckles and cinches some more. She is a kitten in his hands.

Soon, Marshall and I, perched on the wagon's bench, are rattling down the driveway, me at the helm.

"Gee!" I say, self-consciously, my voice deepening to mimic Marshall's. *Gee* means go right in horse-driver lingo, and that is exactly what Belle does, turning onto the dead-end gravel road beside our farm. At the end of the road, I tell her "Haw!", and she turns left. "Whoa," I say. She stops, waiting for my next command.

"Tell her, 'Back,'" Marshall says.

"Back," I shout, and Belle steps backward, the wagon jackknifing like a tractor-trailer. My foot pumps instinctively, searching the floor boards for a brake pedal.

"Whoa," Marshall pipes up.

"Hey, she's even got reverse," I say with a nervous laugh, lamely gripping the reins.

But all he says is "Come UP," and Belle is trotting again.

When we near the house, the horse trader's tone softens. "You got good hands," he says. "You keep 'em nice and steady. You're gonna make a good driver." Whether he means it or not, I am thrilled. Here I am successfully doing what for months I have dreaded. The leather feels good in my palms. Cushioned by three sets of elliptical springs, the wagon jiggles smoothly over the washboard road. With its high spindly wheels and trim bed, it seems to me a vision of elegance, despite the royal blue paint job and fluorescent orange warning triangle dangling in back.

The simple act of taking the reins lifts a weight off my shoulders. It's one thing to swear off grocery stores for a year. Sure, we'll work our butts off to grow our own food, and failure could, technically speaking, mean starvation. But that kind of risk, like procrastinating on your preschooler's college fund, leads to a nagging, down-the-road worry. The thought of steering a wagon tied to a horse, on the other hand, nearly makes me soil my crisp new overalls. Yet, if we are serious about recreating 1900 life, we'll have to master 1900 transportation. "Weren't there cars back then?" a concerned New York friend asked me. Yes, exactly 8,000 among a U.S. population of nearly 76 million. The odds that the average rural American drove one of them are only slightly better than the odds that your plumber has a two-man submarine.

I say goodbye to Marshall after writing him a check for the horse and beam at Heather, who stands in the front yard with Luther toddling around her feet. Luther likes what he sees—a grown-up-size wagon and a real live horse jingling in her harness. Despite my near total lack of experience, I can't pass up this chance for a family drive.

Sitting high on the seat, Luther nestled between Heather and me, we roll back down the lane. Spreading out before us is Trimbles Mill Farm. Our staging ground. After we bought the place, closer inspection of the house revealed that the lovely little front porch was sagging and propped up by steel posts where the brick piers had crumbled. Half of the pickets were missing. Nor was the house free of feces: mouse droppings and rat pellets littered the pine floorboards. Then there was the kitchen floor, rotten from water damage and sinking into the red-clay crawl space. Over most of the plaster walls, previous owners had tacked flimsy faux-wood paneling. And in the bedrooms, someone had hammered up two-by-four closets beside the fireplaces.

But the house has good bones. Beneath the decay and tawdry add-ons, the original walls, wide-plank floors, windows, and doors are all intact. Peeling away the layers, we have unearthed a dwelling that, like Hawthorne's house of the seven gables, seems to have a "life of its own . . . full of rich and somber reminiscences." Its hand-shaped wood, brick, and plaster proudly bear the wounds and wear of time. Even the window glass is original. Today, the bubbled, hand-blown panes distort views of the distant hills just as they did a century ago.

It is an honest house. You see its kind all over the Valley—two-story, red-brick, symmetrical, with a standing-seam metal roof. What little ornamentation these homes dare display is usually found on the porches—here, it's the scrollsaw pickets and brackets that originally grabbed our attention. Sturdy, upstanding, built for the ages by unhurried craftsmen, these homes attest to the success of second- and third-generation Valley farmers. When the first Trimbles migrated to Swoope from Ireland by way of Pennsylvania in the 1730s, they built a log cabin and a grist mill. In 1885, they upgraded by building this brick house. Jefferson favored brick, writing that "a country whose buildings are of wood, can never increase in its improvements to any considerable degree." After the Trimble family sold the farm in the 1970s, ending more than 230 years of continual inhabitation, both the cabin and the mill—a four-story wooden building with an eighteen-foot wheel—were demolished. This house remains.

Heather and I were also smitten by the setting, hard up against the Allegheny Mountains at the western edge of the Shenandoah Valley. The farm lies across the southern slope of a spur leading up to North Mountain, the first of the Allegheny ranges. At the eastern end of the property, the Middle River meanders past bound for the Shenandoah River and, hundreds of miles later, the Chesapeake Bay. Over the course of thousands of years, the river has sheared off the spur, and it is upon this high, steep bank that our farmhouse and its outbuildings perch, within earshot of the purling waters. A board fence and a few trees are all that separate the driveway from the dropoff (yet another Luther hazard) and the shaley shallows below.

Though we originally envisioned a long drive and a private farm hidden behind a stand of trees, we have justified this house's roadside proximity and the dearth of trees—there are six in all, including a silver maple and a massive pecan—with the fact that during our initial visit only one vehicle passed, a green tractor lugging a big round bale of hay. Yes, it is exposed to the road and neighboring pasture, but it struck us as remote, tucked into the grassy folds of the Allegheny foothills.

18

So remote, in fact, that at night a total blackness engulfs the farm, which I learned a few weeks after our first visit when I drove up from our temporary digs in North Carolina to poke and prod and create yet another to-do list, this one house-related (repair porch, replace kitchen floor, etc.). Sitting on the front steps, I dialed Heather on our cell phone and suffered spotty reception while telling her about my walk-through. At one point, I yawned and leaned back against the steps. "Wow!" I said.

"What is it, Logan?"

"The stars! You wouldn't believe how bright they are." Big dipper. Orion's dagger. Everything else unrecognizable to me—except the broad swath of brilliant white arcing across the sky. "Remember that thing I read in the *Times* about the Milky Way?" I said. "Well, we're about to join the third who can see it."

Now, as the wagon trundles along, my eye follows our forty-acre pasture, the first patch of ground we've ever owned, as it slopes gently up to a ridge. On the opposite side of the road, a stream slips through a neighbor's field, thick with spring grass. We round a bend, top a small rise, and the twin totem poles marking the entrance to Camp Shenandoah, Boy Scouts of America, rise to greet us. Beyond that, it's all trees, 18,000 acres of mountainside state forest. If Elim was a little patch of hell on earth, here we've landed in heaven.

We sit without speaking, listening to the rasp of the steel tread on gravel, soaking up the new sensations, enjoying a respite from the squabbling that has threatened to undo both our plans and our marriage.

"I can't believe we're actually doing this," says Heather, her smile stretching from ear to ear. We look into each other's eyes, and our gaze lingers for the first time in a long while.

"I can't either," I say. I glance at Luther, whose chin bobs gently on his chest. He is asleep.

Yet here we are, all the details of our plan nearly in place. In the kitchen is a wood-burning cookstove. A pair of milk goats nibble grass in the barnyard. Half a dozen chickens scratch around a henhouse with southern exposure, exclusive garden access, high ceilings, and the old-world charm of exposed oak and heart-pine timbers—in short, a space to rival our first Manhattan apartment. Looming over it is our 100-year-old barn, as big as a high school gym. The outhouse stands atop a freshly dug hole. Soon the well-driller will come to pull the electric pump and install a manual one in its place. Made of cast-iron, painted fire-engine red, and with a long lever arm jutting to one side, it arrived by mail order the other day looking like a prop from the set of *Petticoat Junction*.

After months of stripping the twenty-first century out of our lives piece by piece, I am beginning to feel the transformation.

Soon after I drop Heather and Luther off at the house and roll up to the barn, my reverie screeches to a halt. It's as if someone holding my own strings screamed WHOA. Suddenly, it hits me that Marshall is gone. Here I am, a first-time horse owner without a manual, and my horse is attached to the wagon beneath my body by a now-cryptic jumble of belts and buckles. In my impatience to get on with the project, I failed to prepare for this moment. How could I have been so foolish as to forego driving lessons or been such a sap as to believe Marshall when he told me that Belle would teach me how to drive? What the hell does that mean, anyway? True, as a well-trained horse, she can obey my verbal commands, but I can't see her turning around and demonstrating the fine points of harnessing and hitching. A moment ago I was an explorer on the eve of an expedition. Now I feel like an irresponsible romantic, and the panic swelling in my gut sweeps me back to the day when, bound for my year-long, post-college teaching stint in Kenya—my first big adventure—I arrived for a layover in New York only to find I had forgotten my passport. Then, at least, I had the reassurance of two relentlessly mocking friends. Now, despite my partnership with Heather, I feel oddly alone.

To make matters worse, Marshall's promise that Belle is "easy-going" now seems more than just harmless horse-trader exaggeration. The guy who put me on to Marshall had called her "bombproof." He was another horse trader whose card I carried around for weeks before getting up the nerve to finally call.

"Bombproof?" I had said into the receiver.

"Yeah, bombproof. You know, one that's not going to kick or buck or turn your cart over. That's what you need. This feller who works for me has just the horse."

That "feller" was Marshall. And now Marshall's bombproof, easy-going horse will not stand still. After finally coaxing her to stop, I jump down, and she nearly drags the wagon over my foot.

20

"Easy, girl," I say, swallowing the fear rising in my throat. In spite of the fact that the largest animal I have ever handled is a golden retriever, somehow I have to get this horse, minus gear, into the pasture. If Belle were a typical saddle horse—tall and svelte—that would be one thing, but she's like two horses squeezed into one. She's a rhinoceros without horns. A single misplaced hoof could crush the bones of my foot. One kick could kill me.

I release the four straps connecting horse to wagon, and Belle steps forward.

The long wagon shafts hit the ground. I decide to tie her, still in her harness, to the fence.

As any horse person will tell you, a halter is one of the most basic pieces of tack there is, a simple configuration of straps that fits one way over a horse's wedge-shaped head, much like a pair of pants fits only one way over your legs. But as I hold the halter up to Belle's head, I can't for the life of me untangle the thing. I throw it down in a panic.

Maybe I can tie her up by the reins. But Belle walks away, the long reins play out in my hands, and I find myself behind her, the *one* place I know I shouldn't be. I tug at the left line and say "Haw!" She steps left and keeps going left, circling around as if she means to trample me. "Gee! Gee! Gee!" I scream, sounding like an eager Beaver Cleaver.

After finally leading her to the fence and looping the reins around the top board, I grab the halter and sprint to the house to find Heather. "What's wrong?" she says, as I enter the kitchen. "Where's Belle?"

"How does this thing work?" I say, holding up the halter as if it were a Wonder Bra. Together, we untangle the straps and sort out the two ends. I grip the strapping tightly so I won't lose the correct position.

As I walk back to the barn, Heather yells after me, "Call Jeanne." Jeanne, the dark-haired Swoope mail carrier who lives one farm over, raises cows with her mother. We've seen her on horseback rounding up bulls. She would definitely know how to deal with Belle.

"No. I can handle this."

"Call her!" Heather says, glaring at me with angry, frightened eyes.

I glare back but don't say a word, swinging around like a door-slam and stomping back to face Belle alone.

Back in the barnyard, I round the shed and there's Belle, untied, backside to the fence, with the reins dragging the dirt. Her head is bowed, and she looks defiant, her eyes saying, *Try me, punk. Just try me.* I stare back, paralyzed by fear, not just of getting stomped by Belle but of the year that lies ahead. What had, during our family buggy ride, seemed so hopeful, so exciting, is now real and frightening and, it seems, doomed.

A voice in my head whispers, *Quit, you fool. Cut your losses.*

CℨꙄꙄ

In New York, I bounced from one story to the next, writing about mountain biking and trekking, brilliant field biologists and the world's great explorers but excelling at nothing in particular myself. While pursuing their passions, my subjects had fought sharks with their bare hands, braved machine-gun-toting rebels, suffered pulmonary edema. Me? I got a repetitive stress injury—typer's elbow. When I travel, I'm a tourist no matter how much I try to convince myself otherwise. This *expedition*, as I have taken to calling it, is how I'll prove myself, how I'll escape my comfortable observer's role and do something tough and intensive and stick with it. This is about self-reliance.

Until lately, things were going pretty well.

After cutting ties with New York, we began laying out the practical steps necessary to recreate 1900, pinning our high-flying plans to earth with bullet points. By January we had a farm and a launch goal: May 15. We rented a furnished apartment in a nearby town and began chipping away at our to-do lists: make house livable *and* period appropriate, dig privy hole, install manual well pump, stock up on old tools, hammer up animal stalls, convert waist-high tangle of weeds into vegetable garden. The more we accomplished, however, the longer our lists grew. After repairing the rotted kitchen floor, I had to dig a twenty-foot French drain to block the run-off that caused the water damage in the first place. Before we could buy chickens, I had to replace the henhouse roof and build a roost and nesting boxes. Soon, the great web of tiny tasks left us feeling as bound as Gulliver.

In between the sledgehammer and crowbar work, the wallpaper scraping, the digging, the hacking and hoeing, we began hitting the books, determined to learn an entirely new (and mostly forgotten) way of life. And in typical twenty-first century fashion, we would do it in a hurry, digesting generations-worth of farming lessons in the equivalent of a college semester. Not only have we scoured history books and century-old magazines and journals for clues about 1900 life—what tools were available, when things were invented, what you could buy at general stores and what you could mail order, daily habits, cooking techniques, holiday customs, and on and on—but we have also studied modern-day homesteading manuals, ignoring the parts about tractors and power tools and animal antibiotics, for survival advice. Though we've read lots of books, our bible has become Carla Emery's *Encyclopedia of Country Living*, which was first published during the back-to-the-land movement of the 1970s and covers everything from "Backwoods Birthing" to "How to Care for Your Dead."

We have visited the county cooperative extension for pamphlets on canning and taken evening horticulture classes. We have eavesdropped on Internet chats among the current crop of tech-savvy back-to-the-landers. Our heads are swimming with facts and figures, dos and don'ts. Take cellaring, for instance: *Do* store carrots in layers of damp sand and apples in a box. *Don't* store them side-by-side or the carrots will taste bitter. *Do* box potatoes in the cellar. *Don't* cellar pumpkins because they'll rot. *Do* put pumpkins in the attic, but don't let them freeze. The best laying hens, we now know, have moist rectums, though how to use such advice remains a mystery.

As former small-town residents, we are also re-learning the ways of rural America. Swoope, population 500, give or take a recent birth or death, spreads out over miles of rolling farmland. Although a canning factory, general store, and post office once stood near a train depot, Swoope no longer has a village center. Coal cars bound for West Virginia and Amtrak trains headed to Chicago still rattle past, building up steam (metaphorically speaking) for the long climb over the Allegheny Mountains. But the depot is gone, as are the general store and factory. The last-remaining vestige of a community gathering place is the post office. Not long ago, Heather called the post office with a request. What transpired helped us realize just how cozy Swoope is.

You see, we had this great idea to move our mailbox from Boy Scout Lane to Trimbles Mill Road, 100 yards away, so that our address would match our farm's name. Trimbles Mill Farm, Trimbles Mill Road, Swoope. How quaint. So Heather asked the voice on the other end of the line what it would take to move it.

"Oh, I'm not sure about that," huffed the postmistress. "You'll have to speak to the mail carrier. And you'll have to call the county's 911 emergency service and ask them to change their records. Why do you want to do that, anyway? The box is right there next to the driveway."

We quickly dropped the idea, but when Heather stopped by the post office a few days later, the postmistress said, "So you want to move your mailbox, huh?" Turns out she knows the mailbox well. Her father used to work as a farm hand at Trimbles Mill. Even after Heather *assured* her that we'd changed our minds—way more trouble than it was worth, really—she nodded toward our mail carrier and said, "Talk to her about it."

"So," an attractive, dark-haired woman said, "why on earth do you want to move your mailbox?" And that was how we met our neighbor, Jeanne.

What *will* the people of this sleepy cattle community think of us and our bizarre plan? I wonder every time I gaze out at the only neighboring home visible from our yard (Jeanne lives half a mile away behind a hill). I can just make it out, a little brick Cape Cod hiding behind blue spruce trees to the north—the first place I'd run if a rattler bit Luther. I can't imagine it would go down all that well, though. My lungs would be burning, hair wild. I'd be wearing dirty clothes and an expression of crazed terror. I have visions of knocking on the door and being greeted by a shotgun-cradling redneck, furious that I interrupted his TV program. *You live where? And you don't have a phone?* By now, the only thing anyone around here knows about us is that we're from New York, which makes me think of that Pace salsa commercial: "*NEW YORK CITY?*" the cowboys yell. "*Git a rope!*"

❧

We have already missed our launch date by the time Belle arrives. A schedule change by the fencing contractor, plus the ever-growing list of last-minute details, has delayed our start. Now, with some of our seeds in the ground and summer fast approaching, we're running out of wiggle room. I've still got stove pipe to install, and if I postpone building the chicken run any longer, our commodious henhouse will soon become a hot box of death.

The pressure is also driving a wedge between Heather and me. We are both exhausted, touchy, and sleep-deprived from Luther's constant night-time waking, which began about the time we left our comfortable rental home and moved to the farmhouse for the final push. Heather and I set out on this adventure as equal partners, just as we tried to maintain an egalitarian relationship in New York, both of us working and sharing childcare duty. But amid the dust and din of renovations, the worries about Luther's safety, and the seemingly insurmountable challenge of getting everything done on time, at some point I started acting like the boss.

One morning, we're spreading compost. The yard is a weedy, muddy mess, and we're bickering about everything—where to plant what, the right amount of space between rows.

"Work the shovel with your foot. It goes quicker that way," I say, tired of watching Heather waste her energy jabbing at the pile. She grits her teeth and swallows her reply. We fill the wheelbarrow, and she begins to push, grunting. The wheel is stuck in the mud.

"Here," I say, sidling in to take the handles. "Like this." But before I can jerk the wheel free, Heather loses it. "I'M NOT YOUR FUCKING EMPLOYEE!" she screams.

"I never said you were!" About to explode, I grab the wheelbarrow and hurl it through the air, letting out a loud roar.

The wheelbarrow bangs to the ground and bounces toward Heather. She does not flinch. Just stands there, feet firmly planted, arms folded across her chest. "Do NOT," she growls, "try to intimidate me!"

Not long after that, we celebrate wedding anniversary number seven—lucky except in marriage.

CRBO

Once again, we push the start date back—this time to June 11.

On the morning of June 10, I am in the kitchen, having just screwed an antique coffee grinder to the wall with a cordless driver.

"Damn this old piece of shit," I say after busting my knuckles on the wall trying to grind a handful of beans. "That's one more thing we've got to do before tomorrow."

"What is?" says Heather.

"Get a coffee grinder. This one's broken."

"We're never going to make it," Heather says, with a huff that seems to heave the blame squarely on my shoulders, as if the broken coffee grinder—and everything else that has gone wrong lately—is my fault.

"It sounds like you never thought we would. Are you even trying to make it?"

"Of course I'm trying, Logan. I've been working my butt off for weeks. I'm exhausted."

"We can't push it back anymore. We said spring, and spring ends in ten days. We have to get started. Let me see the list," I say, grabbing it from her. Triage time. What to do first? What not to do at all? My eyes cascade down the page: mow grass, wash clothes at laundromat, go to landfill, clean house, get stamps, drop non-1900 things (mower, sneakers, strollers, plastic toys, toiletries, cleaning supplies, computer) at ministorage, return rented truck, pick up last-minute supplies (including, I mentally add, a coffee grinder). *Where the hell will I find an antique coffee grinder?* An entry catches my eye.

"*Vacuum floors?*" I say. "Give me a break. We can clean the floor with a broom in 1900."

"Wait a minute!" Heather shrieks. "This is *our* list. You can't start cutting things without talking it over with me first. You're acting like this is your project. That's not fair!"

From upstairs, Luther screams, "Mommmm-ayyyy!"

I storm out and jump in the station wagon, peeling out when I hit gravel at the end of the driveway, barely slowing for the stop sign, bottoming out with an ugly *whomp!* on the bridge hump, thinking, *Who gives a shit? Car's history anyway.* I crank up a rock station on the radio and suck in a deep, manure-smelling breath as the wind beats against my face.

I return, glowering and silent, with yet another paper sack filled with Styrofoam cups of coffee, packets of powdered creamer, a bottle of orange juice, and egg biscuits.

26

"We'll start on the twelfth," I say. Heather doesn't say anything. She doesn't even look at me.

The irony is that our little adventure was supposed to make us closer.

There are other ironies, too. Not only are we stressing ourselves out in order to de-stress, we're rushing to slow down, recreating the past with the aid of modern technology, and replacing our stuff with heaps of period-appropriate stuff (so much for Thoreauvian asceticism). Working out-of-doors was supposed to put a spring in our step and a healthy glow in our cheeks. Instead, Heather is crippled by a painful case of carpal tunnel syndrome.

Blame it on the goats.

Nubian goats, Sweet Pea and Star have broad Roman noses, floppy ears, big round eyes with heavy lids, and saddlebag bellies poking out on both sides of their bodies. A couple of days before Belle arrived, we drove the pair of half-sisters back from the breeder's farm in the bed of a rented pickup truck, me crouching and gripping their collars, wondering if goats bite.

These, at least, do not. Both goats, but especially Sweet Pea, the younger of the two, seem sweet-natured. And sensitive. That day, the farther we drove from their mama—a woman (with eleven children of her own) who bottle-fed them as kids on her living-room couch—the more they panicked, belting out bug-eyed, tongue-lolling screams that sounded almost human. Whenever we slowed for a turn or stopped at an intersection, I squatted lower, worried someone who heard their screams might think I was torturing a child.

That first afternoon, Heather, the designated milker, gathered up pail and lidded tote and bravely marched to the space in our barn we're calling our milking parlor. Other than a few test-runs, she was new at this, and the goats were homesick. The combination was a disaster. Up first on the milking stand, nervous Sweet Pea squirmed and kicked. I grappled with her hind legs while Heather tentatively tugged at her twin teats, milk dribbling out.

At this rate, it would be forever before the swollen bag was empty, but empty it Heather must, twice a day, or the goats would be in severe pain and at risk of infection. In 1900, before the discovery of antibiotics, mastitis (an inflammation of the udder caused by infection) was often deadly. Besides, if we start skipping milkings, the goats will quickly dry up, and we have neither a way to breed them nor the time to wait for them to gestate.

These thoughts raced through my head as Sweet Pea squirmed. Heather shrieked as the goat plunked a shit-covered hoof in the milk pail. I groaned and drove my shoulder into her flank, pinning her against the wall. The whole time, Luther stood five feet away, confused, frightened, screaming for our attention. "Hang on a minute!" I said, through gritted teeth. "Mommy and Daddy . . . are . . . milking!"

When Heather had finished with Sweet Pea, she led her off the milking stand and into the stall. Before we could catch our breath, out barged Star—older, larger, more stubborn—flicking her head suspiciously left and right and planting her hooves determinedly on the barn floor. Grunting, I hoisted her onto the stand and latched her head in the stanchion, and the ordeal began again, Heather milking into a pail of tainted milk that we knew would have to be tossed over the fence.

When she had finished and we had gathered up the pails, I said, "You'll get better with time," the words sounding colder and less consoling than I had meant them to. I lifted Luther, still crying, into my arms and tried to explain why it appeared we were attacking the goats.

While Heather's milking skills did improve over the next week, her hands began going numb from the chore. Searing pain began to shoot up her arms from her wrists. One morning, after twenty minutes of vigorous arm shaking to get the blood flowing, she grabbed the milking pails and walked up to the barn. I stayed with Luther down at the house. Ten minutes later, I heard Heather yelling. "Logan! I need help."

"I can't keep Belle out of the milking room," she said, exasperated, when I entered the milking parlor carrying Luther. "She keeps poking her head in and spooking Sweet Pea."

After luring Belle into her stall with a scoop of grain, I slammed the door shut and latched it. I could hear Sweet Pea bleating and scuffing her hooves on the wooden milking stand.

"No!" Heather screamed. "Stop, dammit!"

Then I heard a new sound and peeked over the Dutch door to find Heather sobbing into her lap while trying to coax the last streams of milk from Sweet Pea's sack.

"They hurt so bad," she said, rubbing her wrists. Luther stood back, fear clouding his face.

"You can teach me," I said. "It doesn't make sense to hurt yourself."

Even after I took over the milking, grappling with the goats twice a day, Heather's pain continued. Knowing that very soon she would not have the chance, Heather visited a doctor, who diagnosed her pain as carpal tunnel. Though the milking triggered it, hoeing, shoveling, wheelbarrow pushing, and wallpaper-scraping have not helped.

The news was a blow to her, since hands-on work is something Heather has craved. In New York, she felt like a cog in her climate-controlled Tribeca office tower, trafficking in the theoretical with grant-hustling intellectuals. Back in college, Heather spent her spring breaks volunteering—teaching English, painting houses for Guatemalan refugees, and serving as an interpreter at a Florida jail. Later, she worked in Cuban migrant tent camps at Guantanamo Bay. Helping people in need inspired her to focus her graduate degree on human rights work. She was used to sore muscles and broad smiles of thanks as signs of a job well done. In New York, on her best days, she got mixed signals from a slave-driving, whiz-kid boss. Her only sore muscles were in her neck, caused by teeth-grinding stress that led her to sleep with a rubber mouth guard.

Heather has never been afraid of a challenge. As a girl, she was a disciplined, dedicated ballet dancer, traveling the country to perform in festivals. In New York, she and I both trained for and ran the New York Marathon (the year before, as I ran the marathon without her, we first said "I love you" to each other in a sweaty, tearful, fleeting embrace when I found her in the crowd around mile eighteen). Hungering again for a challenge that offered tangible results, Heather jumped at the opportunity to relive an era when physical work and daily life were inseparable. Now this.

⌘

On the night of the eleventh, regurgitating thoughts—about Heather's pain, my milking troubles, fear of facing Belle—stir the old demons. I mean, look at us. Our peers are feeding retirement accounts and socking away money for their kids' college tuition, and what do we do? Trade my income—and

29

Heather's entire career—for an isolated forty-acre patch of ground that's starting to feel like a prison. I hide my doubts from Heather, feeling culpable even though we have both come along willingly. Maybe it is my fault. Maybe this is some long-repressed *Robinson Crusoe* fantasy—flee society, survive by your wits, take your wife and child along for the ride. There was the time I flew off to Kenya for a year. Shortly after Heather and I started dating, I convinced her to quit her job and move to Ecuador with me for eighteen months. Sure, those were incredible experiences, but was I also running away from reality? Am I running away now? What have I done?

And here's the kicker. Our adventure, technically speaking, has yet to begin.

CRBO

The power of morning to clear a troubled mind cannot be overstated. I wake on the twelfth refreshed and focused again on unfinished tasks. I hop in the Taurus for one last trip to town. Post office for stamps. Bank to withdraw $1,000 cash. My final stop is an old junk shop on Main Street. In addition to a coffee grinder, we need a pencil sharpener and some dip—pens and ink, since letter-writing will soon be our only means of communicating with anyone beyond shouting distance.

A bell tinkles as I open the shop door and see George, the doddering owner, now dozing in a rocker. I met George on the Valley auction circuit, where Heather and I bought most of our period-appropriate tools.

Feeling like a ghost, I rattle a tin full of rusty skeleton keys.

George wakes with a start. "Well, hello, young man. How's life in Swoope?" That we have a farm west of town is all he knows about us. I have not told him about the project—it just never came up—and now it dawns on me that I won't see George for a whole year.

"Everything's fine," I reply. "Trying to stay on top of the weeds." Leapfrogging over the small talk, I say, "Hey, I'm looking for a few things. You got any old coffee grinders?"

He ambles over to a table heaped with ceramic cookware, crockery, and mason jars and produces a wooden, box-style grinder. The price tag reads ninety dollars.

"Does it work?" I ask.

"I'm not really sure, son," he says, tilting his head and giving me a quizzical look. I can almost hear him thinking. *What kind of question is that? It's an antique.*

Too expensive, too iffy, I think. I'm as sick of shelling out money for old stuff as I used to be shelling it out for new stuff.

"How about a pencil sharpener?" I say.

"Pencil sharpener. Hmm. Let me think about that one." He wanders back toward the doodad-filled glass cases. My clock is ticking, but George has all the time in the world.

"Here's one," he says finally, pulling out a small, cheap cast-metal Model T car with a sharpener built into the rear. It isn't old, only meant to look old, the kind of nostalgic tchotchke they sell at truck stop gift shops. The price tag reads $12.50.

"Does it work?"

George looks at me funny. "Why don't we find out," he says, removing a pencil from a cupful on the cabinet. It cuts a point, but not well.

"I'll give you ten bucks for it," I say.

"Well," he pauses, all the time in the world, "this is a pretty special little sharpener. I don't want to give it away. I'll let you take it for twelve."

"Fine. *Fine.*" I spy a pair of wooden pens with steel nibs in a glass cabinet. "I'll take those two pens, too."

"Now these'll work," he says. "Long as you've got ink."

After handing George a fifty-dollar bill and waiting as patiently as possible while he makes change from his pocket, I grab up my things and prepare to leave.

George says, "You think about that coffee grinder, ya hear. You won't find a better one."

"I will," I say and turn for the door.

"You gonna be at Green Valley this Friday?" he yells, referring to the auction house where I earned both his respect and resentment by out-bidding him one day on an antique tricycle.

I stop and turn to face him, hand on the door. "No, I don't think I'll make that one, George." I smile, taking in the heaps of old tools and country furniture, the old oak ice chest that stands in the window, the hand-crank Victrola I almost bought thinking how nice a little music would be once we no longer have the plug-in kind, the barrel flowering with rusty rakes and shovels and hoes. It is time to go.

"You come back soon, young man," he says.

"I will," I lie.

⚜

I speed back home, bottoming out on the Middle River bridge in front of the house, with $961 in my pocket and our last carton of take-out food on the front seat. I spy Jeanne, our mail-carrying, cattle-farming neighbor, on horseback clutching a bouquet of orange daylilies. Dressed in tight jeans, riding boots, and a western shirt, she wears her thick black hair in a pony tail. Her face is tan from outdoor work. Jeanne, who is probably forty years old, was one of the first people we told about our 1900 project. As Swoope's sole mail carrier—and therefore, something of a community bulletin board—she has helped spread the word, which is fine by us since it has saved us many awkward moments. *Pleased to meet you. Yes, we just moved in. And by the way, did you know we're. . . .*

All last week, every time we bumped into Jeanne, she asked with something more than passing curiosity in her voice what day we were officially starting. "You let me know if it's not going to be Tuesday," she said on Saturday, making it clear she was plotting something.

As I wheel into the driveway, park the car, and join Heather and Luther at the side of Jeanne's horse, I find out what.

"Pony Express!" she says, handing us the day's mail and then the flowers.

"So this is what you've been planning," Heather says. "It's so sweet of you."

Jeanne, more comfortable with gruff than sweet, says, "Yeah, and I told you to let me know if the date changed."

"I know. I know," I say. "It hasn't really. I'm about to park the car for good. I had to buy a pencil sharpener."

"Maybe you should come along with us," Heather says. "Deliver the mail on horseback every day."

"Hell no! I'm not crazy," Jeanne says, tugging reins to keep her horse from nibbling our grass. "Y'all do what you want. I'll keep my hot baths."

I park our station wagon in the pasture on the uphill side of a tumbledown equipment shed cocked at a steeper angle than the tower of

Pisa. We had planned to sell the car but got busy and soon it was too late to take out an ad. Besides, exactly one year from now we will wake up and need wheels again. We have no intention of using it, and though I have a nagging suspicion that there is a proper procedure for mothballing a car, I simply close the door behind me and walk away.

We have no intention of using the telephone, either, so we stash it in a drawer after canceling credit cards, car insurance, Internet account. Yet after much debate we decided to keep the line active. Neither Heather nor I can shake the image of Luther—young, curious, vulnerable— struck by a rattler, bitten by a black widow, crushed by Belle, burned by a woodstove, stumbling two stories out of the hayloft, or tumbling into the Middle River. The heightened risk of death—the child mortality rate in 1900 was fifteen times greater than it is today—is one aspect of the 1900 experience we don't care to recreate. Besides, it won't be cheating unless we plug the phone in.

That afternoon, a guy from the power company—gray work pants, yellow hard hat—knocks on the door. "Says here you put in an order to cut power," he says, sounding confused.

"That's right," I say, cheerfully.

"You want me to cut the power *off?*" he repeats, looking past me at a kitchen filled with food, furniture, and other signs of habitation.

"Yep. Cut it off." He shrugs and walks around back to the meter, fiddles with something, and in five minutes is backing his pickup down the driveway. It seems too quick, too easy for how drastically the change will affect us. I read somewhere that the number of kilowatt hours a typical family uses is equivalent to the work of 100 servants. If true, our domestic army just vanished.

I flip the light switch in the kitchen. Nothing. We are almost there. Soon the darkness will fall.

CHAPTER THREE

Expedition to Nowhere

Bird chatter bursts through the windows. The sun's rays nudge eddies of coolness from the corners. There is something in the air, a sensation that our little compound is more firmly anchored to its patch of ground above the Middle River.

Maybe it is the deep sense of relief I feel lying in bed, Heather curled beside me, Luther sleeping peacefully in the next room. Our preparation period is over and with it, for now at least, the stress. No more errands to run or appointments to keep. No more car. The phone won't ring for a year. It is liberating, and as much as the crotchety Puritan hunkering down in my psyche tries to shatter the peaceful moment, I can't escape the feeling that I am on vacation. A camping trip.

The little Puritan won't leave me alone. He pops up to remind me of all we have left unfinished—garden half-planted, shed heaped with junk, Belle ignored. We could have studied nineteenth-century farming techniques and patched up battered outbuildings indefinitely. Like model railroad fanatics, we could have continued perfecting our life-size period diorama indefinitely, but at some point we had to draw back the curtain and reveal the product of our fevered preparations. That day has finally arrived.

I turn to Heather, whose easy yawn and smile are like a peace offering. "Welcome to 1900," I say. "What's for breakfast?"

"That depends," she replies, "on whether you get the stove going." In our haste, I never put the cookstove through a pre-project test-run. I had been meaning to ever since I cleaned it up, shoveling ash, scrubbing soot with a wire brush, patching holes with stove cement, and scraping out the leathery remains of a family of mice from the hollows beneath the oven box. I slid it into place, but some other job always grabbed my attention. Until only yesterday, the stovepipe lay in sections on the floor.

On my way to fetch firewood, I pass through the kitchen and pause beside the crude box of cast-iron dressed up in white enamel. No switches, dials, or buttons. The cooktop is a puzzle of thick iron plates, with an enamel warming shelf resting above on twin brackets. In back, the black stovepipe juts up and takes a ninety-degree turn into a chimney thimble. The stove sits there, cold and silent.

At the barn, I pause before a towering pile of firewood. Robert E. Lee, when negotiating an offer to be president of Washington College (later Washington and Lee), stipulated forty cords of wood per winter to heat his residence. By my calculations, we have enough unsplit rounds for about thirteen cords, still a hell of a lot of wood. Since we have no trees, I paid a guy with a "Don't Make Me Open This [Can of Whoop Ass]!" bumper sticker on his pickup truck to supply it. He was huge with a mouthful of crooked teeth—it looked like he was given a pipe wrench to suck on as a baby. I must have come off as pretty stupid, since he kept asking me if I was *sure* I wanted the firewood unsplit. "Ain't no difference in price."

As I rock a big section away from the heap, a sliver of oak pierces my palm. "Damn," I say, wincing, the blood swelling at the splinter's tip reminding me that we have just given up our ability to rush to the emergency room. Starting today, I will have to be more careful.

I walk to the shed for a pair of gloves. At that moment, Belle rounds the barn at a trot, ground shaking beneath her hooves, and bellows, as if to say, *Where's my breakfast?*

"Morning, Belle," I say, trying to sound chummy while dodging out of the way. To her, nothing has changed. I am still the same chump in charge of the grain.

She neighs.

"All right, *all right*. I'm coming." I root around the piles of junk—boxes of tools picked up at country auctions, paper sacks of hardware store supplies—until I find a pair of canvas gardening gloves. On the way back to the woodpile, I duck into the milking room and dig a scoopful of Belle's molasses-drenched feed out of a metal, rat-proof can. In the next stall over, Star and Sweet Pea go wild, propping their front hooves up on the half wall and craning their necks for a better view like a couple of children at the candy counter. Their bleats echo inside the barn's deep, dark recesses, setting my nerves on edge. But they'll have to wait until milking time for their breakfast.

Back in the barnyard, Belle drives her nose at the scoop, nearly spilling the grain. I rush into her stall and pour the grain into a metal tub on the sawdust floor. She darkens the doorway, before swinging her huge rump at me and plunging her snout into the tub. I squeeze past legs that could pin my chest to the oak wall like an empty shirt.

Now the chickens raise a ruckus, and I detour down to the henhouse to swing open the flap to their yard. They burst out in a feathery frenzy, each aiming for first peck at the morning bugs. I return to the axe, determined to put breakfast on the table.

The goats scream like babies.

Like most of the skills I need to get by in 1900, wood-splitting is fairly new to me. I have done it here and there, mostly for fun during weekend cabin retreats. Lift, swing, crack. Big chunks fly into smaller pieces. Simple.

Yet as I let fly the eight-pound maul, the axehead overshoots the wood and the handle lands with a pitiful *flump* on the far edge of the upturned log. Like a tee-shot-whiffing golfer, I swivel my head to see if anyone is watching. Belle is, standing in the shadows of her stall peering silently out at me.

"What are you looking at?" I bark, emboldened by the latched door separating us. Inspecting the axe handle, I find dented, splintered wood just below the head.

After ten minutes or so of hoisting and heaving the axe, with at least two more handle-punishing overshots, a small pile of stove-sized billets litters the ground. I gather them up in my bushel basket and trudge toward the house and the promise of coffee.

Heather is waiting for me when I arrive.

"You're drenched," she says.

"I had to split wood for the stove," I say, dropping the basket. "The goats are screaming. Their sacks are about to pop. Once the stove is lit, I've got to get back up there."

The stove. Will it work? Stuffing the long narrow firebox with newspaper and crisscrossing a few of the smaller logs, I light the pile with a wooden kitchen match, shut the firebox door, and wait.

Smoke seeps from the gaps in the iron stovetop. I growl loudly.

"What's wrong?" says Heather, peering in from the washroom, toweling her face.

"It won't draw," I say, waving the smoke away with my hand. I open and close vents on the side and front to improve the draft. I jam the flue lever on top back and forth, but still the old stove wheezes and puffs smoke.

Then I remember the damper halfway up the stovepipe. I open it, and the smoke stops. The wood in the firebox crackles and pops. I step outside and look up. Smoke billows from the chimney.

"I think it's going to work!" I say, grabbing the soap and plunging my hands into an enamel basin, which still holds Heather's leftover face-washing water.

"Great," she says. "I'll put on the coffee."

Luther, who has been clinging to Heather's legs, ambles quietly toward the firebox, drawn by the flicker of orange. "STOP!" I scream, grabbing his sleeve and jerking him back. He starts wailing.

"I'm sorry, sweetheart," I say, lifting him up for a hug.

"NO!" he says, clobbering me on the shoulder.

"Heyyy. The stove's hot. I didn't want you to get burned."

"See, Luther," says Heather, pretending to touch the stove with her hand and jerking it away as if in pain. "Hot! Ouchie! Hot." This is going to be a challenge.

Heather would have preferred a warm-water face wash, of course—and might have it from now on, if the stove continues to cooperate—but she does not complain. She seems as relieved as I that the preparations are finally over. We have reached a milestone, and though it's not quite the same as actually completing our year in 1900, getting started is rewarding nonetheless. Like me, Heather has no real idea what's in store—how much water we will need, if we'll be warm in winter, how we'll clean diapers, what it will take to put three meals on the table. At this point, we have no dirty dishes or grimy clothes to wash, nothing to harvest, no letters to write. We have only the future ahead of us, a future that looks drastically different from the future we faced in New York and a good deal different from what it looked like last week.

Carrying Luther on her hip, Heather walks to the outhouse, head rotating left and right in search of snakes. I follow, filling pots at the water barrel behind the house. She takes Luther inside the small wooden shack with her, not bothering to close the door. As she sits on the seat—still a bit disconcerted by the dark void below—Luther grabs a handful of mulch from an old dented bucket in the corner and tosses it at her feet.

"NO, Luther," she says sharply. "Leave that alone."

He laughs and tosses another handful on the seat beside her.

"NO," she says again, stuck with her pants around her ankles. I stay out of it, watching out of the corner of my eye as I fill buckets.

His face turns stern. "NO," he mimics in his raspy, high-pitched voice.

"Luther, sweetie, do you know what that is?" she asks, trying to distract him. "That's mulch. It comes from ground-up trees. Mommy and Daddy sprinkle the mulch in the hole after we go potty. So it's got to stay in the bucket. Do you understand?"

"Much," he says, trying to say the word.

"That's right, *mulch.*"

Heather and I have been excited by Luther's language skills. He has begun to string words together into sentences. Our favorite so far is "Luther like a pie," which he recently blurted out, face smeared with apple filling.

He looks up at Heather and says, "Luther like a much," and tosses a handful of the dark chips into her pants.

"LUTHER!"

An hour later, the coffee has still not boiled. I once barely survived a ten-day camping trip without coffee. The whole time my head throbbed, and I was as chipper as lichen. If we can't make coffee, I'm calling the whole thing off.

But finally, after I have milked the goats, strained the milk into a gallon jar, and stored it in the cool cellar—fueled by a handful of Tootsie Rolls (c. 1896) from a stash we tucked away for special occasions—the first *pips* and *pops* come from the enamel percolator. Soon the lid rattles, and the heavenly aroma of *Coffea arabica* fills the little kitchen, now sweltering from the stove and hot June sun. Cold and gloppy, the goat-milk oatmeal is surprisingly tasty. It goes down well with the coffee, which we drink from enamel cups so hot you need a rag to lift them, and even still they burn your lips. We've done it—managed to feed ourselves one meal in 1900. Though I don't dare gloat over the achievement, I feel satisfied. Or maybe it's the coffee.

C380

That night, as Heather and I brush our teeth by oil lamplight out back by the board fence, Heather says, "Who came by?" While putting Luther down, she had seen two people out the window. It was the people from the brick Cape Cod, a pair of retired school teachers—not gun-wielding rednecks at all—named Bill and Peggy Roberson. We met them a few days earlier. Bill's an avid gardener. Peggy drives an early-model Subaru with an "I ♥ Ethiopia" bumper sticker.

"The Robersons," I say. "They just came to look. Like rubberneckers at a car crash." Too polite to corner me with questions, the couple had glanced around the yard, from our water barrel to our livestock tank bathtub to the old work bench beneath the maple tree where we scrub dishes, with looks of awe on their faces. They brought us a jar of fresh, shelled English peas.

"This is going to sound silly," Heather says, "but when I saw them through Luther's window, I thought they had come to tell us about a death in the family."

"On our first day without a phone?"

"I know, I know. I can't help feeling like something tragic is going to happen while we're here. It's hard to be so out of touch."

40

I rinse gritty baking soda out of my mouth with a sip of water and spit into the darkness. "Did you know peas don't like hot weather?"

"Yeah, I remember reading that," says Heather. "Why?"

"I mean, *really* don't like it. Hate it. The Robersons pulled their pea plants yesterday. They're done for the season." Our peas, which even today we bothered to weed, are mere sprigs. They'll never make it. "He asked what we'll do if we run out of food."

"What did you tell them?"

"That we'll cross that bridge when we get to it."

We walk to the house, the hollow metal of the oil lamps clanking against the wire handles. The day has been a scorcher—at least ninety-five degrees at one point, according to a thermometer I hung on the tree out back. All day long, I mopped my brow with a bandana. Now I stink. My nest of hair is caked with dried sweat. Neither Heather nor I had time to bathe while the sun was out. Now that the world outside is inky black and beginning to cool, the prospect of a splash bath does not excite us. The well water comes out of the ground at a chilly fifty-five degrees. The stove fire has been out since morning, and it would take a couple of hours to build a new one and heat enough water for a bath. Instead, we dash water on our faces and trudge up to bed, lanterns lighting the way.

Lying on top of the sheet, I tilt my pocketwatch toward the orange glow of the oil lamp. The hands read 9:50. My muscles complain after the long day of splitting and pumping and stooping in the garden.

The pocketwatch ticks loudly in the stillness. Heather gave it to me for my birthday, two weeks ago. I cup its smooth body in my palm, consider the jerky motion of the second hand. The watch symbolizes the era we now inhabit—simple in its technology, patiently wrought, no batteries, no network connection. It runs by our efforts alone. If we forget to wind it one day, it will run down, and we'll have to ask a neighbor for the time. Which reminds me of the Robersons' visit. What if we do run out of food? Too tired to consider the consequences, I roll over and reach for the light.

"I'm gonna blow the lamp out, okay?" I say in a low voice that interrupts only the ticking—no humming fan or refrigerator, no on-and-off cycling AC.

"Heather?"

Nothing. She's already asleep.

⟨ॐ⟩

It only takes a couple days of morning headaches and unintended brunches to realize that if we want breakfast at a decent hour, one of us—me—will have to get up early to start the cooking fire. That means waking before sunrise. Unless the moon lights my way, I am blind for as long as it takes me to strike a match—*if* I remembered the night before to stash the matches on the night stand.

On Day Four, I rise in a room as dark as death. No matches. Feeling around for my shorts and T-shirt, I whisper curses, hoping I don't rouse Heather or, in the adjacent room, Luther, who has been waking up at night screaming for a nightlight. I feel my way out of the room—*easy now, slow and easy*—hands caressing cool plaster along the wall to the stair landing's low walnut railing (it hits me just above the knees). I follow my feet slowly down, down, praying Luther did not leave a wooden train car or stuffed bear on the steps. I continue, around the newel post and into the creaking hallway, around the corner and—*oof!*—I bump the ceiling where it slants to meet the stairs. Easing through the doorway into the sparsely furnished living room, I can *feel* the age of the house, my fingers rippling over the wide, hand-planed jamb.

In the kitchen, I smell onions and curry, hear the *cranch, cranch* of scraping mice teeth. Our rodent problem started as soon as I began chasing away the black snakes. We find nibbled corners on our cheese, little turds on the kitchen table, hear scuffling claws above us in the ceilings. *Where are the matches?* I want to reach for a light switch. Or feel the reassuring click of a flashlight button beneath my thumb. Instead, I shuffle my feet, letting the vermin know I'm here. I stick my hands into baskets and cobwebby crannies, feeling for that familiar rectangular box with the emery strip. My blind arms tip cups and bottles. I brush something off the shelf above the stove. It crashes to the floor with a tinny sound—one of our oil lamps. I stoop and carefully feel for broken glass. It is whole.

When I find a box of kitchen matches in the washroom cabinet, I return to the stove where I righted the lamp and strike a match. The darkness melts.

42

That night, before bed, I walk through the house like a pyromaniac Easter Bunny, hiding match boxes on shelves and in dressers in as many rooms as possible, hoping Luther will not find them.

In more than one way, we feel our way along during these early days. Everything is trial and error, from pinning cloth diapers on Luther to battling the green worms devouring our cabbage plants. I learn to feed a new log into the firebox every fifteen or twenty minutes to keep the cookstove heating consistently. Heather learns to prepare all meals in the morning, letting the fire die before the sun beats down with full intensity. We've stocked up on the dry goods the typical 1900 family would have been able to buy at a general store—coffee, tea, sugar, oatmeal, rice, soap, baking powder, among other things. And we've bought extra, since there is no longer a general store where we can replenish our supply. Using a collection of misfit cookware—cast-iron pots and skillets, chipped enamelware saucepans—Heather makes oatmeal, skillet toast, or fried eggs for breakfast. She boils rice, simmers dried lentils or kidney beans, steams collard greens or broccoli from the garden, and bakes cornbread, covering everything and leaving it on the warming shelf until lunch. Dinner is cold leftovers. We drink well water, ladling it from a crock that stands on a table in the kitchen.

Heather's a vegetarian, so we won't be slaughtering chickens or hogs this year. While it's true that the typical 1900 farm family ate meat, Americans living a century ago consumed far less meat than most people do today. Cured pork and the occasional possum or deer were important for winter survival, but chicken and beef were rare treats. Though vegetarianism didn't really become popular in this country until the 1970s, the practice has a long history. Alexander Pope wrote that "nothing can be more shocking and horrid than one of our kitchens sprinkled with blood and abounding with the cries of expiring victims or with the limbs of dead animals scattered or hung up here and there." Various Christian sects practiced vegetarianism in the U.S. during the nineteenth century. And Thoreau, who ate meat in moderation, famously wrote that it is "the destiny of the human race, in its gradual improvement, to leave off eating animals."

Though we raise no hogs, we do clean our teeth with wood-handled, boar-bristle toothbrushes. We were thrilled to find the brushes in a natural products catalog—and doubly pleased to learn the boars aren't harmed in the harvesting of their hairs. We dip the brushes in baking soda and scrub our teeth out back, spitting over the board fence. As for other personal hygiene, we wash our hands and faces with Ivory Soap (introduced in 1879) using an enamel wash basin. We keep the basin on a beat-up Victorian cabinet—our wash stand—emptying the water by tossing it over the fence and refilling it with a bucket of fresh water hauled in from our water barrel. Bathing is another story.

Nearly a week passes before I take my first splash bath. I ready myself by grabbing a soap bar, a bucket of water, a rinse cup, and a gingham tablecloth for a towel. Because there was no terry cloth in 1900, bathers dried themselves with flat fabrics such as damask, often tasseled along the edges with heavy braided cord. The 1897 Sears catalog, showing a man patting his face with what looks like the dining-room curtain, fails to mention softness or absorbability—towel qualities the modern American takes for granted—and instead touts the towel's coarseness: "A good rubbing down with a Turkish towel after a refreshing bath will put new life and vigor back into your system," the copy reads. "Nothing will create such a ruddy glow to the skin and quicken the circulation quite so well."

Stripping out of clothes so crusty with dirt and sweat they nearly stand without me, I hustle across the grass and hop in the high-sided, galvanized, oval-shaped livestock tank, cocking an ear for the sound of a car. I dip the cup into the frigid well water, raise it above my head, and pour. I yelp and shiver. A second cup. A third. My skin tightens, stands at attention in thousands of tiny bumps. Every part of my body stiffens—except for one part, which disappears like a frightened snapper into its shell. As I whimper, I hear howls of laughter coming from the garden, where Heather is alternately pulling weeds and yanking Luther off the tender bean sprouts. I stand and lather up from head to toe, scrubbing my sunburned neck, rubbing at the dirt caked on my hands and knees, scratching soapy fingertips through the scruff covering my face. I am a Zest commercial in parody, all wild and foamy in a metal backyard horse trough.

One problem is the gummy residue the soap leaves in the hair, the same scum that rings bathtubs. From Heather's first bath, it drives her crazy. She tries castille soap, but that's worse, like using toothpaste. The bar of Old Fashioned Pine Tar Soap is like, well, pine tar. Even glycerin soap leaves the hair sticky. She tries conditioning her hair with olive oil, but finds she needs soap to remove the oil. A white vinegar rinse improves the luster but leaves her smelling like pickles.

In general, Heather struggles with her appearance. Slender, with big hazel eyes and brown hair, she's what you'd call a natural beauty. Though wearing no makeup at all and clomping around in leather boots and soot-smudged shorts may be a little too natural for her and may be contributing to her coldness of late. Heather and I decided against period costumes. Dressing up is not the point. We have, however, sworn off inappropriate apparel, including jogging shoes, high-tech outerwear, bikini underwear, boxer shorts, and anything remotely fashionable by today's standards. The men's briefs and tank-style T-shirt Heather wears—her interpretation of women's 1900-era undergarments—can't make her feel very sexy. ("It's my Archie Bunker look," she says.) Heather *has* looked prettier. But to me, she's still beautiful. And worrying about looks now seems beside the point.

For a farm wife, going without a corset would have been perfectly acceptable. By 1900, mounting evidence showed corsets fractured ribs, collapsed lungs, displaced livers, and caused uteri to prolapse. One report from the period states that a fashionable corset exerted twenty-two pounds of pressure on the internal organs. Feminists staged fierce protests against the shape-altering garment, just as feminists in the 1960s and 1970s opposed the bra (c. 1914) for how it constricted the female form. Heather, a feminist, is soon nostalgic for her bra, however, with the cups and crisscrossing elastic straps that can liberate the active woman.

Then there's the issue of her periods. Upper-class women with domestic staff might have taken to their beds, but a farm wife could not skip even a morning's chores. Although the ancient Egyptians made the first disposable tampons out of softened papyrus and, according to Hippocrates, writing in the fifth century B.C., the ancient Greeks used lint-wrapped wood, the modern applicator-style tampon was not invented until 1929. When Heather's period starts, she skips the Motrin, pins strips of cloth into her undershorts, and goes about her business.

Heather's business—cooking, cleaning, laundry—is the stereotypical chore load of the female, while mine is more traditionally male: wood-splitting, water-pumping, livestock care. Though historically accurate, our setup is more happenstance than planned. We do the jobs we're inclined to do and that will be most efficient. It takes Heather forty minutes to pump twenty gallons of water, and it takes me fifteen. With chores filling our days from dawn to dark, efficiency counts for a lot.

∞

As relieved as we were to find a farm with a root cellar, the void below our house is a constant reminder of the challenge facing us. By summer's end, we will have to fill those shelves with root vegetables and hundreds of jars of food canned on our woodstove. Right now we're focused on growing the food. Canning is something we'll worry about later.

That changes, however, the day a mufflerless pickup truck with "Farm Use" plates roars into the driveway. Out steps Joel Wilson, who lives a couple miles away. With a droopy cowboy mustache, boots, jeans, a plaid snap-up shirt, and a wide-brimmed hat, Joel looks like he took a wrong turn on a Wyoming cattle drive and ended up here.

Joel's wiry teenage son, Tommy, hands us a five-gallon bucket full of cherries. "We can't take these," I say, imagining how much five gallons of shiny plump cherries would cost at a Korean deli in New York City. "This is too much."

"Take 'em," Joel pleads. "We got our hands full running cows. Besides, if we don't give those cherries away, the birds'll just eat 'em."

The cherries are like gold. Before the Wilsons' pickup is out of the driveway, I scoop several handfuls into a colander and rinse them with a bucket of cool well water. Heather, Luther, and I sit around the picnic table, eating one after another, tossing the stones into the field. Luther, who has gone from drinking sippy cups of juice to enamel cups of plain water and from eating the sugar-filled foods of mainstream America—breakfast cereal, peanut butter and jelly sandwiches, fruit yogurts, cookies—to broccoli, beans, and cornbread, goes wild with desire. "More, more, more!" he cries out, his face a red smear. We can't pit them fast enough. Even with Luther's help, however, we don't make a dent.

That night, after Luther is down, instead of falling into bed exhausted about the time most of America sits down for their favorite primetime television show—our routine for the past week—we sit on the screen porch and pit cherries, peeling the flesh from the stones with our fingers. We've decided to try our hand at canning, praying the stove, which takes an hour to brew coffee, will get hot enough to sustain a twenty-five minute boil. Darkness falls, and cricketsong fills the air. The wind rustles the leaves, flutters the flame on our oil lamp. The cool air invigorates us. We sip bourbon from enamel cups—the bottle was a send-off gift from a friend. I squeeze a few cherries in my drink. We smile and laugh together for the first time in a week. The gift of the cherries makes us feel rich. At midnight, nodding into the bowl of pits, our hands as red as a field surgeon's, we turn in.

The next morning, we both rise at 5 A.M. to prepare for canning. I light the stove fire. Quick-burning sticks might just give us the heat we need. There is a hushed excitement to our actions—sterilizing jars, filling the twenty-one-quart waterbath canning pot. Assuming we can grow food, if we can also preserve it, we can make it through the winter.

By six, the kitchen is sweltering. The fire roars in the narrow firebox, gobbling up the slivers of wood almost as fast as I can feed them in. I pry up one of the round burners. Flames whoosh horizontally through the space, pulled by the strong chimney draft, defying the urge to rise vertically through the round opening.

An hour later, steam rattles the lid, and we dive into action, heating jars (so they won't crack), filling them with fruit, topping them off with sugar water, screwing on the lids, and gently lowering them into the boiling water. Our midnight pitting yields four quarts. To sterilize the contents and vacuum seal the jars, we must boil them for twenty-five minutes. I keep shoving on firewood to fuel the blaze.

Totally absorbed in this new task, afraid of goofing up, we must ignore Luther, who is awake now and with us in the hot kitchen. He falls on the floor, banging the wood with his fists and head, screaming, "Mommy, hug. Daddy, hug."

The crude oven gauge reads 600 degrees, whereas before now it had not topped 300. The stove roars. The lid rattles. Steam billows. Success! With the stove hot, Heather rubs three cast-iron skillets with shortening and seasons them in the oven. She also boils water for cleaning diapers.

I work double-time splitting wood. That night, we again pit into the morning hours, until our backs ache from holding our tired heads off the table. With my clanking lamp lighting the way, I carry the covered pot of cherries to the cellar to keep until morning.

The next morning, we can another six quarts of cherries, which we'll use for pies this winter—if Heather learns how to make a pie. When they have cooled, I return to the cellar with the jars of fruit, shining as red as rubies in the sunlight, and proudly arrange them on the shelf alongside our dry goods and a few jars of homemade preserves given to us by well-wishing friends and family. This is our new currency. No more depositing paychecks and spending cash. We sweat and grunt for food—and milk and drinking water and stove fuel. I count the jars, few as they are, the way a miser counts his money. The cellar is our bank, the food lining its oak shelves our security.

For that reason, we obsess over our garden. A plot of gently sloping ground roughly seventy by fifty feet, the garden stands out back, between house and barnyard. A path runs up the middle to the henhouse and the barnyard gate. When we first arrived, thick, knee-high orchard grass covered every inch. For years, cows had grazed there. We worked like crazy to remove the grass, turn the soil, and fold in the old, dried manure we shoveled out of the barn. We're still working like crazy.

The weeds are relentless, far worse than if this plot had been cultivated year after year. Weed seeds can lay dormant in cool soil for decades waiting to churn upward into the topsoil, where the sun's warmth triggers sprouting. With the soil exposed, grass and lamb's-quarter pop out thick as shag carpet. We try to keep up, plopping down on hands and knees to pull plants in the free time between other chores. Before I have finished weeding a row, another row demands my attention, and in the days it takes to make a complete pass through the garden, the weeds in the bed where we started are coming up again. It's like painting the Golden Gate Bridge with a brush.

Gardening is backbreaking work, but it can be deeply rewarding on a number of levels. There's the design work, using pencil and paper to chart out what goes where, walking off the length of rows and distance between them, designating spaces for garden paths. Then comes the soil work and all the rich sensations it involves—the feel of the wood-handled hoe in your hands, the rhythmic scraping of its blade, the rich smell of the turned earth. When it's time to sow, we use a length of twine tied to a pair of stakes as a guide. I'll bang a stake in the ground at one end, and Heather will place the other stake at the other end, eyeing the taut string for straightness before hammering it home. Following the stringline, we poke the bean or corn seeds in the ground and blanket them with soil. It's hard to believe that the contents of these small paper packets will feed us for the year. The seeds seem so insignificant and vulnerable.

In truth, seeds are fairly hardy things, we're learning, as long as they get enough water. But that's the problem. The bug-free, Mediterranean climate that so charmed us at first—every dinner *alfresco*, slack-jawed gazing up at the dome of stars—is actually a drought. Without an electric well pump, we can't water a garden of this size. The best we can do is kick-start newly planted seeds and moisten sprouts with a sprinkle from our watering cans—pumping from the well, dipping buckets, filling cans, back and forth, back and forth. It is so hot and dry by late June—and we are so consumed by our daily chores—that we water at night, once the sun has set, crunching along garden paths by oil lamp or the strobe pops of heat lightning.

⊂⊰⊱⊃

In New York, music filled our apartment: Latin dance music, Brazilian bossa nova, REM, Mahler, Miles Davis. But now, with our supply of music cut off, I am a prisoner to every stray tune that pops into my head. Some are personal favorites. Most seem to have been sent only to torment me.

The first tune that sticks is "Red, Red Wine," by UB40. It surfaces one day while I am cultivating beans, and stays with me for days. I've never liked the song, but something about its simple melody and reggae beat keep it glued there, the rap-like chorus looping: *Red, red wine, you make me feel so fine/You keep me rocking all of the time.* I can't remember any other lyrics, so I invent words to go along: *Red, red wine I want to hold on to you/Hold on to you until my face turns blue.* And so on. *The line broke, the monkey got choked/Bah bah ba-ba-ba bah ba-ba ba-ba. Yeeaah.*

I hum "Red, Red Wine" while hoeing, mouth "Red, Red Wine" under my breath as I kneel to pull weeds, clamp my lips together to keep "Red, Red Wine" from spewing out, and then hear it sloshing around my skull. *Red, red wine make me feel so. . . . Shut UP!* I'm worse than the mumbling crazies we left behind in New York. I try to stop the torture by pretending to end the song, playing it out with an overly dramatic *bum-BAH.* But it comes back like the flame on one of those trick birthday candles. The only solution is to swap it for a better song. *Blackbird singing in the dead of night,* I sing through gritted teeth, holding the tune up like a crucifix. I work my way through as much of the Beatles's *White Album* as I can remember, using "Blackbird" and "Mother Nature's Son" to part the sea of "Red, Red Wine."

But freedom is shortlived. Other random tunes creep in to fill the void: Aerosmith's "Walk This Way" — the rap version. "We Got the Beat," by the Go-Go's. It's maddening. Here we are trying to faithfully recreate the year 1900, and while splitting wood or pumping water I wah-wah the theme music to *Sanford and Son* or thump out the bass line from *Barney Miller.*

Curiously, most of what sticks is from my childhood — sitcom themes, commercial jingles, songs by the Bee Gees, the Commodores, and KC and the Sunshine Band. It's not period-appropriate in the least. If our story had a soundtrack, it wouldn't be some Ken Burns-style collection of haunting mandolin melodies. It would groove, baby. *Do a little dance, make a little love, get down tonight!*

CཞྞO

One day I am weeding the garden when a white sedan pulls up and a tall, broad-shouldered man in a tie, short-sleeved shirt, and wire-rimmed glasses steps out. He flips down his plastic clip-on shades and moves stiffly toward me. Assuming he is another Jehovah's Witness pamphleteer — a carload showed up recently to inform us that the world would soon end — I prepare to politely send him on his way. Instead, he offers me a clammy hand and barks, "Eugene Gibson, Boy Scouts of America."

Eugene Gibson is in charge of the Stonewall Jackson council of the Boy Scouts of America, including Camp Shenandoah, which borders our

50

property. Just stopping by to say hello, he says, but after a minute or so of awkward pleasantries, he gets down to business.

"What are your intentions with this?" he says, motioning up toward the barn.

"Well," I say slowly, "we just had the roof painted. Maybe some day we'll turn it into a woodworking shop or craft studio."

"I mean with the whole place," he says, impatiently.

Has he somehow heard about our project? What is he after? "We're raising our own food," I say, "giving the simple life a try for a while."

"What about the land on the backside of your place? What do you plan to do with that?"

"You mean that wedge of hay field beyond the fence?" I say.

"Nine acres," he adds quickly, as if the acreage is in question. "What do you plan to do with that? Raise cattle?"

"We don't have plans," I say, growing impatient myself. "Why do you ask?"

"Well, to be frank, we want it," Gibson says. "I'm not here to make you an offer, but I'd like you to think about it."

"Why is that nine acres so important?"

"We tried to buy it a couple years ago," he explains, "when we bought the adjoining 159 acres, but the owner, a guy from New Jersey, wouldn't sell. Held on to it as some sort of buffer. When he found out how much we wanted it, he agreed to sell but jacked the price up. We weren't about to pay that kind of money. He was a real Yankee SOB."

"What are *your* intentions with the land?" I ask.

"The camp needs to grow, so we can attract more youth." The plan, he says, is to build a conference center and parking lots. "Plus, we want to add Cub Scout camp sites. Platforms with tents. And a bath house. They'll have to have mom-friendly bathrooms, if you catch my drift." He gives me a wink.

I catch his drift all too well and have heard enough. He wants to develop one of the prettiest patches of ground anywhere. Has he ever bothered to notice the view across that hay field? Every time I'm up there, I feel like breaking into the theme from *The Sound of Music*. "Mr. Gibson, I've got to get back to my garden," I say. "Gotta get more seeds in the ground before the rain comes."

"Oh, sure. I didn't mean to keep you," he says, sticking out the beefy hand again, this time holding a business card. "You just keep in mind what I said. I'm sure we could work something out if you ever want to sell."

"I'll think about it, but I'm pretty sure we won't," I say, pocketing the card and slipping my hands back in my gloves. Something about Eugene Gibson tells me I should take his club's motto—Be Prepared—to heart.

CRSO

For a stubby-legged two-year-old, the trip from our house through high grass to the well pump is a real hike. But I want Luther to get used to it. As I make my chore rounds, I can't carry him everywhere.

Pausing to urge him on, I gaze around at the pasture and mountains, my chest aching with pure joy—*we're finally doing it!*—knowing that instead of being in daycare our son is with me and I am not chained to a computer and we are together, outdoors, walking to fetch water. How simple! Even the pink-blooming thistle reaches for the sun with an innocence that eclipses its prickly reputation.

"Come on, Luther. Daddy's got to water the goats," I say, waiting now before opening the gate. He stops to look at the chickens poking around their pen. *What's your hurry?* I think.

I stop and listen. Back in New York, I tried to imagine what 1900 might sound like compared to the cacophony of our Brooklyn street—car alarms, thundering motorcycles (which set off the alarms), the grinding whine of downshifting trucks, screaming jets bound for LaGuardia, drunks arguing in streetlamp shadows, and backyard dogs meeting at common fences to try to chew each others' faces off. Now that we've arrived? I hear the wingflap of chickens, a chittering of swallows, and the soft drum roll of wind against the metal barn roof, sounds that work on my being like therapy—until the goats start whining for water.

Soon we're there, and I start pumping, while Luther stoops to play with pebbles. It's hard work raising water at a third of a gallon per stroke from a depth of eighty feet below the ground. After fifteen reps, I stop to catch my breath and shake out my burning triceps.

The water I pump for household use travels by force of gravity through a hose to a metal water barrel 350 feet away. The hose was my somewhat unorthodox solution to the problem of a distant well, an alternative to drilling a new well closer to the house (a $10,000, hit-or-miss prospect) or hauling water two buckets at a time. A century ago, Sears sold plumbing fittings and rubber hose. Back then, as today, any farmer worth his salt would have devised a similarly resourceful solution.

I continue pumping and then screw down a valve, diverting the water from the garden hose to the pump's wide spigot. On the next stroke water gushes out into a two-gallon galvanized bucket hanging from the spigot end. This is our drinking water.

The splatter of water catches Luther's attention. He reaches for the bucket, now full. It tips and water splashes on the dirt. "No, Luther," I say. "Daddy's pumping now. We need this for drinking."

"You wanna drink! You wanna drink!" he begs, mixing up his pronouns, the way two-year-olds do.

I lower the bucket and let him sip from the edge. His hands reach up for the sides. Water soaks his T-shirt. He squeals at the coldness. The day is heating up, and I raise the bucket to my lips, letting the cool water pour down my throat and soak my shirtfront. "Feels good, huh?" I say.

"More, more!" he screams, delighted. I lower the bucket again, and his hand catches the edge, this time dowsing him. He shrieks and laughs and jumps up and down.

Back at the house, I open the kitchen door and a blast of heat and cooking smells escape. Flies bump against the wall. I carefully pour the drinking water into a three-gallon crock on a stand in the corner, ladling a glass for myself while it's still groundwater cool. Through the kitchen window I see Heather in the garden, stooping to pull weeds in her wide-brimmed straw hat. Lunch and dinner sit in covered pots lined up on the stove's warming rack. Starving, I grab a handful of Tootsie Rolls from the tin.

On the way to the barn to water the goats, I hoist Luther to my shoulders, where he sits, kicking my collar bones and pulling my hair. In the barnyard, the goats follow in my wake, sniffing my calves. I lower Luther, and we step into the goats' dark stall. Lumpy turds litter the sawdust. The pair lingers at the door, poking their noses in, and when we walk back out carrying two empty buckets, they scatter, romping playfully together on the patch of concrete outside the pen.

We return to the well and fill the goats' buckets. Coming back, Luther trails me, keeping a watchful eye out for Belle, who stands in the far corner of the barnyard indifferently munching grass. He turns to look at her and then scurries to catch me, yelling, "Uhhhh, Daddy!" with a voice that sounds close to tears. I have my eye on him the whole time and am ready to step in if Belle ever shows any sign of aggression. The goats mill about near their stall. When they see us, they lope up to nose the buckets and nudge my crotch, sending Luther into a panic.

"Daddy!" he screams, clinging to the back of my legs. "Up. Up. Carry me."

"They're nice goats," I say, putting down the buckets. "They won't hurt you. See?" I crouch and put my arm around his shoulder while petting Sweet Pea's smooth tan coat. They *are* nice goats, less menacing than most dogs, even though Star, the big black one, did playfully lunge at Luther the day after we brought her home. I didn't think much of it— didn't have the time, really—and since then have been trying to abate Luther's fears. He'll just have to grow comfortable with the animals. It will be good for him.

"Up, up," he whines. I ignore him, turning to unlatch the barn door. Suddenly, out of the corner of my eye, I see Star rear up on her hind legs. In half a breath, she cocks her head to one side and thrusts her body forward. Her bony skull meets Luther's squarely in the forehead with a blow powerful enough to launch him through the air. He lands with a bounce on the rocky ground.

"STAR!" I yell, kicking her hard and running to Luther. His face is scrunched up and red. A scream swells in his lungs and finally bursts from his lips. I scoop him up into my arms and, crazy with rage, chase the goat, kicking at her while hugging Luther to my chest. Coming to my senses, I stop and run to Heather, who now stands at the garden gate.

"Star butted him!" I say, handing Luther to her over the gate. No blood, no broken bones.

"Why did you put him down in there if she butted him before?" says Heather, scowling at me. Then she changes her tone, soothing Luther with soft words while rocking side to side. He keeps screaming.

"I don't know!" I say, breathless. "I can't believe she really did it."

I sprint after Star, trying to kick her again, swinging my leg so hard I throw my body out from under myself. I hit the gravel with a lung-crushing thud and roll. Star runs to the rear of the barn. I follow in a fast-moving linebacker's crouch. She's bleating her head off, tongue wagging in cartoon desperation. I move like an animal. She tries to race past me, but I grab her stubby tail and catch hold of her collar, shoving her in her stall.

Sucking air into my lungs, I go to find Heather and Luther.

They are sitting at the picnic table in the shade of the silver maple, Luther calm now but still in Heather's arms.

"Star butt Luther," Luther says in a pouty voice. "Daddy give Star time-out."

"I sure did," I say, making the words sound upbeat, "a loooong time-out." But inside I feel horrible—for letting it happen and for losing my temper afterward. It must be my exhaustion, I tell myself. I can hardly face Heather. I turn and walk back toward the barn. The goats need water, and so does Belle. I need lunch, but that will have to wait.

When I get there, Belle is eyeing me across the barnyard.

CŞSO

I swear Belle is judging me. It all started with that look.

Before Belle, I never thought much about horses. People form deep and lasting bonds with their horses. Some whisper to them. They're supposed to be smart, sentient beings, and though I am no horse lover, I can already sense a depth to Belle that hints at consciousness. Mostly, she is like a child, basic in her urges and dislikes. She craves sweets, doesn't like to be pinned up or told what to do. She's moody and stubborn. There are times, though, when her stillness, the cock of her head, and those bottomless black eyes suggest a wisdom and maturity beyond the range of a child, times when I would not be surprised to hear words spring from her mouth.

Not long after the butting incident, as I approach Belle's stall, a rat scurries by. Though I've found fat rat droppings and teeth marks on our cheese, I have not encountered a rat since New York, where I once witnessed a scene in a subway station that I'll not likely forget. As I hurried alone late at night through the dark, urine-stinking pedestrian tunnel, black rats started pouring from one side past a row of tiled columns to

55

the other, stuffing their fat bodies into drain holes. They had come from a heap of rags and cardboard lining the wall. With a shudder, I realized the pile was a row of sleeping homeless men. I stopped and yelled—*hey! hey!*—to scare up any rats hiding in the shadows and then sprinted for the exit stairs.

With that scene in mind, I face off with this rat in the barnyard. It is shivering, and I realize it has eaten the green poisoned pellets I scattered around the barn crawl spaces. The broad-daylight sight of its beady eyes and fat hairless tail makes my heart pound. I heave a stone at it and miss. The rat darts, weak but determined, and crouches beside the barn foundation, eyes buggy with fear. My adrenaline is pumping. I don't want to let it get away. I need rat closure. I chuck another rock. It misses. The rat doesn't move. I try again and miss. I finally connect, blood spurting as if from a stomped packet of fast-food ketchup. The rat shakes and then goes still.

Shaking, too, I'm struck by the rawness and violence of nature—the violence of my *own* nature when a creature takes our food or butts our child. Though Heather and I weren't naïve enough to expect a year of pastoral bliss, we were ill-prepared to deal with these primal responses. It's mostly fear, and I'm letting it lead me around by the nose.

I look up and see Belle standing in the shadows, staring at me again with those big black eyes. The day will soon come when I will have to face her, and I damn well better be ready for that.

CHAPTER FOUR

How I Learn to Drive

Two weeks into 1900, something completely unexpected arrives in the mail: a wedding invitation. Even better, it's for a wedding *reception* only two miles away. Cold beer. Live music. We're there! Ignoring the R.S.V.P. telephone number, we respond by mail.

P.S. Where can we park the horse and buggy?

William Willett and Shani Geary, Swoope's resident bohemians, are tying the knot. Recently relocated from Portland, Oregon, they live in a rented bungalow behind the Swoope post office with their four-year-old daughter, Addison. A freelance baker, William works out of a shed behind their house—the Bread Shed—where he keeps a commercial mixer and pizza oven. Shani, who has a tattoo of an orchid (her birth flower) on her calf and drives an old, bumper-sticker emblazoned Subaru similar to Bill and Peggy's, sells William's sourdough loaves at the Saturday farmer's market in town. She is loud and bristling with opinions. William is easygoing, enjoys literature. Flour dusts his soft-soled shoes.

Bearing cold beers and a warm sourdough loaf, they dropped by one day to introduce themselves and find out if the rumor was true—that we were some kind of living history kooks. I showed them the outhouse, the garden, the woodstoves. We hit it off right away.

Still, the invitation catches us off-guard, which may explain our overly optimistic assumption that we can make it there. The truth is, I have hardly looked at Belle, except to fill her feed bucket every morning. The harness still lays heaped in the shed, a strap broken from our tussle during that first encounter.

As luck would have it, our second-nearest neighbor is one of the best draft horsemen in this part of the Shenandoah Valley, a man who folks say can handle any draft horse, no matter how big or how mean.

Clyde Tillman's no horse whisperer. The seventy-year-old fireplug of a man dominates through bullying—yelling, cursing, beating. He wears dentures and a glass eye and spews profanity. At least this is what I've heard. The owner of a shrinking plot of farmland originally settled by his family in the mid-1700s, Tillman clings to a patch of hillside less than a half mile to the south of us, inhabiting a paint-peeling frame house whose limestone foundation and commanding height hint at proud origins. He plows his field by horse, hauls timber by horse, and travels the Mid-Atlantic states competing in horse-pulling competitions. "Clyde Tillman's from a different century," one Swoopian told me, before he knew that we ourselves were heading to a different century.

On the one hand, I can't believe my good fortune to have an expert draftsman for a neighbor. On the other hand, I am totally intimidated. For the first few weeks of our project, my fear wins out. Even though I need Clyde Tillman's help, I can't bring myself to ask for it. He is the ultimate local, a farmer whose family has worked the same soil for centuries. I'm the ultimate outsider, living off a small bundle made off New York real estate while playing at old-fashioned farm life. I'll face him as soon as I have proven myself worthy.

The date of the party approaches, and still I avoid Belle and the broken harness, blaming my procrastination on chores and garden work. Fortunately, Jeanne is my second conscience. She sometimes drives our mail to the kitchen door, the engine of her Jeep Cherokee whining loudly as she punches it in reverse up our steep curving driveway. Her steering wheel is on the right side, and backing up puts her driver's side facing the house so that all she has to do is roll down her window and hand me the mail, which she does the day the coffee grinder we ended up having to order from an Ohio catalog serving the Amish arrives in a box too big for the mailbox.

"How's Belle?" she asks.

"As ornery as ever," I reply, holding the box and a few letters on top. "Still fat?"

"She's not fat, Jeanne. She's just big boned."

"You gotta work her," she says, shaking her head. Jeanne has also been chiding me for not cleaning Belle's hooves. "Are you picking up her feet?"

"Not yet," I reply. Jeanne's icy blue eyes bore into me, her impatient smile shouting, *Wimp!*

"You're gonna have to trim her hooves soon," she says. "I can give you the name of my farrier, but he's not gonna be happy if Belle won't let him work her feet. If she kicks him, it's your fault," she says, her Cherokee rolling forward. "Well, gotta run. It's Monday, you know." And then, as she speeds down the driveway, "You *better* start working that horse!"

"I will," I say, "as soon as I can get a handle on all these chores." But she is out of earshot, speeding off to the next mailbox.

Cₛₐₒ

Without exactly meaning to, I meet Clyde Tillman. I'm walking past his house one day, when I see him taping a hand-inked sign that reads "FOR SALE $1,200 OBO" on the driver's window of a caramel-colored, circa-1975 Thunderbird. Being on foot, I notice for the first time the squalor—sagging barns and metal-sided outbuildings; junk spilling from garage openings like nails from an overturned box; rusty farm plows, discs, and mowers drowning in thigh-high weeds. A brindled mutt, missing an eye and broad patches of its fur, explodes from its nap, barking hoarsely, charging me with hatred in its good eye. Just as I am about to spring to the hood of the T-bird, the dog jerks to a stop with a loud yelp, choked at the end of a chain.

Tillman ignores the dog *and* my reaction.

"Hello!" I say, trying to sound nonchalant.

Dressed in dirty navy work pants and shirt, his skin tan, leathery, and slightly oily, the old man moves about as if I didn't exist. His expressionless ham hock of a face reminds me of Anthony Hopkins playing Hannibal Lecter.

"Hello, Mr. Tillman." Nothing.

Just as I am about to yell out my name, he looks up and flashes a row of perfect white teeth, leaving me unsure whether he's glad to see me or going to bite. In a low, calm voice he says, "I hear you pulled your well pump."

"Yes," I say. "Yes, we did. We put in a hand pump."

He shakes his head, still smiling, drilling me with his eyes. He must have heard about our project.

The silence makes me nervous. "It's a good workout, pumping your own water," I say, instantly wishing I hadn't. What use, after all, would a farmer have for a workout?

"Let me get this straight," he says. "You took your indoor toilet and made it an outdoor toilet?"

"Yes."

He bursts out laughing.

I tell him about Belle and the wagon, but instead of asking him for help, I say, "I hope you'll get to meet Belle someday." After more awkward silence, I decide to leave.

"Nice to meet you," I say.

Tillman says nothing. He just turns and walks toward his house.

⁂

The morning of the party arrives, and it's clear I'm not driving Belle. It's only a couple miles. We'll walk and pull Luther in his little red wagon.

By lunchtime, the heat is crippling. Ten minutes in that red roasting pan would blister Luther's fair toddler skin. We abandon our plan, moping through our chores. At 4:30 P.M., I am splitting wood, when Bill Roberson drives up.

When the Robersons recently had us for dinner, serving us peanuts and beer before the meal in a room decorated with ebony carvings and batik prints—Peggy's "Africa room"—I realized how laughably wrong I had been in my presumptions about the people in the brick Cape Cod. A former high school math teacher, Bill grows daylilies and vegetables, makes applesauce, bakes, feeds stray cats, and takes care of his daughter's horse, Ebony, even though Sarah lost interest in Ebony years ago and is now teaching English in Japan. He is a gentle soul with placid blue eyes and an unhurried demeanor, the perfect foil for his energetic, intellectually voracious wife. Peggy, also a former teacher, reads anything she can get her hands on—that evening, she reached for a volume of Frost to find a poem about scythe mowing—but she's particularly fond of women writers and gushes about the contemporary southern novelist Lee Smith. I could hardly believe it when Peggy explained how after college she flew off to the Congo to teach for a year, and she was just as surprised to hear about my Kenya experience. To have *that* in common with our nearest Swoope neighbor was just plain weird. Drawn by the peace and quiet, Bill and Peggy have been in Swoope for more than three decades. They never knew the family that rented Trimbles Mill for the ten years before we arrived. Within a few weeks, however, they've taken to us, walking over nearly every day to say hello or drop off some treat. When they bake pies, Peggy makes the crust and Bill the filling, a perfect example of their complementary partnership.

"We'll keep Luther," says Bill, as I lower the axe and mop sweat from my face. "You and Heather go to the party." We're on again!

Now all I have to do is toss a bucket of cold water over my head and shave.

It is a mistake to hurry with a straight razor. Taking your time is dangerous enough, as I learned during my first couple of attempts. Fiddling for the proper grip and blade angle, I winced as the blade seemed to tug each hair out one by one, confirming Lord Byron's opinion of shaving as "a daily plague, which in the aggregate, may average on the whole with parturition," or birthing a child.

Now, as I sit at the picnic table facing my gentleman's tableau—shaving soap and brush, strop, razor, basin, face cloth, mirror propped against a bucket—my thoughts race out ahead to the party, where I mentally take my first sip of cool, craft-brewed beer. Back on earth, my hand makes a couple of passes from ear to jaw, and then—*ouch!*—an inch-long slice opens up below my right sideburn. That refocuses my attention but does nothing to steady my hand. By the time I'm done, a collection of fresh cuts have stained my T-shirt and shorts red and turned the basin water pink.

"*Ooowww*," Heather says, cringing at the blood-soaked tissue bits polka-dotting my face. I worry she might faint. The sight of blood does that to her. "Why put yourself through that torture?"

"I tried to grow a beard when I was in Africa," I say. "It didn't work."

"What do you mean it didn't work?" I can almost hear her next thought: *You don't have to do anything. It just grows.*

"It itched—and it was embarrassing," I say, explaining how the mustache-less growth made me look like an Amish farmer, which would actually be sort of fitting. My friends called it the Strip-O-Beard. Strip-O for short.

We hurry into our cleanest clothes, drop Luther at Bill and Peggy's, and we're off, pedaling our bicycles.

The ride is beautiful. As I coast down and around the bend past Jeanne's house, the valley suddenly spreads out before me. One by one, the cows lying along her wire fence haul themselves up and lumber off at the strange sight of a cyclist. A cloud of tiny black birds lift and bank in unison toward the long stretch of mountains. This is the fastest I have traveled in weeks—it's my first time over Jeanne's hill since we got rid of the car—and my heart soars to be free of the responsibilities of the farm.

I am so wrapped up in this new sensation that I don't bother to check on Heather, who I assume is experiencing her own private moments of elation.

Then I hear her.

"Looooogan," she calls faintly. I stop and turn. She is a stick figure on the horizon.

Bicycles in 1900 looked a lot like bikes today. Wheels, spokes, pedals, cranks, frames (the men's version and the women's), uncomfortable seats—all pretty much the same. Gearing up for the project, we searched for bikes that were old, but not yet collectible. Cheap, heavy, and single speed were our selling points, the kind of thing rusting in the corner of half the garages in America. Countless yard sales and junk shops turned up mostly BMX bikes or pink things with streamers dangling from the handgrips. Running out of time, we bought two circa-1970 bikes off eBay that arrived as piles of parts in shredded cardboard boxes. Neither worked very well. At the last minute, after paying considerably more money, I hauled a perky, fully restored 1950s cruiser home. It has whitewall tires and a basket, and because its tall frame better suits me, I pedaled off on it this afternoon while Heather mounted a little blue girl's bike with a rear hub whose ball bearings seem suspended in peanut butter.

"This thing is sticking," she says, exasperated and out of breath, once she catches up. "I had to pedal to get *down*hill."

"Let me see." We trade bikes and I stand on the pedals, pushing with all my strength yet still barely moving them in jerky arcs. She gets on the cruiser and zooms out ahead.

By the time we arrive at the party, I am walking—half pushing, half leaning on the little blue bike, sweat pouring down my face. Soaked, my cotton shirt clings to my chest and back. My khaki pants are tucked into my socks so they won't get gobbled up by the greasy chain. A clump of guests wearing sundresses and pressed shorts swivels to stare at us. From the looks on their faces, I gather we are the first to arrive without a car.

After the biking, I'm thirstier than ever. Searching for the beer, I survey the scene. A party tent shades long tables of food—green salads, Thai noodles, Mexican seven-layer dip, chips, and plenty of tofu dishes. The sweet sound of acoustic music rises from the front porch, where a guy strums a guitar and a woman rubs a washboard to keep time. A group of kids scampering by sends a pang of regret that we could not bring Luther. It's all a bit overwhelming. For three weeks, I have spent every waking hour hauling, splitting, pumping water, hoeing, milking, weeding, or catching snakes. We have only seen a few neighbors, never more than one or two simultaneously. Facing this smorgasbord, live music, and hordes of chatty, well-scrubbed people, I feel like a caveman who has just crashed a garden party.

At last, I'm staring wolfishly at two beers as if I have crawled off the Sahara instead of biking over from our farm.

I quaff half of one cup down and top it off at the keg before finding Heather and handing her the other. "I can't *tell* you how good this is," I say, taking another sip.

"What kind is it?" she says.

"I don't know. Something amber," I say, taking another gulp from the cup and then smiling at her with a foam mustache. I belch. "Pardon me."

"Go easy, Logan. We've only got an hour."

"Then we better get started," I say, taking another gulp. Never has a beer tasted so good, so cool, so rich. I survey the crowd, strangers mostly, and then raise the cup again. "I'm going for a refill."

After a few beers, Heather grabs my hand and tugs me toward a sloped lawn. "Let's go say hello to William and Shani." The newlyweds have just finished talking to an older man in dark shades and a Panama hat, when Heather says, "Congratulations! What a beautiful party."

"Hey, you two made it!" says William, wearing khakis and a powder-blue guayabera. His shoes are flour-free. "Where's the horse?"

"We rode bikes instead," I say, feeling the buzz of the alcohol in the gauzy thickening of my tongue. "Which is probably a good thing. I've never driven a horse drunk before."

"Yeah, drunk biking is so much safer," says Shani, and a guffaw slips from my mouth—a little too loudly, I gather from the look Heather gives me. I catch myself leering at Shani's clingy black dress and at the glitter sprinkled across her cleavage. "I hope you wore a helmet," she adds.

I almost explain that there were no bike helmets in 1900. But I'm here to have fun, dammit. Food, beer, acoustic music—they all existed a century ago. *Relax.*

I peel off to refill my beer, promising to get a plate and meet Heather. But I never make it. I bounce back and forth from keg to conversation, never eating a morsel, losing myself in the effortless plenty of it all. Everyone seems to have heard about our project, and everyone wants to know what it's like. *How do you buy groceries?* (We don't.) *What happens if you get sick?* (Don't know.) *Where's the horse and buggy?* (At home.) Frankly, I'm tired of yakking about it and really just want to enjoy myself. I wander over for another beer. As the sun sinks, the air temperature turns deliciously cool.

For the first time in three weeks I stop sweating.

At some point a train thunders past, a mere thirty yards from the food tent, on the same tracks that families like ours would have taken to town a century ago. Dogs slink away. Kids bolt to the fence to watch. Adults caught in mid-sentence smile self-consciously, pausing until the roar subsides. Closing my eyes, the pulsing thrust of the coal cars filling my head, it is easy to imagine myself in a world without automobiles, where the "iron horse . . . shaking the earth with his feet," as Thoreau once wrote, still electrifies and astonishes, is still the miracle of speed and human conveyance.

The last of the cars passes. I open my eyes. The roar echoes in my head, making me even woozier. *Is it darker suddenly?*

"Logan!" says Heather, appearing out of nowhere, an edge of panic to her voice. "Have you looked at the watch?"

"No."

"It's eight-thirty! We told Bill and Peggy we'd be there before eight. You've got to milk!"

"Shit! What are we going to do about that crappy bike?" I can't bear the thought of riding it home.

"Leave it," Heather replies, taking charge. "William said he'd lend us his bike. He's up in the shed now getting it ready."

A bare electric bulb lights the musty storage shed, which smells of cut grass and gasoline. William leans over an olive green mountain bike, furiously stroking a hand-pump, feeding air into the front tire. Sculpted from some high-tech alloy and tricked out with all sorts of gadgets— pump rack, water-bottle cages, speedometer—the bike has more gears than I can count on two hands. Just looking at it feels like sacrilege.

"Thanks, William, but we can't use that," I say.

"Logan! We've got to," interjects Heather. Outside, the sky is blackening. There is no moon to light our way. The goats are probably about to pop.

William keeps pumping. "Dammit!" he shouts, cradling his hand. Blood oozes from his knuckles where he has bashed them on the spokes. A problem with the pump has the laid-back baker riled. He pops the nozzle and bends to inspect the valve. Sweat drips from his cheeks. Grease smears his guayabera.

I stand there frozen, grappling with our choices. Walk or take the bike. As if emerging from a fog, I come to my senses: This is William's wedding night, and he's busting his ass to help us. We've already ruined his shirt. I don't want to do any more damage.

"William," I say, "Go find Shani. I'll do this." He hands me the pump. Swaying slightly, I fiddle and fuss, pressing the nozzle on and off the valve until, finally, a deeper hiss tells me air is entering the tire. I pump like a madman, sweating once again, racing the ticking seconds.

A crowd has gathered outside the shed. We say our thanks and dash past with the curtailed farewells of Cinderella fleeing the ball, only our piece-of-shit blue pumpkin has miraculously transformed into a swift olive-green chariot. In an attempt to make things right with our rules, I jam the bike into the lowest gear and suffer the slow, thigh-burning pedaling the whole way home.

The cry of the goats hits me when I top Jeanne's hill. I race down Trimbles Mill Road in the dark, navigating by the light of the Milky Way. I feel my way into the house for a match—barking my shin, feeling like I'm going to puke—and gather up my buckets with a clanking that only makes the goats bleat louder.

I milk by moonlight, drenched in sweat, my pants, which I meant to keep clean for special occasions, dusty, greasy, and wrinkled. Still, I've made it.

I put the goats to bed, call Belle into the barnyard, and latch the pasture gate behind her. I peek in on the hens, raising my lantern to cast light against the far wall, and am relieved to find all six huddled together on the wooden roost. I stop and listen. Voices, the rattling of the metal wagon. Heather and Luther on their way home.

♋

Not only am I no closer to driving the wagon, but I had to admit to William and Shani and everyone else I met at the party that, while technically we should have arrived by horse and buggy, I have no idea what the hell I'm doing. This wagon business has touched a nerve, stirring up insecurities about the authenticity—and meaningfulness—of our endeavor. We are, after all, *pretending* to live 100 years ago. After researching the history of technology and rural life in 1900, we created rules, our hunch being that by pretending in as historically accurate a way as possible, we will have accomplished something important by the end of the year. Some exceptions are justifiable—the use of sun screen, for instance, especially for lilywhite Luther, since today's ozone layer isn't as effective at blocking harmful UV rays as it was a century ago. Other exceptions smack of cheating. Not driving Belle is one of them. I can't just park her in the pasture because I'm scared.

Soon after, my chance at redemption arrives in a familiar green pick-up truck with Farm Use plates.

Tina Wilson, daughter of Joel the cowboy, who brought us the bucket of cherries, hands us a second party invitation, this one for her family's annual July cookout. Not only is it deeply satisfying to be included — we're still meeting our fellow Swoopians — but if I can deliver us there in a civilized fashion, not frantically pedaling kiddie bikes, then maybe I can salvage some of my pride. Most of the people at William and Shani's party were townies. The Wilsons' party promises to be a gathering of cattle farmers, including some of Swoope's oldest families. I *have* to drive the wagon.

Three days later — on July 4, a Wednesday — Heather, Luther, and I are eating breakfast outside at the picnic table: cornbread, the last of the oranges stored in the cellar, and eggs that Heather has poached to perfection using a splash of white vinegar and a canning-jar lid for an egg ring. The Wilsons' party is this weekend. After putting it off for a month, today I'm finally going to try to hitch Belle.

Just as I am draining my coffee and mustering up my courage, a white station wagon pulls into the driveway. Two guys get out. One is Chris, a young teacher from Baltimore who is apprenticing at a nearby pastured meat farm called Polyface. The other is a big, wild-haired stranger, and from the looks of his own Strip-O-Beard and clothes — tab-collar shirt, broadcloth trousers, suspenders, wide-brimmed straw hat — Amish. Except that his clothes are all white, and his pants have gaping holes in the knees, with ragged flaps hanging down. His name is David.

I fetch a couple of wooden chairs from the kitchen, and the pair joins us in the yard.

"So I hear you guys made your million in New York City and decided to try your hand at farming," says David with a roguish gleam in his eyes.

"Not exactly," I say, stiffening. I recognize the line. Joel Salatin, who runs Polyface, said the same thing with a grin on his face and a big chip on his shoulder when I first met him. It's hard to blame someone like Joel, who has spent his entire life farming in Swoope, for being skeptical of newcomers like us. But who is this guy? "Yeah, we lived in New York. Now we live here. We're trying to learn something about the old ways."

"This place must have cost you a bundle," he says, looking around. Chris shifts uncomfortably in his seat.

"You're a farmer?" Heather says, turning the attention to David.

"I know a thing or two about farming," he says, sounding like a cocky Gomer Pyle. "And a thing or two about the old ways." He, too, is a former Polyface apprentice, he says, and now he's back to help the Salatins prepare for a big weekend workshop that will draw would-be organic farmers from around the country. He mentions his family, the Yoders, in western Maryland. I peg him for an Amish rebel, out on his own among the "English."

I am not used to loitering in the morning, and today is an especially big day. "I need to go teach myself to drive my horse," I announce, standing and stacking the breakfast dishes. "You guys are welcome to come along if you'd like." As much as I enjoy Chris's company, I hope they will leave me to muddle through this alone.

"You've got a draft?" David booms. "I can show you how to drive."

"You know something about horses, too?" I say, skeptically.

"Sure do."

I look up at Belle, who stands beside the barn watching the goats with a look of disdain as they playfully butt one another, their big ears flopping. I don't like this guy one bit, but what else can I do?

"Come on," I say, and the three of us walk to the shed.

David scoops the neglected harness off the floor, tosses it expertly over his shoulder, and marches across the barnyard to face Belle.

"What's her name?" he asks.

"Belle."

"Hello, Belle," he says, stroking her neck. "We're going to take a little drive." Then to me, "Looks like she could use it. She's a real pig."

In fifteen minutes, Belle is harnessed and hitched to the blue wagon. All those wayward straps now stand at attention, stretched tight and buckled in all the right places. Her lead rope is tied to a fence post. The belly strap that broke during our tussle the day she arrived is fixed, bound with bailing twine fed through holes in the leather that David punched with a nail. Things are looking up.

"Where's your crop?" David asks.

"My what?"

"Your whip."

"I don't have one." He shakes his head and hops the board fence, snapping off a sapling and waving it in the air—*whish! whish!*—like a fencer testing his foil.

I yell to Heather, who is down at the house with Luther. "We're going to drive her! Meet us down front."

It is clear to David how little I know about horses. Still, when we climb up on the springboard bench, he hands me the reins. *Okay,* I think. *Stay calm.* I've done this part. Gee means *go right.* Haw, *go left.*

The problem is the hill. Marshall and I started on flat ground. Now we're pointed down our steep gravel drive, the one that skirts the river bluff. Just on the other side of that three-board fence is a forty-foot freefall to the shallows below.

My hands tremble. "Come up," I say. Belle just stands there. "Come up!" I yell. Nothing.

With a flick of his switch, David pops Belle's big rump. The horse bolts forward, eyes wide, snapping our heads back. We bound down the driveway, the steel treads chewing up the gravel. With no steering wheel or foot pedals, I feel completely helpless. I panic and reach for the brake lever, hoping the rubber-faced mallet pressing on the wheels will slow us, but as my hand shoots out I drop the right rein. Belle veers left, straight for the fence, and I picture us smacking into it and pitching over the edge of the bluff. David snatches up the strap and yanks. "Gee up, Belle!" She swerves right, straightens, and barrels down the paved part of the driveway to the bottom, where Chris, Heather, and Luther wait on the steps.

"Whoa!" I scream. We keep rolling. I hold one line, and David holds the other. We both pull. "Whoooaaa!"

Belle stops. David laughs and lets out a whoop. "I forgot how much fun this could be."

"Forgot?" I say, flustered and still wondering whether I should trust him. "How long's it been?"

He ignores me, focusing instead on a horsefly that has been bothering Belle. It lands on David's arm. *Slap.* "I got him, Belle!" he says with a manic intensity, raising his hand to reveal a splat of blood. Smearing the blood on his white pants, he bellows, "Let's go!"

Chris jumps in the back. Once again, I hold the reins. "Come up," I say, and this time we set off down Boy Scout Lane at an anticlimactic, yawn-inducing walk, just as I had done a month earlier on our family ride. It does not occur to me that you would want to go much faster in a wagon until David grabs the reins. "Here," he says. "Let me show you." With the impatience of a lead-foot who finally breaks free from a clot of traffic, he snaps one of the long leather lines with a flick of his arm. "Trot, Belle!" Every muscle in her body pricks, and she runs, and even I know we're going faster than a trot.

"The guy didn't teach me that command," I say, grabbing the thin iron bench railing.

"You've got to have a way to tell her to go faster." Again, David snaps leather against haunch, urging her forward, as if we are fleeing a posse. Whenever she relaxes, he pops her with the sapling. At the end of the lane, we turn around. Soon, we're crunching to a halt beside our driveway. "Come on, Heather!" I say.

Chris jumps out to stay with Luther. Heather crouches in the wagon's bed. We shoot down the road in the opposite direction, David driving.

"I had no idea Belle could move so fast," Heather says.

David focuses on the road, bantering to the horse. *Trot, Belle. Come on, Belle.*

"Go right," I say when we reach the stop sign at Trimbles Mill Road. "There's somebody I want to see."

The minute we touch driveway gravel, Tillman's dog goes wild. I worry that Belle will spook, but she doesn't let the chained yapping bother her. Good horse.

Inside the house, an old woman peels back a curtain and leans on a walker, peering at us. Ellen, his wife.

And asleep in a lawn chair inside one of his junky garage openings, legs splayed, fingers laced and propped on his chest, is the enigma. He wakes from his Fourth-of-July nap to the strange sight of three beaming people—one dressed like an Amish ice-cream man on the skids—aboard a bright blue wagon. Easing his stiff body out of the chair, the old farmer ambles over to a huffing, lathered Belle.

"Hello, Mr. Tillman!" I say, trying to contain my excitement. "Bet you didn't expect to see me drive up."

He says nothing, instead circles horse and wagon slowly.

"What do you think of her?" Heather asks. No response. Then, as if he might be deaf, she repeats, "WHAT DO YOU THINK OF THE HORSE?"

Ignoring her, Tillman zeros in on the broken strap David lashed together with green bailer twine. "Have you been to see that feller in Dayton who has the buggy shop?" His voice is quiet, almost sweet.

"Burkholder?" I ask, remembering the Mennonite's shop from when we were searching for a wagon.

"I think he makes a single piece of leather you can attach here and run under the horse. You might ask him to fix you up one."

"I don't have a way to get to him anymore. The twine will have to do for a while."

David is mercifully quiet during the visit. He's eyeing Tillman's training sled piled high with slabs of concrete. Even though Tillman's horses are nowhere to be seen, one can only imagine what beasts they must be to pull that load.

I turn to Tillman. "Well, what do you think of her?"

"She's fat."

Belle is getting antsy. It's time to go. Leaving Tillman's, I take the reins, trying out the new command as soon as we are out of his driveway. "Trot, Belle," I say, and she obeys, settling into a nice pace that swiftly delivers us home. David hops down. He and Chris are due back at the Salatin farm.

"I appreciate your help," I say, shaking David's hand, my hard feelings having melted away in the excitement. He feeds me some last-minute pointers: relax, focus, give her commands in a soft, objective voice rather than an emotion-drenched plea. Reinforce commands with the flick of the crop, and soon I won't need the crop. Except for the crop part, it's good parenting advice.

"And carry lots of bailer twine," he shouts, before getting into Chris's car.

Once again, I'm left to unharness Belle. Thanks to David, though, this time I am prepared.

The party is three days away.

捴者

Goat's milk is naturally homogenized. Its cream does not rise to the top. Knowing that, and still needing to make butter, we bought a hand-crank cream centrifuge that draws out the little globules of milk fat by spinning the milk at something like 9000 revolutions per minute. One morning, I oil up the cheap Russian-made contraption and anchor it to the picnic table. Luther stands nearby, watching.

"The milk goes here," I say, pouring six entire quarts into a funnel the size of a big popcorn bowl balanced on top. "And I turn this handle to spin the milk." Luther's eyes widen as the gears begin to hum.

Hunched over the table, I turn harder and faster. Thick cream dribbles out of one spout and skim milk trickles from another. I crank harder. The gears buzz louder, jars and metal bowls rattling on the table. Faster and faster I turn. The milk licks at the funnel's rim. The cream drools. *Why is this taking so long?* I crank even faster, but when I shift my weight trying to get comfortable, my free hand accidentally tips the basin. BLAM! Milk explodes everywhere with 9000 rpms worth of momentum.

"Aaarggghhh!" I scream. Heather rushes through the washroom door, bursting into laughter when she sees me covered from chin to boots in dripping milk. I pick up the upturned cream bowl and slam it on the table.

We have been repeating the don't-cry-over-spilled-milk adage to Luther, who no longer has the security of his spill-proof sippy cups. At lunch, after I've cleaned up, Luther makes a hand-cranking motion and a noise that sounds like ZZZrrrZZZrrr. "Daddy spill milk," he says. "Daddy mad."

"I didn't cry," I say, "but I shouldn't have gotten angry."

That same day, after reading the driving chapters of Henry William Herbert's 1859 manual *Horses, Mules, and Ponies and How to Keep Them*, I prepare for a solo run. I need to practice before risking the necks of my family.

It's afternoon by the time I can hitch the wagon, and I'm hot, tired, and in a foul mood. After the milk explosion, I exhausted myself mowing the grass around the house using our rusty reel mower. Because I waited too long between mowings, the grass was sagging with thick seed heads. I shoved and yanked the mower until the grass was low enough to deter snakes. Then I collapsed into the hammock and fell asleep.

I woke disoriented, soaked in sweat, and not feeling up to the drive.

Now, after haltering Belle, I cannot remember the safety knot David taught me, the one he used to tether Belle to the fence, the one that, if she panics, will slip free with a jerk before she splinters the boards or breaks her neck. My rope fiddling makes Belle nervous. When I return from fetching the harness, the lead rope drags the ground.

"Oh, Belle, you untied my knot," I say, faking self-assurance, bracing for her to jerk away. But she stands as I retie the knot, and stands longer as I heave the harness over her massive head and fidget with the straps.

The tricky part is getting started. Belle stood for David. Now, as I plant my foot on the iron step to hoist myself onto the driver's bench, Belle starts walking. "Whoa!" I yell. Jumping back to the ground, I yank the reins. She fights them, twisting her neck while still walking. I leap onto the moving wagon just before we plunge down the steep driveway. This time, though, I keep my cool, pulling hard and steady on the lines and repeating "whoa" until she stops halfway down the driveway. Good girl.

"I won't be long," I yell to Heather, who pokes her head out of the kitchen door.

"Logan, please be careful," she says. Heather has been worrying about a horse accident ever since learning that the poet Maxine Kumin barely survived a severed spinal cord after being thrown from a buggy by a bolting horse. Kumin's luminous essays about raising chickens, tending garden, and mending fences sustained Heather through our days of preparation. But the horse incident scared the hell out of her. And me, too.

"I'll be careful. Don't worry," I say, though we both know that on these narrow, unpaved country roads, frequented by thrill-seeking teenagers and impatient townies, my safety is not entirely in my own hands. And with Boy Scout camp now in session, traffic has picked up considerably.

I pass Bill and Peggy's brick house at a swift clip. With a snap of the sapling crop, Belle remembers her new command. Bill is kneeling in his tomato patch. He raises his head and smiles. "Can't stop!" I holler.

I cross the Middle River on a bridge with no railings. I prod Belle up and around a steep section of gravel road. Flying down the other side is frightening. "Easy, Belle," I say, tugging at the reins. I pull back on the

73

brake lever and slip it into the first notch, the rubber mallet creating just enough resistance to keep the wagon from pushing Belle. Another trick David taught me. When the road flattens out again, I release the lever.

Suddenly, Belle heaves to a stop in the middle of the road. She rears, tossing her head back and forth. "What's going on, Belle? Come up!"

She balks. The wheels grind and twist on the gravel as she tries to back up. Something is spooking her. But I see no dogs, no cars, no tractors. Maybe it's the old shed looming into view around the edge of her blinders. I urge her forward with the crop, tugging left and right to keep her headed straight. Past the shed, she quiets. A large dark mass so close to the road must have confused her. Bombproof, huh? What about shed-proof? Though my heart thumps wildly, the wagon is soon back in a steady rhythm.

The ride home is uneventful — until I reach Trimbles Mill Road, where a maroon minivan roars up behind me. With my inexperienced hands holding the reins, Belle has gee'd and haw'd all over the road. Now the driver of the van honks impatiently for me to let him pass. Keeping my eyes on the road ahead, I stick my hand out and press down on the air, as if patting a child's head. *Take it easy.* My driveway is in sight. If he would just be patient, he'd be safely past in thirty seconds. No such luck. When I weave right, he hits the accelerator and speeds by on the left, kicking up dust. Belle stays cool, but the move scares me, and I throw my shoulders and arms up in the what-the-fuck shrug I used to give cheeky cab drivers in New York. "Asshole!" I shout as the van tears past, a Boy Scouts of America sticker glaring back at me from the bumper.

Back in the barnyard, tired but satisfied, I begin unbuckling harness straps. Belle stands for me without having to be tethered, and I compliment her in soft tones. Good, Belle.

CRED

The day before the Wilsons' party, David shows up at our place. Same ragged white outfit. Same straw hat. Same horsefly blood smeared on his pants leg. We are headed out for a family walk to gather blackberries, and we invite David to tag along. Grateful for his help, we're also glad for his company.

The wild-eyed stranger seems mellower today. David's edgy, overbearing personality has shrunk into pudgy amiability. With Luther perched on my shoulders, we walk up the gravel road into the woods behind our farm. As we stroll, David teaches us the names of trees and plants and recounts stories about his family, the Yoders, and their horses. Approaching the fence where the berry bushes droop with fat, purple fruit, Heather turns to David and says, "So, what was it like to grow up Amish?"

"The Yoders?" he says. "I didn't grow up with them. I just lived on their farm for a couple years."

"Then where *did* you grow up?" she asks, surprised.

"Me? I grew up in Chevy Chase, Maryland."

David—David Fleig, we learn—is on an extended odyssey not unlike our own. A product of suburbia, he was raised in the tony D.C. bedroom community by an attorney mom ("trusts and wills," he says) and a NASA scientist dad. After reading the entire Wendell Berry oeuvre, Fleig dropped out of college ("my parents freaked") and chose a life of old-fashioned farming as an alternative to a career and consumerism. He is an itinerant laborer, though not in the way an orchard owner—or a Mexican who picks his apples—might define one. Educated, bohemian, accustomed to money (but seemingly broke at the moment), David is a globe-hopping rustic wannabe who has signed on for stints with the Salatins here in the Shenandoah Valley, a farm in Iowa, and a dairy in New Zealand. He once made a pilgrimage to Tasmania to meet Bill Mollison, the founder of the sustainable agriculture movement known as Permaculture. A couple of seasons with the Yoders explain the clothes and his winning way with draft horses.

"What do your parents think of your choices now?" I ask.

"Well, let's see," he says. "I'm twenty-seven, and I've been doing this since I was about twenty, so I guess they've had time to adjust. But they tend to see a graduate degree as a safety net. If you've got one, you can always get a job."

David removes his hat and holds it as a church usher would an offering plate, resourcefully filling it with berries, the way Winnie the Pooh does with his nightcap in one of Luther's board books, when the bear finds himself in a berry bramble with no pail. Come to think of it, now that his hard edges have softened, the ruffled David sort of reminds me of the Pooh Bear.

I ask David what he is currently reading. Munching one blackberry for every two he caches away, he peers at me and says, "You've heard of Peter Drucker?"

"He's an economist or something, right?"

"A management guru," David corrects, warming to the subject. "You see, I've got this idea that thinking is like a math problem. I really like how this Drucker guy thinks, but I don't believe in the numbers he's plugging into his equation. In fact, I disagree completely with what he feels is important in life."

David has a dream, and Drucker, along with the far-flung farming experiences, figures into it. One day David hopes to run a grass-based dairy, which is a more radical concept than it sounds given the predominance these days of mega-dairies, where penned-up cows gorge themselves on dirt-cheap, government-subsidized grain. But that's not all. The dairy would be the cash producer for a craft school. Not an ordinary craft school, mind you, but a craft school for ex-cons. This dairy/ex-con craft school would be close to D.C. (maybe they'd matriculate ex-pols, too?), where there would presumably be a market for the milk, cheese, and butter, as well as the ex-cons' crafts. He'd hire a marketing teacher to instruct the ex-con artisans how to sell their wares. There would be an on-site mall for retail sales. Plus, they would give tours. What a wacky plan. I love it!

"I need start-up money," David says, his enthusiasm dampening. "A lot of it."

As we set out for home, David places his hat, now empty but berry-stained, back on his head. I marvel at how this disheveled, enigmatic stranger's quest reminds me of our own. (Heather and I have even talked about starting our own boutique goat-cheese business when we're back in the twenty-first century.) Even more baffling is how David emerged from nowhere just when we needed him. Who knows if he can turn his romantic vision into practical reality, but you gotta love the guy for dreaming big.

On the afternoon of the Wilsons' party, we take turns bathing in the feed tank under the maple tree. I slice my face all to hell shaving with the straight razor. Heather comes away smelling like vinegar. We pack extra cloth diapers and pins, a cole slaw made from a garden cabbage, and a bundle of bailer twine. And then we are off, the wagon rattling out of the driveway with Luther wedged between Heather and me on the wooden bench.

I sit tall in the wagon, confidently addressing Belle. Since that first day, when I drove Heather and Luther down Boy Scout Lane, I have doubted whether I would ever drive them again. Though I am by no means buddies with Belle, I do feel more comfortable in her presence, and I sense a change in her attitude toward me.

Belle shies slightly at the first Middle River bridge. A scream slips from Heather's mouth as Belle swerves toward the railing, but I coax the horse and wagon safely across. Belle is preoccupied by the flies buzzing her ears. Her tail swishes nonstop, and every time she waves the flies off her head, the wagon veers toward the drainage ditch running alongside the road. Heather tries to mask her nervousness with conversation. Her words pour out. "I wonder who we'll see. I hear it's a pretty serious farming crowd. Lots of talk about the weather and cattle." And then to Luther, "I bet there will be some other children there, sweetie. Won't that be fun?"

It's never easy being the passenger, even in a cushioned, temperature-controlled car interior. But here's Heather, five feet off the ground in a bouncing and weaving buggy pulled by an animal, trying to hold our son while not sliding off the narrow wooden seat. I, at least, hold the reins, which gives me some sense of control. Heather is entirely at the mercy of the horse, a rickety wooden-wheeled box, and her inexpert husband. She keeps looking down and gasping every time the thin wheels skirt the ditch.

Then I see it—the shed, looming up ahead. *Come on, Belle*, I think, edging her to the right, hoping it will escape her view.

Yet when the weathered building leaps into her line of vision, she pitches a fit, stopping dead in her tracks and rearing her head. "Easy, Belle!" I say, tugging at the opposite line to keep her straight in her traces. Whinnying loudly and snorting, she wags her head back and forth as I struggle to hang on to the reins.

"Logan!" Heather shrieks as Belle yanks us toward the ditch.

"Come up! Belle! Come up!" *I have to get her past the shed. No turning. She'll flip us on this narrow sloped road.* "Unnnhhh, Daddy!" Luther cries. The bench is cramped, and as my arms flail, my elbow slams into Heather. She grips Luther to her chest and clutches the side of the bench with her other hand. Belle yanks right. The wheels groan under the torque.

"Come UP, Belle!" I snap the rein against her flank. "Yah! Yah! Get moving." She walks—jerky, snorting, still waving her head—but she moves. "Good girl. Easy, girl." Once again, as soon as the shed is behind her, she calms down. "Good, Belle. That was just a shed. A shed can't hurt you. Everything is alright," I say, gentling her. "Everybody okay?" I say to Heather.

"Logan," Heather gasps. "That scared the shit out of me."

"It scared me, too. I'm sorry. Belle's fine around cars and barking dogs, but for some reason that shed really spooks her." I pause. We've gone too far not to continue. "Maybe we should talk about what to do, you know, if things really go bad." Shades of Maxine Kumin.

"What do you mean?" Heather asks.

"It's hard to tip a big wagon like this, but it could happen. The key is not to panic." The thing to do, we decide, is hang on until the last minute and then jump. Fine for us, I think, but what about Luther?

Keeping Belle at a safe trot, I drive on, praying we see no cars.

φφφ

Because a cattle guard at the Wilsons' front gate prevents Belle from crossing, we're headed for a white cottage down the road, the home of Ishtar Abell and her grown daughter, Leasha.

The first time we visited Ishtar's, we sat on her broad front porch, sipping lemonade, serving ourselves crustless egg salad sandwich halves (peanut butter for Luther) from china platters, and feeling immediately at ease. A plump, jovial woman in her early seventies, whose thick glasses can't hide the twinkle in her eye, Ishtar hails from the family that founded the *Baltimore Sun* newspaper. At some point she and the family fortune parted ways, not that money and social status seem to matter much to this free spirit. Ishtar is a swimmer, a reader of poetry (she named her cat Edna St. Vincent Millay). She has lived all over, including the Australian bush during the 1960s, when her then-husband oversaw the creation of a secret U.S. government satellite tracking station. When she learned of our 1900 project, instead of giving us advice (like so many well-meaning people had), she asked questions. "It's so sensible," she said finally. I could have kissed her.

And then there's her name.

For the first six months of her life, Ishtar had no name. She was simply baby Abell. "I have two older sisters," she explained. "My daddy had been hoping for a boy. When I was born, he told my mother, 'You raise the other two. This one is mine.'" Her father spent much of his time at the family's country estate, hunting and entertaining. One day, he and some buddies were having cocktails and listening to the phonograph. A piece of classical music caught his ear. One of the men recognized it from an opera he had seen called *Ishtar*. "'That's it!' Daddy said. They all carried me down to the river and christened me Ishtar." Babylonian goddess of love.

I make a hard left into Ishtar and Leasha's gravel driveway and hop down, thankful to be back on solid ground. I stand at Belle's head, holding her halter, stroking her nose and murmuring, while Heather climbs down and then helps Luther. "Hello dears!" Ishtar trills. She and Leasha bound out of the house bearing drinks—highball glasses, lemon wedges, tinkling ice—effusive, giggling, full of hugs and warm shoulder pats, as if we were Lindbergh arrived in France. Their festive mood lightens ours, and by the time Leasha and I have unharnessed Belle and latched her inside Leasha's fenced five acres with her horse, Pete, I feel ready to face the party crowd.

The party crowd—five dozen or so people of all ages, half of them wearing big starchy cowboy hats—sits sipping iced tea in aluminum lawn chairs on the Wilsons' oversized driveway. It's clear that unlike us urban transplants, farmers don't like grass. They plant it, fertilize it, run cattle on it, make hay with it, but when it comes to relaxing, they prefer clean, dependable concrete.

This is a B.Y.O.C. party: Bring Your Own Chair. Having nothing at home lighter or more portable than a ladderback, we must borrow extras from the Wilsons, taking our place in front of the three-bay garage. Ishtar pulls two beers out of her cooler. "The label says *Since 1829*," she whispers, "so I figured these were okay." Inside the garage, folding tables groan with dishes. Heather's mixing bowl of slaw looks lonely among all the meat-and-cheese casseroles. Wild with glee, Luther runs after some bigger children, slowing down long enough to gobble down a hamburger and a hot dog. Heather may be a vegetarian, but Luther and I never entirely swore off meat. He is fascinated by the charcoal grills. Despite repeated warnings, he comes away screaming, his hand blistered.

I go easy on the beers, preoccupied about driving us home. And still I goof up. By the time we walk back through the white pines lining Ishtar and Leasha's drive, objects begin to dissolve into darkness. Belle whinnies, nose over the fence. Leasha helps me hitch her. As we are saying our goodbyes, a white pickup truck eases into the driveway. Poking his head out the window, a man faking a hick accent says, "Excuse me, sir, but did you know that your headlights are out?"

It's Michael Godfrey and his wife Victoria, who own a nearby estate called Wheatlands.

"I'll have that looked at," I say, playing along but anxious to get home.

"Seriously," he says, losing the accent. "We're worried about you driving that thing home in the dark. How about we give you an escort?"

"We'll manage fine," I say, tired of feeling like a charity case. The Wilsons' chairs. Ishtar with her 1829 beers. Everyone means well, and I'm grateful, but in 1900, we would have had no escort. *We're the ones who put ourselves in this predicament. We'll get ourselves out.*

Heather whispers, "The ride over was scary enough in the broad daylight. Let's follow them."

"We insist, Logan," Victoria says from the passenger side.

Feeling ganged up on, I'm about to repeat my refusal, when reality hits me. Without headlights—or taillights or dashlights or running lights—how exactly will we manage? We can't walk home. Luther's almost asleep.

"Okay," I say. "Lead the way."

We follow the red glow of their taillights as they creep over the gravel road, up and down hills, around turns. In the darkness, Belle ignores the shed, much to our relief. A car speeds up behind us—probably someone else leaving the party—and then brakes, and I shudder at the thought of what might have happened had we been alone in the dark. At Boy Scout Lane, Michael stops and rolls down his window.

"Can you make it from here?"

"We'll be fine," I say.

"If you guys ever need anything, you know where we are."

As I urge Belle up the road and into our driveway, I hear the goats bleating. I've done it, driven Belle. I'm relieved, but the accomplishment feels diminished somehow—by having to park at Ishtar's and walk, by needing an escort home. How long will we have to rely on the help of those still in the twenty-first century to get by in our pretend 1900? Still facing an hour or more of milking and other chores before I can sleep, I drive Belle up to the moonlit barn and begin unbuckling straps, the cries of the goats puncturing the darkness.

CHAPTER FIVE
Waiting for Rain

t is a July afternoon. I am in the garden with Luther, while Heather bathes herself in the metal watering trough, when the sky to the north turns black and the wind tousles the trees lining the steep riverbank. Gusts stampede through the valley like a herd of invisible animals, shoving cornstalks to the ground, shredding beet greens. As the clouds boil, my body tingles from a mix of trepidation at what could be a tornado—neighbors still talk of the twister that blew through a few seasons back—and desire. I want rain like I've never wanted rain in my life.

The skies have been teasing us. Nights, we lie sweating on bedsheets, the wind building, clouds huddling in constipated clumps over North Mountain, blotting out the moon. Thunder rumbles, fat drops drum the tin roof. I finally doze, expecting a downpour, dreaming of puddles between garden beds. But we wake to find nothing, just the drone of summer insects, a sweltering stinkbug funk. Along our freshly planted rows, the dark evidence of our night-watering is gone, the tender shoots facing yet another day of relentless heat from the sun. We feel absolutely helpless.

Our garden is dying of thirst. The cucumbers and squash are stunted. The corn is tassling prematurely. The tomato plants are brown, speckled, and shriveling, the new fruit ruined by end rot. All our printed sources say our vegetables need an inch of water a week. In the past three weeks, nothing. Bone dry. Before that, the rare thundershower. Though I've been fooled before, these clouds are darker, more resolute. Hope swells.

"Look, a storm!" I say to Luther, who has been following me around, dragging an empty metal bucket. I make the sound of rain and wind and tickle his belly until a smile spreads across his face. Ever since the spring, when the loud cracks and booms and bright flashes of a thunderstorm made him scream hysterically, Heather and I have tried to reassure him any time the thunder growls.

"What does the thunder say?" I ask.

"Here comes the rain!"

"That's right," I say, hoisting him onto my hip. "The plants are thirsty." I turn to Heather, who crouches in the tub, rinsing soap from her hair with an enamel cup. Her eyes are closed, and I stare longingly for a moment at the suds slipping down her neck and back, over her breasts. We've both been on edge lately because of the drought, among other things. Though these days I'm physically closer to Heather than ever before—both of us at home working side by side—in other ways, I've never felt so distant from her. Looking back at the sky, I say, "You better finish up before the lightning hits."

The county is well below the annual average rainfall. Neighbors bring it up whenever they visit, since here in farm country, weather is more than small talk. Now that it matters to us, we've joined the conversation.

Rain worship is new to me. Like most children, I grew up singing, *Rain, rain, go away, come again some other day*. Rain just doesn't matter when you eat out of supermarket cans, boxes, and bags. I believed the weatherman when he badmouthed rain for ruining weekends, spoiling sporting events, and canceling holiday parades. It's part of our sunny American ethos. Who needs rain when you've got sprinkler systems and cheap municipal water to keep lawns and perennial borders green?

Suddenly, *we* do. We're tapped into the ground water, but even with an army of laborers forming a bucket brigade we would be out of luck. Something's wrong with the pump. It quits after lifting a couple dozen gallons.

Inside the house, I rush around in preparation, covering the firewood box on the porch, lowering windows. Glancing at the churning thunderheads through Luther's window, I think, *This time it's got to rain!* For the first time ever, I understand the desperation that could drive people to dance for rain. Instead of watering the sprouts, tonight I hope to go to bed early and let the drumming of the rain on the roof lull me to sleep.

By dinner time, no rain. The wind rattles the tin roof, but no rain. I light the lanterns early. Heather puts Luther down upstairs, and I scrub dishes in the washroom. Still no rain. Then the clouds part, and the sky brightens. By the time I milk at 9:00 P.M., the wind has fizzled, and stars blink down from a polished sky.

"Don't get too comfortable," Heather says, when I plop down at the kitchen table after carrying the strained milk to the basement. "We've still got to water."

"Why won't it just rain?" I say, laying my head on my arms.

"It's got to," she says. "Some day."

⋐⋛⋑

The drought is not our only problem. Critters have declared war on our garden. Tiny green caterpillars are devouring our cabbages. Beetles munch the leaves of our potato plants. Nearly every morning when I step outside to pee, the same rabbit cocks its head and freezes between the rows of white-runner beans. And every morning I chuck a stone to chase it off, walking the rows like bitter old Mr. McGregor inspecting for damage. Dropping to my hands and knees, I stuff dirt clods in rodent holes in the furrows.

"The bugs are killing us," I say to Heather one morning, when she joins me in the garden after cooking the day's meals.

She stares down at my pink-stained fingers. "What *is* that?"

"Bug guts. Look," I say, turning over potato plant leaves until I find a cluster of beetle larvae, squeezing them between my fingers. *Pop.* Pink drops splatter her thigh.

"Gross, Logan."

I am obsessed. Any time I pass by the garden—to milk, pump water, split firewood—I detour up and down the straw paths popping beetle

85

larvae. If I see the striped-shelled adult beetles, I dispatch them with a cockroachy crunch. When the Japanese beetles arrive, I squeeze them, too. But soon the Jap-beetle advance party is joined by thousands of munching, procreating beetles, and squeezing begins to feel futile. It's maddening. First they chew through our two elm trees. Then I catch them swarming the branches of the young pear, apple, and cherry trees we planted. They turn leaves to lace in a matter of hours. Without chemicals, we have to defend our garden however we can, even bare-handed.

Heather, struggling to keep up with the cooking, cleaning, and much of the childcare, is of a different mind. "Do you really think that does any good?" she says one afternoon, as I squeeze a bug between my fingers.

"We've got to do *something*."

"You spend all your free time chasing bugs, and meanwhile there are weeds everywhere."

"If we want this garden to produce," I say, "we've got to find the time to do both—weed and kill bugs."

"There isn't any extra time, Logan. It's not like we're sitting around reading magazines. We get up in the dark and work past dark just to keep up, and I still can't manage to stay on top of the laundry. Do you know that I haven't worn underwear for five days because it's all dirty?"

"You've got to prioritize better," I say. "Set aside an afternoon for laundry. Tell me when you want to do it, and I'll take Luther all afternoon. I'll let you get the laundry done."

"Prioritize! Me? You're the one running around every five minutes squeezing fucking bugs."

I don't help matters by spending an afternoon holed up in the shed making a butterfly net. Ever since I learned that the little white butterflies flitting around the garden lay the eggs that hatch into the green worms that shit tiny green turds—*frass*, it's called—as they blissfully burrow deep into the folds of our cabbages, I've been determined to stop them. Given our plan to store the cabbages for winter, stowaway larvae will mean ruin.

At first I crawled along the rows peeling back the leaves and popping the caterpillars like I popped the beetle larvae, leaving my hands covered in green guts and frass and reeking of soured cabbage. Then I started going for the butterflies, nearly throwing my elbow joint out trying to bat them with my hand. I tried swinging a broom at them, then a mop. Far too slow. I needed a proper tool.

As I exit the shed, bearing a net made from burlap wired to a forked branch, I can't help but feel a little self-satisfied—for the prescience to bring along a roll of burlap (it seemed appropriate and useful) and for my castaway resourcefulness.

Luther loves it. "Mine! Mine!" he screams, grabbing for the crude implement.

"Not now, Luther. First, Daddy's going to get those butterflies," I say, creeping around the garden, swishing wildly, a mad grin plastered to my face.

Heather shakes her head, and I don't want to give her the satisfaction of knowing that I know how ridiculous she finds me, so I continue clowning for Luther.

"You find the white butterflies, Luther. I'll *get* them. We'll be a team."

"Ungh! Ungh!" says Luther, pointing at a white fleck slowly fanning its wings on a cabbage plant.

Swaaat! The butterfly flits away. The cabbage head rocks on its stalk.

Other butterflies elude me, too, jerking away at the last second as if attached to invisible puppet strings, their effortless flight like a winged smile. Soon I'm bounding over the furrows, swinging furiously at fluttering white grins. It's like trying to hit a feather with a baseball bat. My clumsy feet are doing more damage than the larvae. I drop the net in frustration and hurl a handful of dirt at the next butterfly I see, knocking it to the ground. As it lies there stunned, I pounce. *Gotcha!* It's in my fist. Then between my fingers. Pop!

My antics are driving Heather and me further apart. It's not just my lame attempts at pest control that try her patience. It's my compulsive behavior. She grumbles that she's in charge of cooking, dishes, and laundry, and I am in charge of "special projects." The butterfly net. A bathing platform I've begun. Fun, creative work that involves hammers, wire cutters, and fresh air. But I work my ass off splitting wood, pumping water, mowing, and putting up with Belle's attitude and the whining goats. Plus, I do my share of dishes and take care of Luther plenty. She shouldn't complain so much.

Having been without butter now for weeks, I decide one hot July morning to give the cream separator another try. I set up under the maple tree, bolting the contraption to the picnic table and laying out all the bowls needed to catch and hold the cream and skim milk. I crank and crank, bending uncomfortably, switching to the other hand when one gets tired, careful not to upset the funnel again. When the skim milk in one catch basin nears the rim, I reach for the replacement bowl. It's not here. I forgot it.

"Heeaather!"

"Yeah?" she says from inside the kitchen, where she has spent several hours steaming beat greens, frying zucchini, boiling eggs, and baking cornbread and a cobbler with fresh-picked blackberries.

"Grab the bowl by the wooden drying rack." Pause. "You better hurry." She appears, sweat-soaked hair plastered to her forehead, flour dusting her apron, and silently hands me the bowl.

Soon it's time to refill the giant funnel on top. Only I forgot the milk. It's still warming in a pot on the stove.

"I need more milk. NOW!"

"It would have helped to talk about this first!"

"You knew I was going to be separating cream today," I say, still cranking the handle.

"We did NOT talk about it, Logan!" Luther, who has been following her, grabbing at her apron, mimics her roar. She brings the milk and without saying a word pours it in the basin on top while I crank away.

When the separating is done, I take the quart of disappointingly thin cream and disappear into the cool basement for an hour, trying to make butter by steadily shaking the jar. But it doesn't work. All that trouble and no butter. The rest of the day, we move through our chores in brooding silence, nursing grudges.

Though we experience small pleasures—ladling cool drinking water from our crock on hot days, finding letters from friends and family in the mailbox, cutting a crisp stalk of broccoli for dinner—our days are marked by frustration and a growing bitterness toward one another. I was convinced that our animosity during the preparation period would melt away as soon as the project started, but things have only gotten worse. I remember something else Meryl from Heather's office said when she heard our 1900 plans: *You two must really like each other*. We did, once. We worked to build an equal partnership, agreeing that our marriage ideal was to remain best friends. What has happened to us?

Have Heather and I changed so much since we fell in love? It happened at a wedding in her Alabama hometown, a blissful weekend that found us constantly sneaking away from the organized events to swap tales of adventures abroad and stare into each other's eyes. She had lived in Spain and on Lake Atitlan in Guatemala, where each day she walked a rocky path to work with indigenous women. I had taught school in Kenya, climbing mountains and hitchhiking around East Africa. We both agreed that we'd never marry someone without first living with them in a third-world country.

We had other things in common as well. As teenagers, we were both desperate to escape our small southern towns. We both asked our parents to send us to boarding school, Heather to Connecticut, where she quickly lost her southern accent after being told to "say something, just talk" so classmates could laugh at her drawl, and I to an all-boys school in Virginia, where I felt equally alienated by rich kids from Richmond. We both attended the same southern university, where we met and even dated briefly. But it wasn't until we both came back from adventures abroad that we bonded over a mutual desire for escape and a shared curiosity of the world.

That night, during the wedding reception, Heather and I wandered away from the dance floor to sit beside the Tennessee River, where a row of yachts and ski boats bobbed in slips. The August air was warm, and we were young, and as we lay back on the grass, staring up at the night sky, I was flush with love and lust and possibility. As strains of *Stars Fell on Alabama* wafted over from the clubhouse, the sky exploded with shooting stars. Absolute truth! We figured out later it was the Perseid meteor shower, which happens every August around that time. But that night, I lay frozen in awe, tears welling in my eyes, convinced that this beautiful woman and I were destined to share a life together.

The very next weekend, Heather visited me in New York, and we hopped a train out of the city, checking into a bed and breakfast in Connecticut and signing the register as Mr. and Mrs. Ward while hiding mischievous grins. A year later, we rented a tiny apartment together in Hell's Kitchen, with a bedroom so small we had to hop on and off our double bed at the foot since there was no room on the sides. Not long after, I secretly shopped for an engagement ring, and then proposed one August during a trip to the Appalachian Mountains to watch the Perseid meteor shower. And, true to our word (though at the time we had forgotten our pledge), during our engagement we lived together in the third world, subletting our apartment and moving to Ecuador for eighteen months to run the South American Explorers Club in exchange for room and board and $250 U.S. per month. We hitchhiked, camped, bunked on sagging mattresses in two-dollar-a-night dumps, nursed each other through bouts of amoebic diarrhea. When we flew back to the States to get married, it was small-town déjà vu—same Holiday Inn, same clubhouse, same florist from the wedding that brought us together. During the first dance, we swayed not altogether gracelessly to *Stars Fell on Alabama*.

But now we have no music. Literally. Neither of us plays an instrument. We have no songbooks. We remember only a handful of children's ditties—and snippets of pop tunes we'd rather not recall. Filled with chores and childcare, our days plod by in a gray sameness, with flashes of happiness. As much as we had embraced the gritty reality of life in 1900, we had no way of anticipating the work and worry of it all. We had no idea that we would face a drought.

And we're jumpy, having shooed away skunks from the tall grass, felt creatures dart past our legs at the compost bin at night, and stepped over snakes. (I'm still haunted by the old-timer's warning about rattlesnakes slithering down from the mountains in search of water when it's dry.) Our experience has brought to the surface the brutality of nature. Everything, it seems, wants a piece of us. Aphids swarm our tender turnip greens. Houseflies buzz the set-aside food in the kitchen. Rodents gnaw at our cheese. You can't even relax in the outhouse. Wasps paper its corners with nests. Spiders creep in the dark recesses beneath the seat. Doing my business one day, I heard a strange *crunch, crunch, crunch* near my ear— a carpenter bee chewing a hole in the poplar siding. Season after season of bee boring has already collapsed a massive shed on the property by turning its pine beams to Swiss cheese. My guard is always up.

It's the same story all over again. Just like in New York, here I am nervous, preoccupied, unable to focus my energy. Instead of fielding phone calls and e-mails, meeting deadlines, chasing checks, and trying to keep up with the bills, I fret over the weather and insects, feeling frustrated, angry, and inadequate. Watching our thirty-eight tomato plants wither has the gut-punch feel of rejection.

ᘓᘙᘗ

Other gardeners are doing fine. Victoria Godfrey is one of them. Word of her garden has gotten around.

One day Victoria drops by to ask if we want any kittens. Their barn cat has just had a litter. A few days later, I finish my chores and set out for their farm, Wheatlands, and a couple of much-needed mousers.

Standing sentinel at the head of the long straight driveway are twin brick pillars, one inset with a piece of chiseled stone that reads, "Wheatlands 1811." A cattle guard stretches between the pillars, so I steer Belle through a gate and into the front pasture. Michael and Victoria walk out to greet me.

Newlyweds, the pair recently moved to Swoope to try their hand at organic cattle farming. Handsome, fit, with a neat salt-and-pepper beard, Michael is in his sixties but looks a decade younger. He is the son of Arthur Godfrey, the famous early television personality, though he never speaks of his father, and I never ask. An avid naturalist, Michael has written field guides and produced a popular birdwatching video. He plays the dobro (which I'm disappointed to learn wasn't invented until the late 1920s). He thrills at the sight of dried scat. You'll be walking along, and he'll drop to a knee and start picking it apart for bones, teeth, and hair, guessing at what animal deposited it. Closer to my age, Victoria has long dark hair, a welcoming smile, and a sense of humor as off-beat and acerbic as her husband's. She calls our experiment in time travel the Manhattan Project.

"Welcome, neighbor!" says Michael, wearing a beat-up white cowboy hat. The pair hops in and we bump across the dusty pasture toward an imposing, 200-year-old brick manor house. What really catches my eye, however, is the vegetable garden, and after tying Belle's lead rope to a fence post and unhitching the wagon, I wander over for a closer look.

The lush plot—Eden comes to mind—puts our withered experiment to shame. Foot paths padded with a thick straw divide neatly elevated rows of mature plants. Big-shouldered turnips and beets burst from the rich soil, their greens fanning out like peacock feathers. Squash and cucumbers lie on the ground like treasure from a tumped-over chest. Bushy pepper plants sag with long, fat chiles, some red, others green, nature's Christmas decorations. Hoping to one day grow them commercially, Victoria has planted 225 pepper plants. She runs me through the numbers—x plants per acres, y pounds of chiles per plant, z dollars per pound—so quickly my head spins. Plus, it's hard to pay attention when I'm mentally working through just how many delicious meals stand at my feet. *Drought?* I think. *What drought?* If only we could use a sprinkler.

"How's your garden?" asks Victoria.

"Oh, it's coming along," I say. "We got a late start."

"We have way more than we can eat," she says. "Will you take some things home?"

Even if her extra veggies *will* get tossed into the compost heap as she claims, there is the matter of self-sufficiency. We're living this way to see if we can—and to see what that feels like. It won't do us any good to become the equivalent of a 1900 welfare case. Then again, I'm sick of cabbage. And dried pinto beans. I've eaten so many eggs lately, I can almost feel my arteries hardening.

"Sure," I say, "but only if you promise to stop by for goat's milk."

Victoria hands me a paper grocery sack and tells me to have at it. And I do, stuffing turnips, beets, carrots, several varieties of colorful Andean potatoes, Swiss chard, mustard greens, green beans, onions, cukes, and a big funky head of fennel into the sack. She hands me basil and parsley and a bunch of fresh-cut flowers—sweet pea, I think they're called—which I tuck into the top of the veggies.

I drop the sack in the wagon, and we walk to find Michael.

"Step inside. I want to show you something," he says from the doorway of one of four neat outbuildings lined up along the gravel farm road. I see stacks of dusty barn boards, a workbench, and—floating amid a froth of wood shavings—lots of antique hand tools. He points to a big wooden *thing* in the corner, ancient and hand-hewn out of a tree. "I

92

made it back in North Carolina. It sat on my porch for years. That's why it looks so weather-beaten."

"What is it?" I say.

"Why, that there's a *gen-u-ine* shaving horse," he says, putting on his hick accent, clowning out of self-deprecation. He demonstrates, straddling the crude bench, inserting a piece of pine, and clamping it tight with a swinging mallet, which he operates with his foot. Using a two-handled blade—a draw knife—he deftly shaves the pine, pulling toward his belly (dangerously close to my inexpert eyes) as chips fly, occasionally easing up on the mallet, flipping the piece, and resuming the determined scraping.

Then Michael stops, eyes the piece, complains, swears under his breath, and mumbles something about leaving his *damn* dowel saw in his *damn* truck. He looks up. "Logan, pretend you didn't see this." Then he flips a switch and a table saw roars to life. He makes a furtive cut and then flips the switch again. The saw whines down. More shaving. More sweat and flying slivers. "Close your eyes again," he says, getting up. All this trouble, I think, smiling, for rules Heather and I created for ourselves. I turn around to humor him and for a few seconds the saw shatters the silence.

"Voilá." Michael holds a wooden spoon, smooth and pretty as can be, smelling like the old heart-pine floors in Trimbles Mill. "This is only a spoon, but your basic man of yore would have used a shaving horse for making shingles, axe handles, wagon spokes. It's a lost art."

Victoria pokes her head into the shop. "Maybe you better catch those cats, Michael," she says. "Logan probably needs to get home."

"Yeah," I say, remembering Belle tied up alone in the pasture. "I should check on the horse."

But Victoria says she'll do it on her way to the house. A few minutes later, just after we finish putting a pair of kittens into my basket, a faint yell draws us out of the barn. We jog toward the house. Standing in the pasture, Victoria throws up her hands.

"Belle's gone," she says when we reach her. In her hand is the lead rope—or half the lead rope. One end is frayed where Belle snapped it.

It doesn't take long to find the horse. She's behind a row of trees fiercely tearing at the long grass and pausing to chew before bending and tearing again. She hardly looks up as I inch toward her, speaking in soothing tones, trying not to be self-conscious, though I can feel Victoria's stares at my back. "Can I help you?" says Victoria, who has experience with horses.

"No, I've got to learn how to handle her myself."

When I reach for the end of the rope dangling from her halter, Belle jerks away. I reach again. We struggle like that for a few minutes, until she submits, like a sullen teenager. I connect the two ends with a simple knot, tug on it to check its strength, and walk her back to the wagon.

Michael has gone to fetch one more cat, this one full-grown. We had not asked for a third cat, but saying no seems rude after their generosity. Victoria runs to get something in the kitchen while I hitch Belle to the wagon. She returns with another gift—two ice-cold beers wrapped in newspaper. Michael walks up from the barn holding a writhing pillowcase at arm's length. Cursing and red-faced, he's bleeding from a long scratch on his forearm.

"Logan," he says, handing me the bundle. "Meet Mudflap."

Mudflap was once a housecat named Mittens, enjoying a pampered existence with Victoria's cousin in Short Hills, New Jersey. When divorce divided her household, Mittens was shipped off to Wheatlands (confirming that some pets actually do wind up on farms), where Victoria rechristened her Mudflap for the folds of flesh behind each leg.

Though her new name suits her, country life does not. Once Mudflap springs from the pillowcase back at Trimbles Mill, she darts away, skulking along the fencerows, scowling at us as we laugh and play with the kittens, which Luther names Banjo and Pick.

We now have a dozen animals in our care: six laying hens, two milk goats, a horse, and three cats. As the primary caregiver for this menagerie, I am beginning to feel like Dr. Dolittle. I soothe Belle with words, chatter with the chickens, coax the goats onto and off the milking stand. They come to me for security and to beg for food. I feel the weight of responsibility for these animals. Which is why I grow alarmed when the animal feed starts running out.

Though our farm produces grass for the horse, grass and slop for the chickens, and milk (and mice) for the cats, it's not enough. And without a grain crop and a protein-rich legume hay, like alfalfa, we can't keep our goats milking. So we decided early on to supplement the animals' diets, making an agreement with a feed store on the other side of the county—the closest one we could find that delivers—to show up on the third Thursday of every month. We didn't explain why we would have no phone or car. And Chad, the polite but taciturn driver, hasn't ever pried. But now he's long overdue, and he won't answer the letters I've sent asking about our feed.

The goats notice immediately when I begin to ration their food, belligerently scraping their snouts back and forth in the empty grain tray. When it's time to dismount the milking stand, they plant their feet and raise their heads, locking into the stanchion and scowling.

One day, Star, the bigger and surlier of the two, simply refuses to leave the stand. I've got milk to strain and a day's worth of chores staring me in the face, and I'm not in the mood for taking shit from a goat. I yank on Star's tail, and she lets out a frightened bleat. Hoofs scuff wood as she scrambles for footing on the planking. She missteps, pedaling for purchase, and slams onto the rough concrete floor head first. I feel horrible.

It wouldn't be so bad if our goats would eat like goats. Tin cans? Old shoe leather? These two turn their noses up at grass. The goat lady, their former owner, sent them off with explicit dietary instructions that included sweet grain, dried beet pulp for fiber, alfalfa hay and pellets for protein, and powdered sea kelp for extra vitamins and minerals. I drew the line at the kelp. It sounded healthy enough—so healthy, I considered taking it myself—but it was prohibitively expensive. They're spoiled rotten.

I try latching Star and Sweet Pea in a small grassy paddock behind the barn where there's nothing to do but eat grass, and they scream like they're being tortured. *Ngheeeelp!* If I'm nearby, they contentedly nibble weeds, popping their heads up to check on me. The minute I walk away, they squeal again. I am now their mama.

The two of them are like a pair of monkeys—curious, mischievous, springy with energy. If I'm doing anything in the barnyard, they'll nose around until they screw up something, like the time Sweet Pea climbed over the woodpile while I was splitting wood. She kept picking at the kindling in my wheelbarrow until she dumped the whole thing, skittering away, ears flapping. When I pass through the barnyard, they file in

95

ahead of me, stopping suddenly to cock their heads, to make sure I'm still there. If I'm hauling anything heavy, like buckets of water, I'll bump into them à la The Three Stooges, stumbling and spilling my load.

The chickens completely snub me. They scatter warily when I approach, as if at any minute I might snatch one of them up and toss it in a boiling pot. But at least they eat—anything and everything, gobbling curdled milk, which I dump in an old bedpan, and kitchen scraps. They attack their metal feeder, emptying it in a frenzy of dipping heads and scattered mash, and then charge out the chicken door to scalp the grass in their yard and dig in the dirt for insects. Their pen is now a moonscape, but I refuse to let them out for fear that they'll decimate the vegetable garden.

We have six hens, and they consistently lay two or three eggs a day between them, giving us fewer than two dozen a week. It's not enough. We're hungry from the physical work and eating in a period-appropriate fashion—like people who have never heard of cholesterol. A single breakfast might wipe out half a week's worth of eggs.

We need more chickens.

ભ્ઠ

One day, I decide to get more. I harness Belle and drive to the Salatins' farm, Polyface, where we got the first six. On the way, I stop for a pickup chat with a local farmer. He's headed in the opposite direction, which puts the pair of excitable Labrador retrievers in the bed of his truck face to face with Belle. They light up, barking and cutting tight circles. He settles them with a gruff, "Shut up!"

"I seem to recall Clyde Tillman carrying a bigger whip than that," he says, smiling, looking at the switch in my hand.

But just as I'm about to answer, Belle jerks forward.

"Whoa, Belle!" I yell. But she doesn't listen. I tug hard on the lines. Her head kinks, but she stubbornly pushes on.

Swiveling around, I say, "Talk to you later," trying to hide my embarrassment. And then, "Trot, Belle."

A few hundred yards from the Salatin farm, I remember the bridge. It spans the Middle River at the entrance to their property. The bridge's heavy oak timbers are intentionally spaced six inches apart to prevent cattle from crossing. No horse could manage it.

I ease off the road opposite the entrance and find just enough space to park a fifteen-foot long horse and buggy. As I'm tying her lead rope to a tree, Belle won't stop jerking her head, stepping nervously, as if the ground were on fire. I'm angry and hot and operating under an increasingly short fuse. My hand shoots up and clamps onto her nose bridge, a move I learned from our farrier. "Don't fuck with me, Belle. I'm not in the mood." Her ears perk up. She stands at attention. I finish my knot, grab a basket and some chicken wire from the wagon bed, and carefully step across the bridge, peering through the gaps at the brown water slipping past. I almost turn back. I can't leave her alone like this, I think, hitched to her wagon and tied to a tree with a slipknot. But I have no choice. I'm here, and we need the chickens.

When I return, carrying a squawking, dust-boiling basket full of Rhode Island Reds, she stands quietly beside the tree.

"That's a girl," I say, stroking her neck. "Didn't mean to get rough before."

On the way home, I top the hill and am relieved not to see the farmer. Alone for once, I look up to see North Mountain's long ridgeline standing fiery in the afternoon light. I see Buffalo Gap, the passage used long ago by pioneers trundling west in their wagons. This time last year, I might have been elbowing for space on the C train to Brooklyn, I think, in a sudden burst of elation. Instead, I'm clip-clopping home with a basket full of chickens and a horse that just might be starting to respect me.

Up ahead, Clyde Tillman walks slowly down his driveway. *He's coming to see me*, I think, sitting up a little straighter in the wagon. But the old man sticks his hand in his empty mailbox and turns for home without even glancing my way. He stops under a tree and waits. Sure enough, when I get closer, he returns to the roadside. I ease the wagon onto the shoulder, far enough to be out of the way of passing cars but not so far that I'll be in the weeds if Belle decides again that she wants to walk.

"How ya doing?" I say.

Instead of a greeting, Tillman clacks his top set of dentures and says, "You need to get you a black hat."

Just then Jeanne roars up in her red Jeep Cherokee. She stops beside the wagon and hands Tillman his mail. He stands between us, leaning his arm on top of my left wheel. *Please, Belle*, I think. *Stand still.*

Shifting more weight onto the wheel, as if it were his kitchen counter, he launches into a story about attending some sort of Mennonite service. "Never seen so many of 'em in my life. They was all dressed the same—black pants, white shirts, black hats, no jackets. It was pouring rain, but they didn't have no umbrellas."

Jeanne, hidden behind a pair of dark Ray-Bans, listens patiently. My attention drifts to Belle, and I catch myself cringing. *Don't move. Please don't move.* She stands, stiller and more attentive than she ever has, making me wonder if it's respect for me—or for Clyde Tillman and some mysterious power he holds over horses.

Tillman finishes his story, and Jeanne speeds off.

"Boy," he says, as if that were my name, "you must have found a lot of dirt roads to have gotten yer wagon this dusty." *Well, what do you know?* He noticed my wagon. Then he turns and walks back to his house.

"Come up, Belle," I say, pointing her toward home. "Good girl, Belle."

∞

The drought wears on. Some of the earliest vegetables we planted—cabbages, a row of beans, squash—are producing, but the others wither, and the pasture grass turns brown. Tomatoes die on the vine. It's blight, says Bill Roberson, who gave us the tomato plants as seedlings. "You've got to pull all the sick plants and burn them to keep the blight from striking next season." I can't bring myself to do it.

One plant seems oblivious to the water shortage. Tall and prickly, dotted with handfuls of soft pink flowers, thistle merrily grows inches each day, it seems. Proud national plant of Scotland, thistle is a favorite food source of the goldfinch. Its branches play a supporting role in Audubon's portrait of the bright-yellow seed-eater in his *Birds of America* folio. Yet, judging from the reactions of the cattle farmers of Swoope, you would think thistle sprouted from the very follicles of hell.

They poison it with sprays, decapitate it with their brush mowers, hack its roots with stone-sharpened hoes—anything to keep it from multiplying and choking out their pasture grass, which it does with alarming rapidity. As first-time landowners, we fenced off an acre or so of our pasture beside the house, deciding to let nature reclaim it. A wildflower meadow would be nice there, we thought. Thistle, which would draw goldfinches, is just the sort of wildflower we had in mind.

The problem is, thistle does not respect borders. As those pretty pink puff balls dry up, clusters of downy, seed-bearing parachutes burst forth onto the breeze to infiltrate new territory, fulfilling the weed's manifest destiny. Thoreau quotes an unnamed source who mathematically calculated the plant's potential for destruction: Assuming a 100 percent germination rate, this person figured that the fifth year's crop from a *single thistle seed* would beget "a progeny more than sufficient to stock not only the surface of the whole earth, but all of the planets in the solar system, so that no other vegetable could possibly grow." In a season or two, unwitting aesthetes such as ourselves could undo years of toil by a neighbor bent on eradicating the plant.

Ever since our head-high thistles grew rank with seed, our neighbors have started to grumble. Standing on our front porch recently, Michael Godfrey, wearing his trademark white cowboy hat, said, "I don't mean to poke my nose into your little history experiment, but if you don't do anything about that thistle over there," pointing to the tangle of weeds we were calling our meadow, "it's going to bite you in the ass." Did I have a plan, and if so, what was it?

One day Jeanne, whose mother's pasture stands immediately downwind of our meadow, asks the same thing: What do we plan to do about it? Between struggling to get the wash done *and* weed the garden *and* trim the grass nearest the house—a haven for snakes—with my rusty reel mower, I explain, I simply do not foresee tackling the acres of thistle in and around our meadow with my hand tools. Sorry. Can't do it. Survival first. "So," Jeanne says, in a mock-serious tone that is really quite serious, "they just blow over to Mom's field, and she'll have to get out there with her hoe."

The next Saturday, a sweltering July morning, I spy a figure in the pasture across the road swinging a long-handled tool amid weeds that dwarf her. It's Jeanne's seventy-year-old mother, Jean, chopping thistle with a hoe.

Jean works all morning, felling plant after towering plant. Then she takes a break and walks up to our house, eagerly accepting Heather's offer of fresh well water ladled from our crock. Tilting her head back like a thirsty athlete, the tiny gray-haired woman guzzles, while Heather and I stand quietly by. I glance down and notice her feet. This woman has been whacking thistles in her espadrilles!

Resting now on our porch, Jean can't stop gushing in her wispy southern drawl about how *good* our water is, how *awfully nice* we are to give it to her, and how *surprised* she is to have polished off two whole glasses of it. She never complains about the thistles—or about the next generation, in the form of our downy seeds, that will force her to defend her acreage again next summer.

After rehydrating, Jean marches back to her field to brave the snakes in her canvas sandals. Maybe it's because Michael's and Jeanne's earlier criticism raised my hackles, but did I detect a hint of disingenuousness in Jean's sweet manner? Was her display of gracious stoicism meant as a guilt trip? Complicating matters, it turns out that Jean is a Trimble by blood. The land she owns across the road was once part of the same farm we now own, making her the seventh (and Jeanne the eighth) generation to farm it since the original land grant was deeded more than two and a half centuries ago. When Heather and I planned our wildflower meadow, we had not considered the neighbors. What for? It's our land. Now that we're getting to know the people of Swoope, I'm confused about our place in this community and what's expected of us.

Interacting with neighbors at all is new to us. After growing up in claustrophobic small towns, where everyone seemed to know everyone else, Heather and I both relished the anonymity of New York. We had plenty of friends. If we wanted to get together, we made appointments. That's what busy New Yorkers do. Here in Swoope, where we are anything but anonymous, we have had to adjust to the Drop-In.

The joke among neighbors is, *We knew we'd catch you at home.* They can't call, and they know we're basically stuck here. So people drop in. They come to us in trucks, by all-terrain vehicles, on bicycle, and on foot. Once, I hear the clip-clop of hooves on the driveway and find two women on horseback beside the screen porch. "We heard about this wonderful thing you're doing," says a woman with brown riding boots and gray hair curling out from a helmet. "We're envious!"

Accustomed to my privacy and uncomfortable feeling indebted, I don't always handle these visits so well. We're busy preparing for winter, which makes me feel a bit like Aesop's ant, set upon by a crowd of grasshoppers. As fond as I am of Bill Roberson, for instance, sometimes it drives me nuts when he shows up and I'm in the middle of chores. A grin plastered to my face, I'll wave from behind my mower and keep pushing, or remain sequestered in the barn with the woodpile, letting Heather be hospitable.

But I'm learning—we both are—to relinquish our hoes and washboards for a porch sit, learning to be grateful for the company, learning that the work isn't going away. It will still be there when our friends leave.

We're also learning how to handle their generosity. Drop-Ins never come empty-handed. In Swoope, every day's a potlatch. The Godfreys might bring fresh bread, Bill and Peggy home-canned beets, Ishtar and Leasha potato salad. Though we never ask others to follow the rules we've set for ourselves, many do voluntarily, making homemade mayonnaise or taking care to cover a bowl with period-appropriate wax paper. We reciprocate by giving away goat's milk, eggs, oatmeal cookies, and the delicious cheese Heather's been making. But keeping up is hard. One day (before the thistle episode) Jean gave us shortbread cookies, and we gave her milk. But the very next day, the milk came back to us as a quart of cool sweetness called "drinking" custard. Ishtar loves our goat's milk and stops by twice a week to fill her half-gallon jar, but she insists on leaving a tiny manila envelope filled with four quarters. "For Luther's college fund," she says, against our protests.

Eventually, Chad drops in, too, with the sacks of animal feed. We remind him we have no phone, and he promises to show up on time next month.

There's one person I can't summon to our farm no matter how hard I try. That's the well driller. For weeks I've been sending blotchy ink-well letters begging him to pay us a visit. The pump has been acting up. You'll pump forty or fifty times, and suddenly the resistance will increase, grow springy, like you're pumping against the force of a giant rubber band. When that happens, the water stops flowing.

One day, a big panel truck rumbles into the driveway. It's Ben Law, second-generation well-driller. When I greet him near the side porch, he gives me a funny look, and I grow self-conscious at how things have changed since he came to pull our electric pump. Then, Heather and I were clean and well-groomed, and the garden was an orderly grid of turned rows and fledgling broccoli plants. Now, both garden and its care-takers have gone shabby. Heather, sweating in the kitchen, waves a soot-blackened hand out of the porch's screen door. My hair is a wild tangle, my face dirty with a five-day shadow. I wear ragged cut-off jeans and boots and am shirtless, since Luther vomited on me after breakfast.

"I'm sorry about how long it's taken me," Ben says. "I figured if it was a big emergency, you would have called."

I throw on a shirt and lead Ben up to the pump, where he confirms my worst fears.

"Your pump's fine," he says after inspecting it. "But your well is dry-ing up. It's not the only one around here." That's why it took Ben so long to stop by. He's been working overtime to drill new wells for farmers who are afraid of losing entire herds of cattle. His quick calculation reveals that the water level in our well has dropped by more than twen-ty-five feet. Fifteen feet more, and we're out of water.

CBSO

We enter the hottest and muggiest stretch of days so far. Even at night, the temperatures hover in the upper eighties. Even our breeze has failed us. Sick with the sniffles for the first time since we started, Luther is try-ing our patience with contrariness, fits, and the impossible wish to be held by one of us every minute of the day. As the heat and humidity mount, so does the tension between me and Heather.

We're in the garden one afternoon, when Heather says, "What hap-pened to my flowers?" She is bending over a bed of freshly turned earth.

"Oh, no," I groan. "What did they look like?"

"They were cosmos, tall, about to bloom."

"I pulled them yesterday," I say. "I thought they were weeds."

"What a waste." She buries her face in her hands and sobs. These were her flowers, the only flower seeds either of us had sown, one tiny indulgence in a garden dominated by utility. Wearied by our challenge, she had planted them in a gesture of hope. Focused on surviving the year, I recklessly uproot-ed them. The cosmos were Heather's cave art, and by killing them—even if accidentally—I had rubbed out her expression of freedom and beauty.

"I'm sorry." But my apology is not enough.

For a whole day after I uprooted her cosmos, Heather won't talk to me. She plods through her chores, lips tight, eyes dark and brooding. She hardly looks at me.

When we do begin speaking, it's to utter perfunctory work-related comments—"More wood for the fire?" or "Did you pump water?" After moving some hay bales one day, I enter the kitchen, sweaty and itching from where the hay has scratched me, and find Heather sitting, defiantly reading a *Wall Street Journal* from a stack of fire-building papers a neighbor brought. I plop down nearby.

"Can we talk?" I say. "I really am sorry about your flowers." I also want to tell her that I'm starting to get it—that simply avoiding starvation for a year isn't our only measure of success.

"This isn't just about the flowers," she says, laying down the paper and facing me. "It's the big-picture problem. Our relationship."

"Why do you have to be so fatalistic about our relationship?" I say, feeling myself in familiar territory. "Why can't we just have an argument about a stupid mistake and then get over it?"

"I feel like we don't know each other, Logan. I feel distant from you. We never communicate."

"I'm still trying to figure out the best way to communicate with you. I know I've got a bad habit of trying to solve your problems. But I'm trying to change. Like right now."

"We hardly touch anymore," she says. "We're like two single people passing each other. I walk around all day stewing about you, bottling things up."

"Think about how long and hard we work. Luther takes up nine-tenths of our waking hours. It's not like we have time or energy for much intimacy."

"That's what we said in New York! That's what we said when we were busting our asses to get ready for this damn project. That was supposed to end as soon as 1900 started."

I return to a troubling thought: Maybe this project is a terrible mistake. In trying to avoid the settled, circumscribed life, we answered our restlessness not with some overseas adventure, but rather by yoking ourselves more tightly to adult responsibility and tedium. We did it partly because we had a child. Our *at-home* adventure, we called it. An expedition to nowhere. Back when we were living in Ecuador, during a tense time between us, Heather had a deep-seated urge to fly—off to Chile, alone—though she never went. Maybe a relationship founded on a mutual desire for travel and adventure—for escape—is inevitably doomed?

When Luther wakes up, we have resolved nothing. We awkwardly play with him, although foreboding lingers like match smoke in the space between us. In our preoccupation, we have failed to notice a bank of black clouds moving in from the north. Now a chill licks at the last of the sweat stinging my scratches, grabbing my attention.

"Look," I say. "Rain!"

We rush outside, Luther on our heels. At first, a few fat drops thump the henhouse roof. Then the rain spills as if from a tipped bucket, slapping at our heads and shoulders, battering the hard earth of the garden, and instantly gathering itself into brown rivulets to rush down the driveway. We weren't expecting rain. No weather reports. No news from neighbors. In our brooding, we missed the signs.

Heather breaks into sobs. I hug her and cry, too. Letting go is easy in the deluge. Luther stands looking up, confused. "Luther hug Mommy, Daddy," he says. It makes us laugh, and I lift him, holding him between us as we laugh and cry and rock back and forth. Then he laughs. "Happy Mommy! Happy Daddy!" he says.

"Yes, happy Mommy," says Heather. And then to me, in a whisper, lips at my ear, "I love you, Logan. I never want to lose you. We'll make it work." And in between sobs, my arms locked tight around her, all I can say is "Yes. Yes. Yes. I love you."

PART TWO

Seasoned

CHAPTER SIX

Picking, Cleaning, Shelling, Shucking

As if the crack of thunder were a starting gun, the plants in our garden explode with new growth, guzzling water in their race to the first frost. The sky springs a leak during early August, blessing us with one life-sustaining downpour after another. The potatoes and beans bush out. The squash and cuke vines curl and creep over the ground, vying for sunlight. Corn stalks rocket skyward.

The rains palliate our worries over the garden and well level, and with clearer heads Heather and I work harder at our partnership. We are talking again and touching, though gingerly, as if afraid of breaking something that can't be fixed.

Daily life is still a grind, with chores demanding most of our time. I'm still only four pages into the first book I've opened, *The Red Badge of Courage*. Each night I prop up a pillow and lay back to read by the soporific glow of the oil lamp. Each night the book whacks me in the face within minutes.

But we've been at it now for eight weeks, and we're growing more competent. At first the crudest necessity drove us. If we needed water, I would pump. A cooking fire? I'd rush to split wood. Meals were pretty monotonous—oatmeal for breakfast and lots and lots of cabbage. Edgy, always a few steps behind, we stumbled through our days. Now, we're more efficient, soaking dirty dishes and washing them twice a day, pumping extra water the day before laundry day, adding to the reserve woodpile every time I take axe in hand. With the garden producing more variety, Heather has been preparing big, colorful meals with four and five different vegetables vying for space on our plates. Those meals are what we're sweating and slaving for, and we've learned to savor them. And every so often, we'll free up an hour here or an hour there, rewarding ourselves with a quiet moment for letter writing, a walk with Luther, or a hammock nap.

Just as I'm feeling more in control, I'm also learning to admit that I'm powerless over some things—the Japanese beetle plague, for instance, or the weather. When I feel frustration and fear welling up, repeating a simple question—*What's the worst that can happen?*—helps settle my mind. Sure, the worst that can happen to us pales in comparison to the worst that could have happened to a farm family 100 years ago. They were stuck in 1900. We're not. But I'm not convinced our situation's all that different. Everyone faces uncertainty. At some point, you've got to let life run its course, surrendering control in the face of overwhelming events. Wrestle giants, and you're bound to lose.

So after eight weeks, do I feel like an authentic nineteenth-century guy? On a strictly superficial level, no. As hard as we may try, keeping the twenty-first century at bay is impossible. But when I look beyond the cars, beyond the plastic and occasional out-of-season melon brought by the neighbors, I do feel transported. Perched on the wagon bench in my overalls and straw hat or splitting firewood, I feel as though I'm finally finding my rhythm. I face each day with more patience and confidence. The same is true for Heather as she perfects her goat's-milk cheese and further masters the subtleties of woodstove baking.

If she and I were still in New York at such a critical juncture in our relationship, we might see a marriage counselor. Instead, we work out our issues over a hot woodstove in August. It's canning time.

We try our best to estimate the amount of food we'll need to preserve for winter. It's a complicated equation, involving lots of guesswork—how

much our summer plants will yield, when the first frost will kill the garden, what (if anything) we'll be able to grow in a fall garden, what we'll be
able to preserve (can, dry, pickle, or cellar), and when next year's spring
garden might produce. Oh yeah, and how much we—and any surprise visitors—will consume.

We set our goal at 300 jars of food, which will give us about ten jars
per week from early October to May. Plus, we'll cellar potatoes, store
winter squash and pumpkins, and dry limas and field peas. As the days
grow shorter and colder—with a killing frost liable to strike at any
moment—the clock will be ticking to get it all done on time.

I am *sous-chef* to Heather's *chef de cuisine*. I pump extra water for the
canning pots and split mountains of wood to keep the stove roaring all
day like a blast furnace. I wash quart jars, arrange lids. Meanwhile,
Heather simmers sugar syrups, adds herbs to pickle recipes, and slices
piles of peppers, beans, squash, okra, and cucumbers. Much to our
amazement, the tomatoes have bounced back, shrugging off their end
rot and yielding twenty-five pounds a day—enough ripe red fruit for
sandwiches, sauces, salads, and quart after canned quart.

Day after day, the fire roars and the canning pots bubble. Food-filled jars
line the kitchen counter, glowing in the sunlight. As soon as they cool, I
carry them in baskets to the cellar, where I sometimes have to rearrange to
find the space for them all. No matter how exhausted we are, we've got to
keep pushing ourselves during the window of ripeness. We're behind on
the green beans. The last few batches have been tough and stringy.

One afternoon, as I'm setting the last hot jar on the counter to cool, listening for the telltale *pop!* that signals a proper vacuum seal, I say to
Heather, only half in jest, "So what do you want to do on your birthday—
besides canning?" Her birthday is tomorrow.

Like a lot of guys, I tend to procrastinate gift-shopping so that when
the day finally arrives, my efforts are hit or miss, usually miss. I buy
books that never get read or bath salts that clutter the cabinets. I pick
out sweaters, knowing she'll return them—big fuzzy gift certificates to
Banana Republic. It may be the thought that counts, but too often my
gifts are an *after*thought.

Heather's birthday begins drizzly but soon the skies clear into a cool
bright preview of early fall. Sure enough, we put water on the stove for

canning green beans. As we work, Ishtar and Leasha show up to pick up milk and drop off a basket of goodies—flowers and a birthday card for Heather, homemade mayonnaise, spoonbread. Then Bill and Peggy bring pink champagne and a vase of flowers. "We had a bottle of that last night for our anniversary," says Peggy. "It's wonderful." Despite the chores, Heather is in a great mood.

I have something I need to do in the kitchen—a surprise—but just as I'm about to kick Heather out, Jeanne knocks on the door. "Logan, I need your help," she says, a serious look on her face. "Bring a pair of gloves."

Bloated and flyblown, a dead calf lies in her field. I breathe through my mouth to avoid the stench. Together we hoist the rotting carcass into the bed of the truck. She's going to dump it in the woods for the vultures. "I can meet you at the top of the hill," I say, hoping she won't ask me to get in her truck. "No, I only needed help lifting it." Her words are clipped, all business.

Back at the house, I can't shake the sight of the dead calf. It gives the day a hint of gravitas that only enhances its importance. But the unexpected chore has left me short of time, so I dash around readying things for this evening. Luther's napping. Heather has gone for a walk.

We dine on the screen porch, bathed by a cool breeze. Atop a clean blue-checked tablecloth stand a vase of black-eyed susans, candles—*de rigueur* in 1900—jelly jars of warm pink champagne, and my attempt at pasta with fresh basil, tomatoes, and goat cheese. Luther is content to slurp his noodles without sauce. Heather enjoys the food simply because she didn't have to cook it.

"I'm afraid it's all you're getting this year," I say, handing Heather a small package wrapped in kraft paper, decorated with Luther's crayon scribbles, and tied up with sisal twine.

She opens it and gasps. "Did you *make* this?" she says. I nod, trying not to look too pleased with myself. It's a bracelet, braided from Belle's mane.

"How did you know how?" she says.

"Like I knew how to do any of this. Like you knew how to make *chevre* and cook on a woodstove."

Heather smiles. "When did you find the time?"

"I've been sneaking off to the shed when you weren't looking." The bracelet took me weeks to weave. Then I needed a clasp. With time running out, I thought and sketched and then one day something green-tinted and round surfaced in a turnip bed I was turning. I grabbed a handful of dirt and slowly, dramatically opened my palm, sweating out the moment. And there was an old copper washer—just the thing I had envisioned—like some inscrutable Asian coin, perched on a pillow of earth.

Heather slides the bracelet onto her wrist and holds it away from her, admiring it. "I love it, Logan. This means more to me than anything you have ever given me."

I want to remember this feeling forever. I never again want to take Heather for granted.

A car putts up the driveway: Ishtar and Leasha are back. They hustle in with hugs and good wishes, cradling something wrapped in a dish towel: homemade vanilla ice cream in a wax-paper-lined cookie tin. It's the perfect complement to my surprise chocolate layer cake—my first cake ever—made from recipes I found in two vintage cookbooks.

"Ice cream!" says Heather. "It's been so long. What a treat!" Luther, face smeared with the thick dark icing, is kicking and beating his wooden high-chair tray, his whole body gyrating with joy. "I can't get over the fact that all of this is homemade."

Leasha squirms uncomfortably. I'm about to ask about what kind of ice cream maker they have, when Ishtar looks at Leasha conspiratorially and says, "I'm glad you put the *mmmm* in the *mmmm*." Leasha quickly adds, "Yeah, Mom, that was good." So maybe it's not homemade. Why pry? I decide. After all, it's the thought that counts.

CREASO

Heather and I are walking out of the driveway, pulling Luther in his red wagon, when we see a white station wagon speeding toward us from the Boy Scout camp. It's traveling too fast for the gravel road, which turns sharply at our mailbox. That's just where we're standing when the driver hits his brakes and skids straight at us, losing control on the gravel and fishtailing for fifty yards. Just as he is about to plow into us, the driver regains control and makes the turn, rolling to a stop at the intersection at Trimbles Mill Road.

"Hey!" I yell. Approaching the car, I'm just able to get the license plate number before it squeals off, spitting gravel at me.

When we were negotiating to buy Trimbles Mill, we considered the Boy Scout camp a real asset. The totem poles marking the entrance, the lake, with its dock and roped-off swimming area, only enhanced the fairy-tale nature of our new environs. Kids from all over the state come to the place where we *live* for wilderness camp. We imagined pleasant exchanges with boys and their counselors. They might even be interested in our 1900 project. Better the Boy Scouts, we figured, than some land developer.

The neighbors laughed at our naiveté.

"The Boy Scouts? Good neighbors? Just wait," said Jeanne, who once discovered a carload of counselors in her pasture. They had just crashed through a section of wire mesh fence. No problem, the counselors said. Everything would be fine, since the owner of the land was a friend of theirs. They had no idea they were talking to the owner. "You'll see."

Since the start of the weeklong camp sessions in June, Boy Scout Lane has been like Flatbush Avenue in Brooklyn. Three days a week—Sunday drop-off, Wednesday parents night, and Saturday morning pickup—minivans and shiny new SUVs barrel down the narrow farm roads. Tractor trailer trucks emblazoned with "Pepsi" and "Cysco" force locals into ditches. Gangs of late-night strolling counselors heckle the cows. And though no one has proof of it, everyone around here is convinced the counselors are to blame for a rash of baseball-bat mailbox bashings. Our box is spared, but Bill and Peggy find theirs dented and discarded beneath the Middle River bridge. Peggy asks me to climb down and fish it out for them.

The day after the skidding incident, Heather walks to the camp, pulling Luther in his wagon. She plans to report the incident and ask for something to be done about speeding parents and counselors. She wants to let them know there's now a child playing at Trimbles Mill Farm. Surely the Boy Scouts, with their oaths to remain courteous, friendly, and kind, will respond favorably.

They do not, which I learn from Heather when she returns.

"The car that almost ran over my family is in your parking lot," she told the director, a distracted man in khaki shorts and Boy Scout neckerchief whom she met inside the camp's office cabin. "The license plate number matches the one my husband gave me."

He hardly seemed to care, though a younger man in the office, who had followed her into the hut and rummaged around in a corner, spoke up when he heard Heather read the plate number. "That was me."

As if the problem were solved, the director turned to Heather and said, "Well, then, there's your man," and walked away, leaving Heather and Luther facing a tall blond counselor, probably twenty years old. "You don't understand, lady," he said, an edge of cockiness to his voice. "When we get out of here, we just want to have fun." Besides, he said, he was being egged on by the other guys in the car. And he was in control the whole time. After several minutes of back-and-forth, Heather left, without even an apology.

Not long after, on a warm, moonlit night, Heather and I meet on the front porch. Luther is sleeping upstairs. The goats have been milked. The dishes are clean. We're alone together and in good spirits. Rocking on the porch swing, we start kissing. Heather pulls off her shirt.

"Should we?" I say and am surprised by her answer, which is wordless yet unmistakably clear. I lower the wick on the oil lamp.

Soon our clothes lay in piles on the porch, and we've moved to the steps leading down to the yard, not the most comfortable spot, but who cares? Being outdoors in the quiet dark with only the occasional lowing cow to break the silence exhilarates us.

And then, in the distance, we hear a low rumble and see the bouncing beams of a car's headlights. It's coming from the Boy Scout camp, down the long straight gravel road.

I lean over and blow the lamplight out. "Don't worry about it," Heather pleads. But I can't help it. The magic is lost. Even if the driver won't be able to see us in the moonlight—and I'm not convinced they won't—I'm distracted. The rumble grows louder. More headlights. A caravan of cars and trucks grinds toward us in a procession of glowing dust. They roll through the intersection and continue over the Middle River bridge in front of our house. And then I remember: It's Wednesday. Parent's night.

Even as we harvest, we defend against new garden threats. Joining the assault alongside the Japanese beetle and the cabbage white, which hails from Europe, is the Mexican bean beetle. Our garden now feels like an embattled front in a new world war. The bean beetle's larvae are soft and bright yellow, a yellow that blends with the wormy green and potato-beetle pink to stain my fingertips in a rainbow of bug guts. *Pop!*

When the corn and beans begin to mature, clusters of blackbirds loiter in the trees above the river. Their chatter reminds me of a third-world bus depot. I'm not sure if they're looking for insects or plan to pick at the plants themselves. I take no chances and shoo them away.

Just the other day, a groundhog moved in across the driveway from the mailbox. One morning over oatmeal, we debate what to do about it.

"We could trap it," Heather says.

"The farmers don't trap groundhogs," I reply. They shoot them or train their Australian shepherds to root them out and break their necks. Groundhog holes can snap a cow's leg or tip a tractor. We don't have a tractor or cows, but we do have a horse. Besides, this groundhog is threatening to turn our vegetable garden into a breakfast bar.

"Peggy says you're supposed to release them at least fifteen miles away," I say, "or they'll come back." And even then, you're dumping your problem onto somebody else's property. How fair is that? Though I don't mention it to Heather, Michael Godfrey, who has a groundhog problem at Wheatlands, suggests gasoline. Pour, light, BOOM!

"What if I shoot it?" I say, picturing the rusting 16-gauge pump shotgun I borrowed from my father, the one wrapped in kraft paper and hidden on top of a tall pine wardrobe in our spare bedroom.

"Where would you shoot it?"

"I'd trap it and carry it up on the hill."

"What would you do with it once you shot it?"

"I don't know."

"I don't like that idea," Heather says.

I don't like it much either, but I feel like we need to do *something*. I remember something David Fleig said about farming: *You've got to learn when to kill.* So far this summer, I've done my share—the snake, the rat,

114

dozens of mice, and countless insects—and frankly, I'm not feeling too good about it. (Well, I'm losing no sleep over the Japanese beetles.) Adding to my ambivalence is the story Jeanne's mom told us about Oscar, the orphaned groundhog raised by her children.

"Oscar had such personality," recalled Jean in her wispy drawl. "She was the friendliest pet we've ever had." Oscar loved Gaines Burgers and made the cover of a local newspaper eating a honey-glazed Krispy Kreme donut. Oscar chewed away the shoe molding in their house, burrowed into a plaster wall, and nested in the insulation. "She must have itched, poor thing," said Jean. In the fall, Oscar hibernated in a burrow beneath the barn. "My son would call to her, 'Oscaaaar!' and Oscar would call back to him with this high-pitched noise, like a screech owl—*ooh, ooh, ooh*. He could hear Oscar getting closer in her underground tunnel—*ooh, ooh, ooh*." Jean, hardly the typical cattle farmer, forbade anyone to kill groundhogs on her land—until she broke her ankle in a groundhog hole. After that, groundhogs were fair game.

It would be just our luck: Our groundhog crosses the road, digs a hole in Jean's pasture, and Jean breaks another ankle—while chopping thistles that came from our meadow!

"The farmers shoot groundhogs," I say.

"Yeah," says Heather, "but the farmers also raise animals for slaughter. They're used to killing. We have no reason to kill."

So we don't kill the groundhog. Instead, we try to stink him out. I start by dumping a half gallon of sour, clotted milk down the hole. I boil hot peppers and toss them in. I pour chamber-pot piss through his front door. A green mold sprouts at the hole's mouth, which seems to suggest that Mr. Groundhog's gone, but he always seems to pop up again by the mailbox or in the front yard, where the grass is now knee-high. It's a mystery—until one day, when I'm tromping around near his moldy hole and nearly snap my ankle in his back door.

Everybody wants a piece of our garden, even our own goats. One day, I catch Sweet Pea greedily munching young corn stalks. Somehow she has escaped. "Hey!" I scream, "Outta there." And she darts along the fence. I chase her down and dive for her hind legs, hanging on, taking a few kicks in the jaw. I work my way up to her collar and drag her back to the paddock, where I wedge a few large stones in the rain-washed gap beneath the gate to keep her from shim-mying under again.

As bad as it is to have the goats eating our plants, it would be worse if they snuck into the feed room. Too much grain could kill them. For that reason, I always make sure to latch the feed-room door. Because goats are said to have prehensile tongues, which they use to open gates, we've installed special goat-proof latches on most of the gates around our farm. The latch on the feed-room door—high and seemingly out of reach—never crossed my mind.

Sweet Pea, the younger of the pair of half-sisters—slight, tan, smooth like a fawn—has a habit of sneezing when she eats grain. I think she lit-erally inhales her food, which leads to loud, wheezy explosions that have, on several occasions, covered my face and hair with goat snot. Sometimes, the sneeze will trigger a simultaneous fart, like the trumpet of a baby elephant. She'll be on the milking stand, with me perched on a stool at her side, when out of nowhere—HEEEZ-PRUUUMPH!—I'm caught between the two exploding ends.

It is one of these sneeze-fart eruptions mixed with the banging of metal lids that grabs my attention one day. I have just stepped into the garden with the intention of pulling the grass sprouting between the corn rows. Heather's inside the kitchen. As I detour down the row of beans inspecting for Japanese beetles, I hear the sounds and look up toward the barn. The feed room door is open. "The goats are in the grain!" I yell.

I bound through the garden, throw open the gate, and rush toward the barn, yelling "Out!" as I vault the two steps and land in the dark room. When ruminants, such as goats, sheep, and cows, eat too much grain, they suffer a malady known as bloat. The rich food ferments inside the animal's rumen, swelling its sides with gas and squeezing the lungs until the animal suffocates and dies. The treatment for bloat is both simple—release the gas—and horrible. First, you try shoving a hose into the animal's mouth, all the way into its belly, praying for a sudden rush of foul air. But you can't use a garden hose on a goat (the only kind of hose we happen to have) because it can split the esophagus and kill the animal.

If you don't have a hose, you've got one last resort—to drive a knife into the gut, a technique called "sticking." You stick the animal on the left side right behind the rib cage in the swayback spot below the spine.

116

Point the blade forward, toward the right front knee, stab, and then twist. But remember to cover your eyes, since the gas may blow food and digestive juices at your face. Even if you're successful, and your goat lives, it's still at great risk of peritonitis from the unsterile blade.

"Get out!" I say, my eyes adjusting to the dark, and Star tucks tail and darts past my knees. Sweet Pea skitters off to a corner. Then, to my horror, I notice a big black mass crowding the small space. "Belle!" I scream, and she jerks up from deep within the grain barrel. "OUT!"

Instinctively, I clap my hands loudly. Belle jumps and rotates her huge body, spooked. *She'll crush me*, I think, throwing up my hands to stop her. She backs loudly into the barrel. I leap to one side, and she thunders past me. "Get out!" I say to Sweet Pea, and she scampers past, like a skulking dog.

All afternoon, I watch the animals for symptoms—anguished cries, floundering. But the goats are soon playfully butting each other, and Belle is moody and grumbling. Same as always.

C33O

A thunderstorm's brewing, and I'm trotting up to Belle's paddock in the sprinkly precursor to let her back in the barnyard after a foray in the big pasture. No Belle. I check her stall, thinking she's hiding from the flies and mid-afternoon heat. The stall is empty.

"Oh, shit!" I scream. *I left the gate open.* I dash to the barn for Belle's halter and lead rope and sprint through the garden, past the picnic table and into the front yard. When I reach the mailbox, I see her. She's trotting toward me on Boy Scout Lane. Behind her, moving this way, the rain falls in sheets over North Mountain.

I race toward her, bracing for an encounter. Despite my recent headway with Belle, the huge horse still scares the crap out of me. It's all I can do to manage her in the calm barnyard setting. Now, the 2,000-pound animal is running right at me. I have never seen Belle from this perspective, and I realize she runs at an angle, like a dog. No wonder she pulls left, I think. I know that I should have played it cool. But it's too late. "Belle!" I yell. "Get back in that gate!"

When we meet, she stops with a jolt, rearing her head back, nostrils flared, eyes wide and peering down at me. Here's my chance. I lift the

117

halter, nervous, fiddling, and am thrown back to that first encounter. The split second of hesitation is all Belle needs. She tears off past me toward the stop sign and the intersection of Trimbles Mill Road. "Belle!" I scream. And then, "WHOA." She just keeps running.

Belle jogs north, across the bridge and through the tunnel of sycamores, cloppity-clopping on the pavement. I run behind, losing ground, yelling, whistling, clucking impotently. The rain dives from the sky, pummeling my head and shoulders, meeting the ground in a million tiny crowns, frothing the milky brown Middle River. I'm struck by how graceful Belle is, tackless, wagonless, riderless. I wonder how this will end. Will I have to knock on Jeanne's door? Will I have to jump in her truck?

As Belle climbs the hill, running down the middle of the narrow road, I think of all the Boy Scout vans that have raced over the top. "Belle!" I scream, but she only picks up her pace.

Lately, faced with a terrible-two contrarian streak in Luther, I've learned to fight fire with fire. When he won't follow me to the well or sit in the outhouse, I now say, "Okay, don't do it," and I turn and nonchalantly walk away. It usually works. Now, just as Belle tops the hill, I stop and turn for home. "Fine," I say loudly. "Keep going if you want to." Belle stops. I pick up my pace toward home, peering at her out of the corner of my eye. She turns and follows me. When I stop, she stops. So I walk, and she gets nearer. When I turn and slowly walk toward her, she turns and trots away. I head for home again.

Eventually, Belle's at my shoulder. I stop, bending away from her, feigning indifference, casually wiping my arm. I take my time, close enough now to speak reassuringly to her, saying, "So, you're done with your little adventure? Did you enjoy yourself? Get some exercise? Good. Good. Now, it's time to go home." I loop the rope over her neck and hold it at the bottom, where the two ends meet, while I slide the halter over her head. The rain pounds, and the thunder booms. I worry that Belle will spook and bowl me over, but she stays calm. With lightning popping all around, I feel incredibly vulnerable, especially as we pass beneath the rows of sycamores and across the river. From the bridge I can see straight down the valley to Clyde Tillman's house, laundry soaking on the line. I wonder if he can see us, and if so what a sight we must seem, a man and his horse out walking in the rain.

118

☙❧

After much back and forth, I decide to bump thistle-eradication to the top of my to-do list. We may have arrived in Swoope expecting to live our 1900 year in isolation, but we are learning that despite the distances between houses, folks are pretty close. They count on one another. And that includes us. Besides, if a grandmother like Jean can do it, how hard can it be?

One day, I grab a hoe and, unlike Jean, don overalls, work shirt, gloves, and leather boots to armor my flesh against the spines. Starting near the house, where the plants grow sparsely, I chop every one in a ten-foot-wide swath across the meadow and then double back doing the same. I sever the stubborn taproots by stabbing the blade into the ground at their bases and prying sharply up.

At the low end of the meadow, the thistle grows thicker and taller. Single plants sprout up in boxwood clusters of a dozen or more stalks, each as big around as a young oak's trunk. I raise the hoe high overhead and heave with all my might. It crashes to the ground, sometimes slicing crisply as if through iceberg lettuce, other times bouncing dully, rattling the bones in my arms and pinballing my brain against my skull. The plants lunge at me on their way down, clawing my neck and back as I squirm to get away. The thicker they grow, the angrier I get. I hack furiously, swinging the hoe now like a broadsword, dropping the spiny soldiers as they clamber to grab me. Stopping to catch my breath, I survey the surrounding fields and am crestfallen to find that the thistles seem to have suddenly regenerated. They rise up everywhere.

By the time I quit, after a few hours, I am red-faced and huffing, covered in grass, and stinging where the thistle has pricked through my clothes. Espadrilles? What is she thinking? Without some skull-and-crossbones-labeled spray, the plants may swallow us whole.

☙❧

During the last week of August, we're expecting visitors from Brooklyn. They pull into the driveway one morning at 3 A.M. Heather and I light lamps, shake off sleep, and go downstairs to greet them: David Weinraub and Meryl Schwartz, their children Elias, eight, and Lily, five (both asleep in the back), and their senile husky, who bolts from the black Volvo station wagon with a burst of youthful zeal and trees Mudflap.

Heather hugs Meryl. "Welcome to the good old days," she says.

This is Heather's former supervisor, the one who called Heather "fucking crazy" for wanting to live like a dirt-farmer's wife. Now she's come to find out if she was right.

Funny, self-assured, occasionally overbearing, Meryl is 100 percent New Yorker. She grew up in a house overlooking the Grand Central Parkway in Queens. Both she and David are scrappy lawyers with big hearts and a shared passion for public-interest work. Their kids have spent their entire lives in Brooklyn. Which makes me wonder what we're getting ourselves into. They're here for eight days. Do they expect us to entertain them? Because we've got to keep canning. This may be their vacation, but it's not ours.

The next morning, as if having read my thoughts, Meryl, pouring coffee, says, "We are *not* going to be a burden on you guys." And her family's actions match her words, making it perfectly clear that they came to work. They don't shilly-shally over unfamiliar chores but plunge into the garden to pull weeds and fill basket after basket with green beans. They insist their children pitch in, motivating them with the family's one indispensable twenty-first-century treat—gummy worms.

But even the gummy worms get put away, and at one point, Elias pops his head up from between rows and, holding up a green bean, says, "Hey, these things are better raw than cooked!"

They dive in, unafraid to make mistakes, which they do—uprooting half our herb garden while weeding, breaking an axe handle—but who cares?

They even share their piss pot.

Let me explain. The raccoons have begun to strike. Night after night, row by row, they've nearly destroyed every ear of Bill Roberson's sweet corn. Once our corn began ripening, the raccoons started targeting us. Mornings, I would find stalks down and ears ripped open and partially chewed. I have been looking forward to sweet corn all summer. What could I do to stop their nighttime raids? How did they know, to the day, when our corn would ripen?

Sense of smell, of course.

When the deer nearly decimated our young apple trees, a neighbor said coyote urine would keep them away. Great if you knew any coyotes. I began to wonder if human urine would drive away the corn thieves.

By the time David and Meryl arrived, I was peeing around the perimeter of the corn patch at least four times a day and emptying our chamber pot every morning at its corners. Though the garden now smells like a men's room at Shea Stadium, the tactic is working. We're harvesting enough tender corn to give extra to the Robersons. (Peggy, as earnestly as ever, said, "Do you pee *on* the stalks, or next to them?") Now, we've got reinforcements. Good rich New York City lawyer urine!

In more ways than one, our Brooklyn friends are reinforcements. They give Heather and me just the boost we've been needing to make it over the last hump of summer. Our small farm is like a factory, and they're helping us pump up production quotas—picking, cleaning, shelling, and shucking; splitting wood, pumping water. David and Meryl each try everything at least once; goat milking, scythe mowing, laundry. They take cold splash baths and use the outhouse without complaint.

On our friends' last night, we join them in a Friday-night Shabbat dinner. Having bathed and donned clean clothes, everyone is in high spirits. We've spread a gingham cloth on the picnic table and set plates and two bottles of red wine at the corners to keep the warm breeze from lifting the cloth. David and Meryl have cooked dinner—rice, carrots, steamed green beans (raw for the kids), and a whole chicken bought from the Salatin farm and roasted in the woodstove oven. The bounty is breathtaking, even more so for its connection to this place and our hard work.

It has been many years since I said a blessing before a meal. It got to the point where I no longer knew who I was addressing. At such a meal, following such a summer, however, it's impossible not to feel grateful. When curly haired Lily, in her precious doll's voice, leads us in a Hebrew song of thanks, with Elias chiming in, concentrating hard to get the words right, I am struck by the song's humble beauty. "We thank God," says David, translating, "for light, for food, and for wine."

"Amen," I say, raising a glass, choking down my emotions with a gulp of red wine, thinking it isn't so much *who* we pray to but *why*.

121

After finally getting the children down and cleaning up by lamplight, we adults head to the front porch for what has become a nightly ritual this week—sipping Scotch and well-water in the dark. Heather and I take the rockers, Meryl and David the porch swing. We talk and laugh and pause to hear screech owls call to one another across the river bottom.

"You know," says Meryl, "when I told my friends where we were spending our summer vacation, they said, 'Why?' Frankly, I didn't know what to tell them. Now I do."

CRBO

Fall has always been my favorite season. In the City, though, fall's subtle charms are lost amid the concrete and steel. Summers there always seemed to slip straight into winter. Now, having basically lived outdoors for three months, we are attuned enough to notice the changes heralding the season's arrival: a shift in the angle of the sunset, the smell of the wind, mice on the run. And one morning while milking, I look up and notice the swallows are gone. No circlers or swoopers, no figure-eighters, no wire-sitters, no barn chatterers. I'll miss their company.

Led by the seasons, we're in transition, too. We decide to pull the limas to make room for fall spinach, beets, and turnips. It's hard at first. We raised these plants from seeds, and now they're thick-stalked and strong, with waxy leaves and coin-purse beanpods drying on the branch for winter storage. Looking more closely, I see bug holes and scars, leaves nibbled to nothing, the signs of survival, but also buds and tiny new pods. Still producing! I give a sharp tug and am surprised how willingly the plants go, roots snapping crisply. They did their duty. They die with honor, not like the weeds that cling to the soil.

One day our farrier, who drops by every couple months to trim Belle's hooves, says, "I hear it's going to be an old-fashioned winter."

"What does that mean?" I say.

"I don't exactly know," he chuckles, "but it sounds cold." Like the old-timers, he watches the wooly bear caterpillars for a sign of what's to come: the more black they show, the colder it will be. Or he notices the placement of the hornet nests: the higher they are in the trees and barn eaves, the more snow you can expect. Not long ago, I would have scoffed at such

122

prognostication, but now I'm not so sure. I've learned to respect the kind of country wisdom that gets passed down generation to generation by people who live close to the land. Clyde Tillman, who understands horses the way a bird understands the wind, has helped change my views.

I'm not sure of a lot of things I once assumed were true. I'm convinced, for instance, that we have a guardian angel. One afternoon in early September, our angel's little white station wagon pulls up. Out hobbles Ishtar.

"Here's your milk money, dears," says Ishtar, handing Heather the tiny manila envelope and me the empty bottle, "and something for you two." A couple of 1829 beers clinking in a brown sack.

But there's more. Goodies emerge from her basket like clowns from a VW bug: a box of raisins for Luther, a crock of homemade mayonnaise ("I didn't bring much, because it won't keep"), bananas ("these will prevent you from getting scurvy"), a fist-sized loaf of pumpernickel wrapped in wax paper and bound with a string, a small square of fruitcake ("my dear friend in Maryland made this from a family recipe; it *will* keep"), a metal bowl with a wedge of cherry pie ("can't seem to finish the pie"), and a little pink blanket ("if Luther ever gets chilled, you can wrap him up in this—it's yours to have"). In addition to filling her milk jar, Heather hands her a mason jar of goat ricotta and some still-warm oatmeal cookies.

It's not only Ishtar's generosity that leads me, confirmed skeptic, to actually believe she is somehow bewitched. There's the cherubic face, the permanent cheer, the twinkle in her eye, the odd name. Most disconcerting is her knack for uncanny timing. Not long ago, Luther, who had never asked for anything from our previous life, blurted out that he wanted bananas. Five minutes later Ishtar drove up with bananas. During the farrier's first shoeing, he said I should keep Belle's hooves clean. "With what?" I asked. "A hoof pick," he said. I had never heard of a hoof pick. The next day, without any way of knowing about that conversation, Ishtar arrived for milk. She had brought her father's brass hoof pick, a family heirloom. "I thought you might need this," she said. In her eye was that twinkle.

Now, as Ishtar turns to go, Heather, arms laden with gifts, says, "Can't you come in and have some tea?"

"Oh, I can't stay, dears," she says, tottering down the gravel slope toward her car. She pauses, tilts her head and exclaims, "Look!" pointing up at a sky crowded with chunky clouds, like monuments towering to the heavens. One cloudbank shimmers orange. Opposite, a long tubular cloud in a luminescent aquamarine rolls across the sky like an ocean wave.

Ishtar's face lights up. "Look at *that* one!" she says with a schoolgirl glee, "and that one!" We stand silent for a few minutes, watching the colors deepen.

Ishtar sighs and then says, "I'm partial to clouds."

The next morning the clouds are gone. The sky is brilliant blue, and the air is cooler. I walk to the water barrel to fill a bucket and find a single dried maple leaf twirling gently on the surface.

Autumn.

CHAPTER SEVEN

News from the Future

I am sitting on the screen porch shucking corn, with Luther at my feet tugging at the husks, tossing hairy, half-shucked ears in with my clean ones. Heather's in the kitchen making soup, trying to use up our beans, squash, tomatoes, and okra before a freeze hits, which could be any day now. Our sense of urgency was brought on by the arrival of cooler, crisper air. Though the average first frost date is a rough guide, there's no way of knowing when a killing frost will hit.

An engine growls up the driveway, and a Jeep Cherokee skids to a stop. It belongs to Wesley and Crystal Truxell, who live beside Jeanne. They approach with grave faces.

"Have y'all heard?" Wesley says, and my first thought is, *My God, something's happened to Jacob*, their son.

"Heard what?" says Heather, who stands now in the kitchen doorway, drying her hands with a dish rag.

"It's all over the TV," Crystal says. "Terrorists are flying planes into the World Trade Center."

"Man, they're everywhere," Wesley interrupts, words tumbling out. "They blew up the Pentagon. There's a plane down in Pittsburgh. Car bombs going off. This is big time."

Within twenty minutes, three cars line the driveway, and we're huddling with the Truxells, Jean, and Peggy, trying to fathom events possible only in a nightmare. Peggy wears a stoic I-refuse-to-cry grin, lips tight to stop the trembling. Oblivious, Luther runs to her—"Peggy!"—and she forces a smile. *How will this change his life?*

"They're doing triage at the twin towers," Peggy says. "Osama says it wasn't him. A Palestinian group is claiming responsibility."

"Man, this makes me so mad," says Wesley, a tall, bearded man about my age. A welder by trade, he hunts deer and bear and keeps a kennel of hounds, which we hear yelping on still nights. "I'd never want to kill a person," Wesley says in his thick drawl. "But if I could get my hands on the people who did this"—he holds out his hands and shakes two clenched fists—"I'd gouge out their eyes."

Then his eyes widen. "Y'all used to live in New York," he says. "I bet you know lots of folks who live there."

Plenty of people, I think. My brother and his wife. David and Meryl, who both work within a few blocks of the World Trade Center.

"I bet this will make you want to watch television," says Wesley.

Yes. No. Hell, I don't know what I think. This is all so strange and sudden. "I wonder if we should call anyone," I say to Heather.

Before she can answer, Wesley speaks up. "Come on down and use our phone," he says. "You don't really care about your little project enough to not call, do you?" It's a challenge, bolstered by misguided anger. "It's not that big of a deal. You can always go back to it when you want."

All day long I wonder if maybe Wesley's right. Maybe watching the news and using the phone are not that big a deal. In the shadow of such enormity, the whole project suddenly feels "little," as he called it. Don't we have a responsibility to our families and friends? Shouldn't we tune in, like the rest of America? Are we turning our backs on our own era during a time of need?

On the other hand, would we feel any less helpless if we did? If I were still in New York, I might volunteer somewhere, carrying relief supplies or giving blood. Here, we can only imagine what the rest of the country is going through. We can only live our lives.

Which we do, with the same regularity as before, going through the motions feeling empty and strange. The peacefulness of the farm seems pregnant with irony. How can New York be reeling from death and fiery destruction, when here all is innocence and calm—chickens clucking in their nests, cats trailing me for milk as I clink down the path with a frothy pail, Luther jabbing a spade in the dirt?

At night, we try to write letters but the words fall flat, and we give up. Instead, we sit opposite one another on the chilly side porch, sipping bourbon and taking turns reading *Pride and Prejudice* aloud to one another.

Ishtar stops by on the morning of the thirteenth with roses and four large, speckled turkey eggs, oddities that distract us momentarily. While we're snapping beans and shucking corn on the porch, up roars a big white pickup driven by Deb, a concert flutist and former pig farmer who moved here from Iowa ten years ago to work with horses. She drops a stack of newspapers on the table. Staggering color images stare up at us: fire, dust-coated Manhattan canyons, subway walls posted with pictures of the missing. Hundreds and hundreds of posters. We give her and Ishtar eggs and milk and green beans. Exchanging these simple gifts feels good.

Rather than calling or watching TV, we stick to our humdrum routine and watch the mailbox. *What's the worst that can happen?* I'm not sure whether it is resignation or faith, but something helps me abide. I get by without the crutch of technology, the false sense that minute-by-minute news coverage or phone contact puts us in control. I have never been a very patient person. And yet something in me has changed. Over the past few months, I have been calmed by the lack of twenty-first-century distractions and humbled by the power of nature. Like the weather, the terrorist attacks were beyond my control. All I can do is cling to the simple assurance of daily chores.

Like building the cooking fire. One morning, as I shovel aside the ashes and lay on sweet-smelling cherry wood, a strange sensation washes over me. Looking out the window at the mountains, the barn, the chickens scratching at their cratered yard, our spent garden, it's as if the apocalypse has already come, and—technologically speaking—we've been blasted

127

backward in time to some pre-industrial age. And here we are scratching seeds into the earth, cooking with wood, hauling water in buckets.

What *will* become of all this? There's talk of economic hardship, nuclear terrorism, the start of World War III. The stock market had already begun to unravel by the time we launched our project, with the NASDAQ plummeting thousands of points, and now the so-called forces of evil have attacked the U.S., felling the twin symbols of American economic might. For the first time, our project feels practical, in the most distressing of ways. What did Ishtar call it? *Sensible?* Might we actually need these skills to survive some day? I remember the ghastly bomb shelter at Elim and shiver.

And yet, though our mission once seemed to parallel that of the Elim family, our course has long since diverged from theirs. A dark impulse seemed to drive them as they hunkered down, bracing for the world's end. We've come here in search of renewal. As my frightful vision ebbs, it leaves behind a residue of purposefulness and resoluteness. *Of course* what we're doing matters. The attacks have forced people everywhere to re-evaluate priorities, and many are putting things like family, friendship, faith, and good deeds above crass materialism. That's what we've tried to do from the start, even though to some it may look like a game. For the first time, I understand why Heather's grandmother, Christine, cans so much food every year, storing hundreds of jars under the beds and in the closets of her cellarless ranch house, giving much of it away. "You never know," she explained, when I once asked her why she does it. "There could be another depression tomorrow." At the time, I politely nodded my head, finding the idea a bit loony. And I still don't think her little breakwater could withstand a deluge as devastating as the Great Depression. But she's doing what's in *her* power to feel more secure—honing her resourcefulness, staying focused on life's essentials, helping others. Mamaw, as Heather calls her, may be eighty-four years old, and she may live on a quarter acre in town and no longer on her family farm, where someone with rural know-how might stand a chance if times got tough. Nevertheless, she's staking out her independence as a way of making sense of the world, a world that just got a lot crazier.

CƷ&Ↄ

We aren't the only creatures preparing for winter. The rats have been stirring in the barn, leaving little turds in the milking stand's grain box, and scuffling away when I enter at night to milk. Mice have girdled the young fruit trees we planted, so I spend one morning fashioning protective skirts out of some wire mesh I find in the barn, pin-cushioning my palms with the sharp points in the process. Mice are also gnawing our cellared apples, cheese, and a summer sausage David and Meryl left us. I've even found tooth marks on our dinner plates, where they were sharpening their teeth on the enamel.

One day, after gingerly sliding a cheese-baited rat trap into the barn rafters—careful not to let the beefy spring-loaded bar break a finger—I hear a mewing coming from behind the shed. Peering over the fence, I see Mudflap twenty feet up in a tree. "What's wrong, girl? Can't get down?" Not that I'm surprised: Mudflap's a terrible climber. She got stuck twice on the porch roof, where I had to rescue her by reaching through Luther's bedroom window.

When I hear Mudflap calling again the following day, I realize she's really stuck. I hop the fence and carefully slide down the crumbling riverbank, where the tree hangs out over the river shallows forty feet below. *Careful*, I think. And then I call, "Here, kitty. Come on down, Mudflap." *Buzzzz!* Out of nowhere, something dive-bombs me. I duck. *Buzzzz!* Another. I cling to a sapling. Then I see them—red-and-yellow hornets as big as my thumb swarming out of a hollow tree trunk. I duck and swat and scramble up the hill. My left foot slips, driving me to a knee, and then I'm back up, batting and clumsily vaulting the fence. I sprint toward the barn. When I stop—huffing, flustered, but unstung—they're gone.

The next day, I have an idea. Sneezing from the dust, I sort through some ancient siding boards stacked up in the barn. Sawn from lightweight poplar, they're at least twenty-feet long. I hammer a couple of sixteen-penny nails into the end of one, see-saw it over the fence down to the riverbank, and then clamber over myself, being quick about it, expecting the hornets to stir any minute. I hike the board up until it's resting on the lowest limb, held in place by the nails. I lay the other end on the bank.

129

"Here, Mudflap, here's a nice ramp. Come on down now," I say in a syrupy voice. The first hornet burrows into my hair. "Git! Gat!" I say, spastically flapping my hand across my thick mop. I rattle some dry cat food in a can. Beside me, the hollow tree hums to life. "Get on the board, dammit," I say, jigging my hips and waving my free hand. She doesn't budge.

The next day, Heather carries one of our kittens, Banjo, up the hill and lowers him over the fence. "Go get Mudflap!" she says, and the young tiger-striped tomcat darts up the trunk to the limb where Mudflap is marooned. As if demonstrating, he slowly backs down. "See, Mudflap, it's easy," Heather says. Banjo does it again, climbing up, backing down, but the hornets soon emerge. Mudflap paces the limb, mewing pathetically, and then curls up in the notch where limb meets trunk.

After six days in the tree, Mudflap's skin hangs in loose folds over her frame. Her eyes are edgy and ringed in black. She just sits there, curled up like a turtle in its shell.

Hornets are said to sleep at night, so just before midnight on Day Seven, I strike out on a Mudflap rescue mission. It's the darkest night in recent memory. I arm myself with an oil lantern and one of our precious few cans of salmon from the cellar. I've barely made it over the fence and safely down the rotten slope, when I hear something—not the hornets but leaves rustling along the bank. My imagination goes wild, racing up the critter chain from possum to skunk to raccoon. Wesley Truxell has seen bear in these mountains. And bear love salmon. I raise the lantern and squint into the four-foot halo of light. Balancing on the riverbank, I imagine whatever's out there crunching closer, closer, closer. I can't shake the image of a bear: the idiot's grin of fangs looming into view, the stench of foul breath and—*SWIPE*—the beast himself, clawing for a fishy treat, batting me off the cliff and onto the rocks below.

Crunch. Crunch.

"Ahhhh!" I shout. My foot slips, and my arm—the one holding the lamp—shoots out for a handhold. I drop the lamp. It bangs on a rock and goes out. Blackness swallows me.

"Oh, shit!" I scream, dropping everything and scampering uphill on all fours. The rescue mission is a bust.

The next day, I find no signs of bear. No signs of anything.

Heather thinks it was a possum.

"I don't even like that cat," I say to Heather. Mudflap bullies the kittens. She's standoffish and spoiled. Turn your back, and she'll snag a fresh pillowcase out of the laundry basket or a shirt you've set aside, nestling into the cloth like some exiled princess. Unlike Pick and Banjo, who are bright and friendly and always playful, Mudflap is grumpy, hissing them away from the milk dish. "I know she hates it here, but you'd think she'd come down by now."

"Maybe this is some kind of hunger strike," says Heather. "Or maybe she's afraid of the hornets, too. All I know is we can't just let her die."

"I know," I say. "Whenever I get near the barn I hear that pitiful cry."

On Day Eight, a green SUV pulls into the driveway. It's Will Moore, who lives in town, dropping off eight bushels of what he calls "nineteenth-century apples," picked from an abandoned orchard on some land his family owns in southwestern Virginia. Spilling from cardboard boxes, the fruit is small and deformed—unperfected by the genetic tinkerings of man. Next week, he and his family are coming back to make apple cider using a nineteenth-century cider press my father gave us. In July, as an experiment, Will brought us three blocks of ice, frozen in baking pans, which we stacked in a sawdust-filled box in the basement. On the third day, there was still enough left to ice a pitcher of tea.

Will, my age, was the first person we met after we bought Trimbles Mill. A commercial pilot and father of two, Will once nearly chucked it all to move to Alaska with his wife, Kathy. Instead, they stopped in Seattle. Now, having returned to Will's hometown, they raise hens in their backyard for a taste of homesteading.

"Where's this cat Heather was telling me about?" says Will, who is tall and wiry and, today, dressed in crisp tennis whites. He's got a tennis match in half an hour. "Not that I could do anything. I'd just like to see her, poor thing."

On our way to the barnyard, I give an abbreviated version of the story.

"So you see," I say, as we approach the fence, "that tree is hanging over the . . .," but before I can finish my sentence, Will vaults the fence in a flash of white, a court champ hurdling the net. "Watch out for the hornets," I say, but he's no longer listening. Surfing down the embankment, he's focused on the tree.

"Hey, this tree is climbable," he says, stretching his fingers over the lowest limb, planting his feet on the trunk and quickly swinging up, oblivious to the void yawning below. "Hey there, kitty, nice kitty," Will says, peering up at Mudflap, who has sprung to the tree's highest fork. Maybe it's because he's now above the level of their nest, or maybe it's the blinding Wimbledon whites, but the hornets ignore him. He climbs another ten feet. Five more. Mudflap mews pathetically. Easy does it. He's got her! He cradles the cat in one arm while using the other to climb down, but Mudflap squirms to his shoulders and digs in, making Will wince.

I'm at the base of the tree, and by now the hornets are buzzing us. Will quietly hands the bony cat to me and leaps from the branch. I don't let her out of my grasp until we're back at the house, where Heather looks at Mudflap and then at Will's dirt- and bark-smeared whites. "You did it!" she says. His arms and neck are bloody with scratches. Mudflap is a sack of bones, eyes sallow, mudflaps drooping more than ever.

Will, embarrassed by the fulsomeness of our praise, heads for the driveway. "I better get going," he says, "or I'll miss my game." As he speeds off, I am reminded of what Lord Nelson, the famous English admiral, once said: "Never mind maneuvers. Go straight at 'em."

☾⚬☽

In the weeks that follow the terrorist attacks, the necessities of daily life prevent us from dwelling too much on the tragedy. We are relieved to learn from letters that my brother and his wife and David and Meryl are fine. Like the rest of the country, our little corner of the Valley mourns. Neighbors occasionally drop off newspaper updates about the aftermath. Other mail from New York trickles in. Any time we see a New York postmark on a letter, we open it slowly, not sure of what we'll find inside. We read harrowing details from friends about the smell of burned flesh and the greasy ash that fell like snow. We read about friends of friends who died. "I still wake up in the morning and turn on the radio expecting to hear somebody blew up the Lincoln Tunnel," writes Meryl. "It makes me so sad to think of our kids growing up under a cloud of fear." Her son Elias is confused and cries a lot. Three of his Park Slope classmates lost fathers.

Luther is too young to understand what happened, and in many ways that is a relief to us. We've got our hands full steering him through our year-1900 version of normal two-year-old development challenges, like feeding himself and using the toilet. One night, Luther wakes up crying. "Outhouse," he says, but it's pitch black, and the last thing I want to do is get dressed, put on my smelly boots, light an oil lamp, and travel all the way out there, where the skunks loiter at night licking the leftover milk from the kittens' bowls. "Here's the chamber pot," I say. "You can go poopy here."

Big mistake.

"Poopy in outhouse!" he says, defiantly.

"No, Luther," I say. "At night, we use the chamber pot." Groggy with sleep, I'm not thinking about parenting consistency or fairness. I only want to crawl back into bed. The chamber pot's right here. What's the difference?

The difference is that Luther's two. Experts spend entire careers trying to unearth the secrets of the two-year-old brain. All they can do is theorize. Whatever's going on in there, he is determined to go potty and to do it in the outhouse. I can hardly blame him, since that's where we've taught him to go. So at the word no, he screams and wails, throws himself on the floor, kicks and hits and bangs his head against the wide pine planks.

Nights may be a struggle, but Luther's transition out of diapers has gone well, even without all the plastic Fisher Price potty-training aids. Nevertheless, we have experienced the unavoidable accidents. Once, while my attention was on the chickens, Luther squatted in the grass beside the henhouse. Before I realized what he had done, he was happily patty-caking his own poop. Another time, he squeezed one out on the washroom floor, fascinated by this object he alone had produced, with no help from a grown-up.

Like many two-year-old boys, he revels in life's coarser pleasures. One night, we are having dinner with Michael and Victoria Godfrey, enjoying fascinating and wide-ranging conversation by the warm glow of oil lamps, when Luther shatters a momentary silence—everyone chewing—by ripping a fart across the seat of his wooden high chair. I'd compare the sound to a chain saw, except that chain saws didn't exist in 1900.

Which reminds Michael of the time he asked a Native American friend what the Navajo say when they pass gas at the dinner table. We all lean in to hear Michael quote his friend, repeating a Navajo phrase that lifts and falls with a succession of soft vowels and guttural consonants.

"So what does that mean, Michael?" Heather asks.

"It means, *I farted!*"

છ80

Luther was named for a bootlegger who sold moonshine to the coal miners of north Alabama, tucking bottles in a secret compartment in his pickup bed beneath a pile of pick handles. The legendary Luther Helms, born in the late nineteenth century, once allegedly fought his way free from a pair of handcuffs and a carload of deputies. Another time, he shot a sheriff in the jaw. Heather knew the man personally. He was her great-grandfather. In fact, his daughter—Heather's grandmother—is due for a visit any minute.

Edith Lavelle Helms Reid arrives dressed in black—black shoes and socks, black pants, a black ribbed turtleneck sweater, and black rhinestone-studded glasses. Stretching her legs after the long car trip, she swivels her head thoughtfully from farmhouse to barn. At eighty-five, she is old enough to remember privies and wood cookstoves and life without electricity. The world has changed since then, and from her look I gather that she's either wistful or having second thoughts. Maybe both.

Heather steps through the screen door: "Hey, Granny."

"Well. . . ." Lavelle replies, holding out her arms for a hug.

Somehow, Heather's mother, Ginnie, has convinced *her* mother to accompany her on an eleven-hour road-trip—a sentimental journey back to a way of life both would probably rather forget.

Lavelle is hard of hearing yet too stubborn to let anyone fix her faulty hearing aid. As a result she shouts a lot and gets shouted at a lot, and for the first half hour after their arrival, she and Ginnie bicker loudly over why they got lost on the way from Alabama.

Soon, though, Lavelle's back on her trip down memory lane. One of the first things she notices is our washroom. "We washed on the back porch," she says. "When you finished, you sloshed the water right over

134

the rail." Once a week, she and her sisters had to scrub the cedar stave buckets with sand. "It was hard work. Didn't care for it at all." When I clank out to milk the goats, she comes along, her eyes exploring the barn's cobwebby timbers. "My daddy kept three or four milk cows," she remembers, though she has no desire now to milk a goat.

Her daddy, the infamous Luther, whom Heather remembers as an upright, Bible-clutching man with blazing blue eyes (we learned of his checkered past *after* we named our son), was many things, including bootlegger and farmer. In the 1930s, he drove mule teams while clearing land slated to be flooded by the great dams of the Tennessee Valley Authority, which brought electricity to the south at a time when 90 percent of the urban population had it but only 10 percent of rural dwellers did.

"One Christmas, Daddy told us girls the weather was too bad for Santy Claus," Lavelle says that night at dinner, Luther's eyes locked on her wrinkled, lamplit face, "so I didn't bother putting my stocking up. On Christmas morning, all my sisters' stockings were filled with goodies. I felt terrible." Lavelle pauses, sipping from her water. "Daddy told me to go get my shoes on. When I did, I found all sorts of dolls and presents in my shoes. That was about the greatest thing that ever happened to me. I couldn't believe that Santy knew where *my* shoes were."

Mystified, Luther says, "Granny Reid was a little girl?"

"You bet I was," she says, bending closer to Luther. "I was a mean one, too." She grabs his foot. "Gotcha!" Luther jumps, and Granny erupts into laughter.

Though she's enjoying her stay, Granny is a creature of habit, and her habits include electric lights, store-bought food, and television. She keeps looking around absently for a light switch. While putting Luther down one night, Heather finds Lavelle stumbling around upstairs with a candle. In the dark, the forty steps to the outhouse are treacherous.

With babysitters on hand, Heather and I plan a drive. Rolling down from the barn in the wagon, a pair of pitchforks rattling in the bed, I pick her up in front of the house. She takes my hand as she steps into the wagon. Our eyes meet. It feels like honest-to-goodness nineteenth-century courting.

"You know," Heather says, sliding closer, "You haven't taken me for a drive since the Wilsons' party." Without Luther in her lap, she seems more relaxed, even as Belle stutter-steps at the sight of the bridge. So much is behind us now—the summer garden, the canning, the awkward early days of the project when worry and fatigue turned each of us darkly inward. If the terrorist attacks helped crystallize the importance of our 1900 project, it also reminded us both how lucky we are to have one another.

Heather leans her head against my shoulder. Belle trots steadily. A broad V of geese flies over, their calls dissonant and brassy, like some modern composition for reeds. The trees lining North Mountain Road throb with the rust and yellow and burnt orange of autumn.

Passing Bill and Peggy's house makes me think of our neighbors. And that reminds me of something I've been meaning to ask Heather.

"Remember what Meryl said when she was here?" I say. "Her comment that people love to share what they know?"

She nods. When Heather and Meryl worked together, they ran highly successful justice-reform projects on shoestring budgets. Their secret was recruiting experts eager to share their knowledge, often for free. Meryl used their experience to help explain our magnetic draw on the residents of Swoope. We need help, Meryl explained, and the neighbors have the know-how. Gardening, baking, horses, you name it.

"She was right," Heather says. "Everybody likes to feel needed."

"But there's got to be more to it than that. Think about all the drop-ins! All the gifts! I know they're not doing it for the goat's milk." In addition to many, many loaves of zucchini bread, people have dug through their basements to bring us long-forgotten relics—walnut crackers, a pair of laundry tubs, even the complete set of *National Geographic* magazines from 1900. We've stirred something in them.

"It's not about give and take," Heather says. "You should have heard Ishtar get all huffy once when someone called what goes on in Swoope 'bartering.' To her, keeping a tally ruins the joys of the shared experience."

"Yeah, that makes sense," I say. "But it's tough being on the receiving end of so much goodwill. Makes me feel needy." I smile when I think how misguided my visions of self-reliance were.

"They want to be a part of what we're doing," Heather adds. "We've become the nucleus of this community. You saw how many people showed up after September 11th. And they keep showing up. I think the simplicity of our lives reminds them of what really matters in life."

We reach our destination, a barn standing alone on the far side of the Godfreys' farm. I hop down and roll the big door to one side. The hayloft is stuffed with bales of straw, which we need for mulching our fall garden. The rats have chewed through the twine on a couple dozen bales, littering the floor with loose straw. Michael said we could have as much of the loose stuff as we wanted. *Mutually beneficial*, I think, *and neighborly, to boot*. We begin forking it into the wagon's small wooden bed. Soon our straw pile towers, pokes out from beneath the bench, and spills off the sides.

On the return trip, we see a bald eagle, a rare sight in the Valley. We stop to watch as the giant bird lands in a tree, takes off again, and disappears over the hill. "Come up," I say to Belle, making a clucking sound with my tongue. "Let's go home." Mentally, I try the word on again. *Home*. For the first time, it seems to fit.

Home is on Granny's mind as well. After two days here, she's still getting her bearings. With failing hearing, sight, and mobility, she is dependent on modern technology. We should have realized that sooner. One night, it becomes painfully clear. As Ginnie leads her to the outhouse, Lavelle trips and falls. "What are you doing!" she hisses, "bringing an eighty-five-year-old woman to a place like this?" We are relieved to learn she's okay—no broken bones—but the fall frightens her. It frightens all of us.

The next morning at breakfast, Ginnie has an announcement to make. "We're leaving early," she says. "Mother needs to get home."

Trying to sound upbeat, Ginnie asks her mother, "Do you think we could stop by Monticello on the way?"

Lavelle looks across the table at Heather and silently mouths the words, "I don't give a *shit* about Monticello."

"Well," says Heather, out loud, "you didn't want to come here at first either. But I bet you're glad you did."

"I *did* want to come," Lavelle says. "I couldn't wait to get here. I knew there were going to be hardships. But now I'm too far from home."

One day during a visit to the Godfreys' farm, one of the wagon wheels shatters. Leaving the slumped wagon, I walk Belle and the busted wheel home, wondering if my driving days might be over after having just begun.

The next day, I swallow my pride and walk to Clyde Tillman's with the broken wheel slung over my shoulder. I have no choice. Despite my embarrassment over breaking the wagon so soon, I have no idea how to fix the wheel. I lay it against the tree and knock on the door, amid the yelps of his dog.

The old man opens the door, and I follow him into the squalid kitchen. In the adjoining living room sits Ellen, behind her walker, a plastic tray duct-taped to the front spilling crumpled tissues and pill bottles.

"Where's your horse?" Tillman says, flashing his dentures at me in a wicked smile.

"That's why I'm here. I've got a little problem," I say, pointing out the window. "Wagon's got a flat."

When he sees the broken wheel, his face grows serious. We go outside to take a look.

"What'd you do, wedge it in something?"

"I don't know."

"I've broken spokes turning on this driveway. It can happen any time to anybody. You never really know."

I can hardly believe my ears. Is Clyde Tillman trying to make me feel better?

"I'll tell you what," he continues. "I'm doing a job up near Dayton, burning brush for a feller. I'll drop by Burkholder's," he says, referring to the Mennonite buggy shop, "and talk to him about how much it'll take to fix that wheel."

Two weeks later, on a bright October morning, Clyde Tillman parks his pickup in the driveway and sits. When I step out of the kitchen, he pokes his head out his window. "Burkholder called. He's got your wheel ready." Dentures clacking, the old man's in a good mood.

"He's fast," I say, pleased at the prospect of getting back on the road. "You still working up there?"

"Nah, but I need to get me a haircut," he says, looking in the rearview mirror, tugging on his white locks. "I could run you up there right now, and I could stop in at the barber shop."

Pause.

"Well, Mr. Tillman," I say, trying not to seem rude or ungrateful, "part of this whole thing of going without a car is not accepting rides."

He shakes his head and chuckles. "If you've got somebody who can pick it up, fine."

"How much did he say it was?"

"He didn't say. He just told me it was ready and hung up the phone. Burkholder don't like to talk much when it's long distance."

Bill Roberson teaches a math class at a university near Dayton. Two days later, he brings me the repaired wheel, with new spokes and felloes made of smooth, unfinished ash. Total cost: $136.50, about as much as a new car tire.

Not long after, I pedal over to Clyde Tillman's with a sack of apples and find the farmer in his front yard working his team of horses. He ties them to a hitching post beside the driveway and approaches me.

"Thank you for helping me get the wagon wheel fixed," I say, handing him the apples.

"What's *that*?" huffs Tillman, pointing at my bike, with its sissy bar, basket, and chrome fenders, leaning against a tree. "Where's your horse?"

"She's at home," I say.

"Gettin' fat," he grumbles.

By contrast, his horses are noticeably unfat. Tall, rippling with muscles, and much bigger than Belle—a thing I had not imagined possible—they blow and paw the ground. Trace chains and a double whiffletree link them to a contraption he's made for training them to pull: a sled with steel I-beams for runners and a green vinyl bus seat bolted to a floor of weathered oak boards. It is a piece of work, and I gaze admiringly upon it the way a car junkie might let his eyes linger covetously on a neighbor's vintage pickup truck.

"Get on," he says.

I ease into the bus seat, trying to keep a lid on my excitement. Tillman sits down beside me.

"Come up," he barks. The horses step to the left, and the sled swivels after them on the grass. Trudging along, they dig their iron shoes into the clay and churn up clods that rain back down on us. We are riding low, so low that my head is below the horses' exhaust pipes, which makes it awkward when one of the animals shits, the wet green lobes oozing out, *bbvvvfaaaart*, and plopping on the ground.

Tillman guides the pair with two fat leather straps, which he holds close to his body, bending his elbows just so. His stubby arms are dark with sun and grime, more machine part than muscle and bone.

For a while neither of us speaks. In place of words are the clomping of hooves, the jangle of chains and deeper *clunk, clunk* of the iron double tree, the hiss of the steel runners on grass, and the slurred, wet breathing of the horses through their bits. Although dozens of questions—about horses, equipment, training techniques—spring to mind, I keep my mouth shut. Getting information out of Clyde Tillman requires patience and skill. Emerson once wrote of Thoreau: "He knew that asking questions of Indians is like catechizing beavers and rabbits." With Tillman, it feels the same.

"What are their names?" I ask finally, feeling like Aladdin wasting one of his three wishes.

"Bob," he says, nodding his head toward the left horse. "And Amos."

A silent minute or so passes.

"Amos came from an Amish feller up near Dayton," Tillman offers, unsolicited. "He didn't want him no more. Said the horse jerked his arms too much."

That sounded odd, a bit trifling, like selling a car because the windshield wipers slapped too loudly. Besides, Tillman's arms looked steady.

"What do you mean, Amos jerked his arms?" I say.

"Whoa," says Tillman, almost whispering. He hands me the straps. Before I can ask any more stupid questions, he adds, "Come up," and we heave to a start. Quickly, the horses are trotting, the sled fishtailing in their wake.

"Make 'em walk," Tillman grunts. "Make 'em work."

I pull hard on the straps, and the horses slow, rearing their heads and scooping up more sod with each step. My arms feel awkward—out too far, now too close together—but I don't dare loosen my grip. Clods fly with impunity into my hair, pelt my face. My triceps and biceps burn. Soon the pain is exquisite. This is no Sunday drive with Belle.

After a lap down and back with me at the reins, Tillman mercifully stops the horses with a quiet *whoa.*

"I see what you mean," I say, handing over the lines. We sit on the bus seat in awkward silence for probably ten minutes. Then he drives the team back toward the barn, where he halts beside another sled.

Instead of a bus seat, this sled holds a stack of seven concrete weights totaling 4,000 pounds. This is what Clyde Tillman lives for—draft-horse powerlifting. Each summer and fall, he and Ellen trailer his horses to competitions in Virginia and neighboring states to see who can drag the most weight a total of twenty-five feet.

When I first heard about his hobby, I was unimpressed. Dragging concrete across a patch of dirt? How dull. But after four months in 1900, I am beginning to understand that draft-horse pulling is more than just an old-timey tractor pull. It's about a deep relationship between man and animal that's rapidly fading. Thanks to tractors, little if any real work remains for these four-legged titans, who once cleared an entire continent for farming. A man might love his tractor, but he'll never gaze into its eyes, secretly convinced it has a soul. As I get to know my own draft horse better, I am beginning to feel connected, however tenuously, to this man and this age-old tradition.

We step off the bus-seat sled. Holding both straps in one hand, Tillman reaches down to lift the iron ring off the sled's hitch. Speaking quietly to Bob and Amos, he walks them into position in front of the other sled, the one with the two tons of concrete, letting the ring drop over that sled's hitch. The transition looks effortless.

"Most fellers can't do that without help," he says, the furthest I have ever heard Clyde Tillman stray from modesty. Using his magic touch—brute intimidation, say some who know him—Tillman has managed to create a pulling-circuit anomaly, Herculean beasts who are as calm as lapdogs.

I step back, eager to see what will happen next. He lets the animals stand a while. Then, with no fanfare, no horse-pulling equivalent to *on your mark, get set, go,* he quietly bids the team, "Come up."

The horses clearly know what lies behind them, because they take off with such a force that had they been hitched to the bus-seat sled, the acceleration would have pitched us backward. But hitched as they are to two tons sinking into the soft earth, the horses dig and stomp with all their might, barely inching forward in a fury of churning legs, flying spittle, and dust. Only Tillman is motionless, perched along one side, his cap brim dipped ever so slightly to deflect the flying divots. Etched onto his face is a Mona Lisa smile, one of the few expressions he wears other than blank. Driving that rig, he looks like something very old, much older even than 1900. Timeless, in fact, like a figure carved for the ages out of stone.

CBEO

For two days now, the wind has howled through our little corner of the Valley like a ghost train, snapping maple branches, rattling the tin roof, spooking the animals, whistling through gaps in the house. It hectors us, tugging hair and crowding the mind with sound. I'm in the kitchen when I hear a crash from the washroom. I rush in to find shards of glass strewn across the floor. The wind has ripped the window out of its frame.

That night, before bed, I carry a lantern to the backyard fence to brush my teeth, a nightly ritual that continues even now that it's getting colder. The moon is not yet up, and in the blackness, the hollow wuthering and crashing of limbs is even more menacing. Even under glass, the lamp flame gutters. I brush quickly for fear of getting clobbered by a falling branch. When I glance up, I see lights in the pasture.

Three beams wave side to side, search-party style. At first, I assume they're coming from the Boy Scout camp, but our hill blocks all sight of the camp from here. Whoever is holding those flashlights must be on our land. But why?

I consider approaching them, but the wind is about to snuff my lamp, and I don't want to get stuck in the dark.

That night, I sleep fitfully. Every creak and groan, every thump of door or tap of limb sounds like a stranger entering our house. Boy Scout camp is long out of session, and we have seen no signs of off-season Scout activity. Michael Godfrey once caught some teenagers swilling beer after midnight on Jeanne's property, but her place is vast. Our forty acres feels as intimate as a big backyard. As a one-time small-town beer-swilling teenager myself, I never would have parked so near a house. Or carried a flashlight.

Why, on such a blustery night, would someone be poking around our pasture?

CHAPTER EIGHT
Under Fire

A few nights later, I am in the kitchen blowing out lanterns before bedtime, when two trucks rumble up the driveway. The first truck is lit up like a Christmas tree, with yellow running lights trimming the cab. A man steps out and approaches.

"It's been a while!" he bellows, stopping in front of the kitchen door, not entering and not letting me close it. "We're gonna run the dogs behind the barn."

I raise my flickering lamp for a better view of his face. Beefy, it's framed by stringy, shoulder-length blond hair. The guy's probably thirty years old and reeks of beer and cigarette smoke. Beyond, laughter from the second truck rises above the throaty idle of the engines.

"Mike moved out," I say, realizing he has mistaken me for the previous tenant. "What do you want?"

"We want to hunt 'coons, man," he says, as if I were stupid.

"You may have been able to hunt before, but we own this place now."

"Is that right?" he says. "You must have just bought it, 'cause I've been hunting 'coons here for ten years. Carl Cox said I could." Yelps burst from the trucks. He jerks his head toward the cages built into the beds. "Shut up!" The hounds keep barking.

"Carl isn't manager here anymore. The farm got split up and sold."

"Hell," he says, "all we want to do is park behind the barn and take the dogs down to the creek." Swiveling again, he yells, "Shut UP, goddammit!"

From behind me, I hear Heather's voice. "What's going on?" she says. In one hand, she holds a lamp by the bail. The other arm curls around Luther, hugging him to her hip. His head rests on her shoulder, and with a tiny fist he sleepily rubs an eye.

"These guys want to hunt racoons behind the barn," I say. "Carl used to let them when he was in charge of this place." I turn back to the hunters. "I don't think so. We've got a horse in the barnyard now. And a couple of milk goats."

"Aw, we won't hurt your goats," he whines.

"Listen," I say, realizing how ridiculous this is, arguing in a dark kitchen at ten o'clock at night. "Now's not the time. Come back during the day and we can talk."

"Do you own the creek?"

"No. I don't know who owns it. A farmer named Joel Wilson leases all that land. You'll have to talk to him."

"Joel? He's a friend of mine. You got his number? Let's call him."

"We don't have a phone."

He eyes me suspiciously. Like a kid, he won't give up. "Come on, man, we ain't gonna hurt nothin'. We just tree the 'coons. We don't kill 'em."

"What's your name?"

"Donnie."

"I tell you what, Donnie," I say, wanting him out of our kitchen, thinking maybe he's not so bad if he's a friend of Joel's. "There's a set of gates at the back of the property. You can enter there," and as I describe the spot, outlining where they can and cannot go, he nods impatiently, as if to say, *Yeah, yeah, asshole.*

Later, I lie in bed for a couple of hours, ears pricked to the comings and goings of the two mufflerless trucks. Every so often, headlights crawl up and down the walls of our bedroom. At one point, I get up and see the group searching the field opposite Bill and Peggy's house with flashlights. *Those were the guys the other night with the lights.*

Finally, I drift off.

BOOM!

I bolt upright. I jump out of bed and bound across the room, foot bumping the chamber pot, piss dousing my leg and spattering the floorboards. As I reach the window, heart drumming my ribs, I hear an accelerating roar and see yellow running lights racing down the road and out of sight.

"What was that?" hisses Heather.

"The 'coon hunters."

The next day I discover their target—the big brown State Wildlife Management Area sign at the edge of our front yard. The aluminum is dented. Pock marks radiate out from the center, the result of a shotgun blast at close range. I had almost forgotten my earlier fears about firearm-loving rednecks. Everyone in Swoope has been so *nice*. But this incident reminds me that we're still in gun country. And we're still outsiders.

CRBO

Luther and I are filling the screen-porch wood-box a couple days later, when the Robersons' green Camry pulls up. Bill gets out, leaving Peggy in the passenger seat. I stoop to wave, and as she waves back, I notice she's wearing more makeup than I've ever seen her wear. *Too much of a face on,* I think. She picks distractedly at some cut flowers in a vase.

"Thank you for feeding our cats," Bill says quietly, handing me a jar of pear preserves. He and Peggy have just come from parents weekend at their son's college. They both look worn out.

"We talked about tomorrow for dinner," I say, "but if you guys are too tired. . . ."

"I'm not too tired," he shoots back. He turns to Peggy then and mouths something. She cocks her head and gives him a wide-eyed look that silently screams, *Bill!* I am about to assure them that we'd be happy to postpone, when he turns back to me with a pained look on his face.

"We've got a little bad news," he says, looking straight at me with moist but unflinching eyes. "I had a growth removed. It was malignant."

"Oh, Bill," I say, holding tight to the preserves.

145

"I'm going back tomorrow to make sure they got it all," he says.

I think back to a dinner at their house not long ago, when Peggy told us about a close friend of hers who was recently diagnosed with cancer. "She's a fighter," said Peggy, her fierce Scottish pride showing through. Her friend had gone public with her cancer battle, cracking jokes and soliciting prayers. "She has the *best* attitude. That's the way you've got to be." Standing there, unsure of what to say, I wonder how Bill—such a sensitive, private soul—will handle this.

Not long after, we set out to visit Bill and Peggy. It's Halloween, and we've decided to take Luther trick-or-treating, a practice that originated in Medieval England, when the poor went door-to-door asking for treats (in Shakespeare's *Two Gentleman of Verona*, Speed accuses his master of "puling, like a beggar at Hallowmas"). Though we're not sure if rural Virginians in 1900 donned costumes, we can't pass up this opportunity for some family fun.

Luther is Peter Rabbit for the occasion. Like the mischievous little storybook bunny, he is smartly dressed in a blue pea coat with gold foil over the buttons to resemble brass, a ball of wool for a tail, cloth-covered pipe-cleaner ears, and rabbit whiskers and a pink nose painted on his face. The outfit, all Heather's doing, is adorable, far superior to last year's store-bought pumpkin suit. He's so cute, we are dying to show him off, so the three of us set out on foot, bundled against the cold and carrying a paper sack for candy.

Not knowing if rural Virginians *today* trick-or-treat, we have given advance notice to a couple of neighbors that we might knock on their doors. One is Jeanne, and we set out for her house first. We walk the road, sticking to the shoulder. A perfectly round orange moon, tailor-made for the occasion, rises in the sky over Jeanne's hill. Soon, we are standing beside her house, rapping storm-door glass, straightening Luther's ears and reminding him of what to say.

"Trick-or-treat!" he screams, when Jeanne opens the door. Then he raises a grubby orange stub he's been gnawing and says, "I have a carrot."

"You sure do," says Jeanne, smiling. She reaches in a basket, pulls out a handful of candy, and drops it in Luther's sack. We chat for a bit and then walk to Bill and Peggy's in the dark, Luther riding on my shoulders. Peggy wears a black, wide-brimmed pointed hat. Bill does not mention the word cancer, nor do we. Instead, we focus our attention on Luther, who has stuffed his carrot into his pea-coat pocket and is now tearing into his treats. Heather and I decided months ago that while we can't use a camera, we can't stop others from taking pictures. So Peggy pulls out her point-and-shoot and snaps a few pictures of Luther and his carrot. Then she stuffs candy into his bag by the fistful, since he'll probably be their only visitor this evening. Soon we're off, Luther propped on my shoulders, the full moon, gray and higher in the sky, lighting our way.

"Let's go to the Tillmans'," Heather says. "They'll love seeing Luther."

"Do you think they'll be expecting trick-or-treaters?" I picture Ellen zonked out in a chair behind her pill-bottle-cluttered walker.

To our surprise, Clyde and Ellen are both in lively spirits, making a fuss over Luther and stuffing candy into his sack. When we finally get home, I'm exhausted. To knock on three doors, we walked nearly two miles, me with a thirty-pound rabbit on my shoulders.

⊂Зᙠᴑ

A week after the run-in with the 'coon hunters, Joel Wilson drops by in his Farm Use pickup with his wife, Edie. When I mention the 'coon hunter's name, Joel screws up his face and fingers his droopy mustache. I describe him, and Edie says, "Oh, what's-his-name's son. Lives up the road."

"Yeah," says Joel. "Drives an old gray pickup with running lights and a dog box." In addition to hauling dogs, Joel says, poachers use those boxes to conceal deer.

"He made it sound like you two were old buddies," I say.

"Oh, Lord," Joel groans.

"What's his story? Is he bad news?"

"He's not bad news. He just doesn't do much. Can't hold a job. Probably gets by on you and me, if you know what I mean." I assume he means a welfare check.

Joel says the guy borrowed his horse trailer once. Then, he "borrowed" it another time without asking—and without bringing it back. Joel finally had to call Donnie and ask him to return it. Another time Edie caught him and a buddy skulking around the posts and rolls of

147

wire mesh stored near their barn. He seemed edgy and said, "I need some fencing. How much will Joel sell it to me for?" Edie replied, sternly, "It's not for sale." The whole time, he and his friend were ogling all the expensive farm equipment. "It gave me the heebie-jee-bies," Edie says.

To me, that sounds like bad news. The guy sounds like a thief.

Every once in a while, late at night I'll catch sight of a truck with running lights thundering past the house. No more gun blasts, at least for now. I figure the first was drunken sport or maybe a warn-ing shot, a cowardly way of saying, *Don't fuck with me.* I've changed my mind about the back gate, but I can't call to tell him. I feel like we're sitting ducks.

CO380

Winter marches at us. A few cold nights in September stunned the sum-mer garden. A hard frost in early October knocked it out for good, send-ing a rich smell rising from the blackened plants like a final breath. The drought is back with a vengeance. The dryness and the grasshopper plague it brought on have devastated our fall garden. Now the pasture grass is so dry that when I rake around the pecan tree, clearing a ring to make harvesting the nuts easier, static electricity sparks and pops, and I wonder if I might start a brush fire.

With the garden gone, I let the chickens out to feast on the grasshoppers. They've devoured every bug and blade of grass inside their pen, and though they get plenty of layer mash and curdled goat's milk, nothing excites a chicken like a live snack. They especially love a crunchy grasshopper. I know because earlier this fall, out of frustra-tion, with our turnip plants nubbed to nothing, I snatched the insects off the dried cornstalks and tossed them into the dusty arena where the birds pounced like lions on the tiny armored creatures. Now that the chickens are free, they run wild, cackling for joy over the hopping abundance of it all.

Abundant may have aptly described our summer garden, yet we are now on the gastronomic equivalent of a fixed income. We surpassed our goal by preserving more than 350 jars of food, including corn, squash,

148

okra, pickled cucumbers, dill-seasoned pickled green beans, and more than 100 quarts each of tomatoes and green beans. We made three dozen jars of blackberry jelly, put up fourteen gallons of apple cider, dumped a bushel-and-a-half of potatoes in the bins, stored pumpkins and winter squash and onions. We put up a half-gallon each of dried lima beans and field peas. To save time, we let the beans and peas dry on the plants, and then pulled the plants whole, picked the shells, bundled them in a sheet, and whacked them with a stick to pop them from the shells. Sometimes I'll step into the cellar, close the door behind me, and just stand there looking. As proud and fortunate as we feel, however, there's no way to know if we have enough. If we keep our goats and chickens healthy and producing, we've got eggs and milk, but we can't grow any new vegetables. Cracking that first jar of tomatoes a few weeks back launched a half-year of rationing.

Despite our concerns about having enough food and water, about the looming winter, and the 'coonhunters wrecking our peace of mind, Heather and I are feeling more comfortable than ever with our 1900 life. As the neighbors bring news of war in Afghanistan and anthrax scares — one friend saw men in what looked like white space suits in front of a cordoned-off office-supply store in town — I realize how lucky we are to be here together on these peaceful forty acres. Not only do we now cook, clean, split wood, and tend the animals with brisk efficiency, but the pressures of summer have eased. No more watering, weeding, and battling critters. No more harvesting and canning. We return from the cellar lugging a basket brimming with food and a half gallon of apple cider, all of it put up by us, feeling proud and secure. The food is *better* than money in the bank.

I can't contain my feelings of gratitude. For the first time since my boyhood, I offer silent prayers of thanks without getting hung up on the theological details. Heather and I sometimes make love in the afternoons, during Luther's nap. Since our bedroom adjoins his, we meet in the living room. And since we have no couch, we peel off our clothes and lie on quilts on the rug, listening out for Ishtar's *yoo-hoo* or a knock from a pumpkin-bread-bearing Bill Roberson.

One afternoon (when we are fully clothed) Michael Godfrey drops by for a visit. We are standing on the screen porch, when he says, "Hear that?"

I cock my ear, expecting a bird's song. Michael often interrupts conversation to identify the cry of a pileated woodpecker or the *fee-bee, fee-bee* of a chickadee. But this time I hear only hammering, and not the hammering of a woodpecker's bill. The banging stops, and a chainsaw whines to life. It's coming from Clyde Tillman's house.

"Yeah," says Heather. "I hear that racket a lot. Sounds like we live down the road from the Brooklyn Navy Yard."

"That's precision cutting, my friends," Michael chuckles. "Mr. Clyde is putting up another shed."

That afternoon, I walk to Tillman's house, where I find him sitting in an aluminum lawn chair sipping a Dr. Pepper. His thumb is wrapped in bloody tape. He banged it with a hammer, Michael said. Clyde just grimaced and kept hammering, blood dripping and eventually clotting in a glistening, sawdust-flecked bulb of red.

"I heard the hammering," I say. "Need any help?"

Tillman smiles his inscrutable smile, a smile neither of pleasure nor derision. "I'm wore out," he says. "This here shed's more work than I figured on."

I take that for a yes and stand around while Tillman drains the Dr. Pepper. He tosses the can beside the chair and hands me a hatchet and a handful of nails. Self-conscious in front of the old workhorse, I use the flat back-end of the hatchet to hammer scraps of corrugated roofing metal to the sides of his crude frame. The tool is awkward, and I worry that if I hit my thumb I won't be so stoic. But soon, I've found a rhythm, pounding the nails home with a half-dozen or fewer blows each. A little while later, Tillman sucks down another soda. "You wanna cold drink?" he asks. I politely refuse.

The shed shelters a wood-burning boiler that supplies hot water to the house through buried pipes (which explains the billows of woodsmoke we often see coming down the valley on little cat feet). It's a purely functional structure, built entirely out of salvaged materials, except for the nails, which are store-bought. For corner posts, Tillman ripped a telephone pole lengthwise into quarters using his chainsaw. His whole ramshackle collection of outbuildings seems to have sprouted from the soil like weeds.

Having trouble starting the nails on the slick, curvy metal roofing, Tillman bangs his taped thumb again, pausing to hold it trembling in mid-air, a twisted look on his face. He's like a preacher under the spell of God but for the foul language issuing from his lips. The boiler beside us belches smoke.

By the time I leave, there are five Dr. Pepper cans scattered beside his aluminum chair. When I tell him I've got to be getting back, in typical fashion, he does not thank me or say goodbye. I simply walk away, heading for home.

CRBD

One night around dusk, the crack of a rifle rattles the windows. With deer season upon us, we've been hearing sporadic shots coming from the hills and neighboring farms. It's like we've suddenly landed in a war zone. But this blast is the loudest yet. Heather and I burst onto the porch. I can barely make out a small, black pickup truck, headlights dark, easing down Boy Scout Lane. The headlights blink on, the truck accelerates, and then it speeds through the stop sign. No running lights. Whoever it was probably stuck his rifle barrel out the truck window.

"That makes me so mad," says Heather.

Later, clanging back from the milking parlor, I see a pair of headlights searching the wooded hill opposite our farm. I drop the pails in the washroom, grab a lantern, and march toward the road. The truck—probably the same—zooms off before I reach the driveway, but they've seen me. At least they know I'm watching them.

The next morning, I'm standing in the yard when the same small black pickup passes our house on its way up Boy Scout Lane. I jog past the mailbox and start walking down the dead-end road. This time, I've got them.

I haven't gone 100 yards when I see three men and a dog in our field. I hoof it across the pasture, trying to maneuver the high grass quickly without running. I don't want to scare them away. I'm nervous—heart racing, breath shallow. Seeing me, they split up, leaving one to meet me.

When I'm fifty feet or so away, I say, "Hey, what are you doing?"

"My friend shot a deer yesterday around dark, and it ran this way."

"Yeah, we heard the shot," I say, trying to catch my breath, my anger building. "He wasn't shooting from his truck, was he?"

151

"Naw. He has permission to hunt that land over there." The guy's probably forty-five, and he speaks softly, in a gloomy, high-pitched drawl. I'm trying to stay composed, but weeks of built-up fear and anger—at poachers, at rednecks like the 'coonhunters, at myself for not standing up to them—boil to the surface.

"Whose land is that?" I ask, testing him.

"I don't know," he whines. "My friend can tell you."

"What's your name?"

"Tim."

"What's your last name, Tim?"

"Deaton."

"Tim Deaton," I repeat.

"What's your buddy's name?" I say.

He loses his cool. "Now, I'm just going to let you ask him," he says.

"You can't tell me, Tim?"

"I feel like I'm getting interrogated."

"You're acting like you're guilty of something."

"I'll get off your land," he says, "but don't ask me any more questions." He starts jogging down the hill and leaps over the barbed-wire fence. His two buddies are already on the road, standing behind the pickup. My eyes search the group, and I'm relieved to notice that none of them is carrying a gun.

I don't want them to pile in the truck and leave, so I yell out, "Can I help you find anything?"

A guy dressed in quilted camo coveralls, who looks like a long-haired Sonny Bono, stops. "Yes," he says, his voice earnest. "We're looking for a deer. . . ."

"Who shot the deer?"

"Me," Sonny Bono says.

As I question him, I hear some sort of speech impediment. And his eyes—when he talks to me, they drift strangely off to one side. He reminds me of a guy I once knew with brain damage from a construction accident. Hard as I try to stay angry, I can't.

"Listen, guys," I say. "My wife and I heard the shot. It scared us. And then I see you wandering around our property. It would have been nice if you had knocked on the door and asked permission."

They apologize. And then we're all just standing there, awkward as hell. I start walking down the road.

"Jump in," Sonny Bono says. "We'll give you a ride."

"No. I can't," I say. "I mean, I'd rather walk."

CR80

Just when I think we're rid of hunters, an unfamiliar blue pickup truck pulls up while I'm milking. I notice a dog box, and my nerves sit up. I latch the goats in their stall and walk down, hands in pockets. Two guys get out: the driver, with a hint of black stubble on his shaved head, and another man, with a fleshy face and shaggy blond hair.

"Donnie, right?" I say, aiming my hand like a pistol at the long-haired one.

"Yeah," he says. "You ain't heard a 'coon dog this morning, have you?"

"No."

"We was out last night and lost a Walker named Clipper. He ain't mean."

"I'll keep my eyes open," I say.

Donnie, taking in the sweep of the farm, says, "So you bought this place, huh?"

"Yeah."

"You from around here?"

"No. We moved here from New York." Changing the subject, I say, "Listen, Donnie, I talked to Joel Wilson. He said no hunting on that land. That means you'll have to find a different place to run your dogs."

Later that day, the guy with the shaved head returns. He has an angular face, hungry eyes, and a couple of scars chiseled into his jaw. "Still no sign of Clipper?" he asks. "Damn dog cost 1,000 bucks." He has been out most of the night looking. "The name's Dale," he says, sticking a hand out the window. Shaking it, I tell him again I'll keep my eyes open.

CR80

The same day another pickup roars into the driveway. This one's red with a neat little camper top on the back. Recognizing it, I smile.

153

"You eat chicken?" asks a kind grandmotherly woman stepping out of the truck. Short with gray hair pinned into a topknot, Liz Cross wears purple jeans and a hooded sweatshirt in a different shade of purple. With her is an olive-skinned boy of about twelve.

"I don't eat *our* chickens, if that's what you mean," I say. "They're layers."

"No, that's not what I mean," she says. "Are you vegetarian?"

"Heather is. Why?"

"Would you help my friend Dot Makely slaughter some roosters? She'll give you one for every three you kill."

Liz, who lives with her husband Jack on a few acres nearby, stands like a farmer, leaning back, hands stuffed in pockets. In the middle of her sentence, she shifts her weight slightly and farts, clearly but not loudly, with no blushing or begging of my pardon or comments about frogs, as if passing gas during a neighborly chat is the most natural thing in the world, which, arguably, it is. "Dot's blind," she says. "Well, mostly blind. She has crescent vision out of one eye and her colors are all messed up. It happened about five years ago, after her heart surgery."

A highly capable woman, Liz never seems in a rush. Though she stays busy—teaching university cooking classes, counseling prison inmates about nutrition, and raising and preserving nearly all her family's food— Liz always has extra to give, whether it's onion sets or "punkin'" bread or her time. The boy with her, whose name is Nigel, is deaf. He helps her on Sundays.

Liz and Jack are the Helen and Scott Nearing of Swoope. Rugged, resourceful, committed to social justice—just like the homesteading authors of *The Good Life*—the Crosses came here from the Midwest decades ago to build a life for themselves away from the mainstream. They are practical people, saving and recycling almost anything. Piles of pipe, posts, and plastic containers, and rolls of rusty wire lay weed-tangled on their property, next to hothouses and broken-down sheds. Jack is an electrician and a tireless tinkerer. The day he met Luther, he drove home and returned a few hours later with a broomstick horse—clothesline bridle, scrap-leather ears, white plastic bottle-bottom eyes. The brown wood stain on the head was still wet.

"But I don't know anything about killing roosters," I say.

"You'll need to go at night because that's when you can catch them," says Liz, ignoring me. "She's got a son that lives with her, but he won't do it. Says he's too busy, but I doubt that."

I have no way of seeing in the dark, so I visit Dot Makely's during the day, pedaling over one afternoon with a pair of canvas gloves in the basket and a nervous stomach. A big, boyish man, probably forty, wearing a grimy mechanic's uniform, answers the door, scowling. I realize I'm dirty, too, and wild of hair. "Is Mrs. Makely here?" I ask. "I'm your neighbor. I came about the roosters."

"Mommm!" he calls, turning and shuffling into the cramped house. I follow. He points at a woman sitting at the kitchen table and then plods into an adjoining room. I hear television voices and laughter and see blue flashes, like dull, boomless fireworks, lighting up the dark room.

"Liz Cross said you needed some help," I say, introducing myself. Unlike her son, Dot Makely is perfectly charming, launching into conversation as if we were old friends and had been sitting over lunch since noon. We talk. Actually, she talks, and I listen. She talks about her chickens and the coyotes that come down from the mountains to stalk them, about her land, which she kept after her divorce, about her spring, which is still flowing despite the drought. It's as if her mouth, rather than her ears or nose, has compensated for her blindness. Which is fine with me, since the talking postpones the killing. All I can think of are the neck-wringing stories I've heard. Now that I have chickens—and know how big they get—I can't imagine ripping the head off one.

"Listen to me, gabbing on and on," she says. "You've probably got things to do. Let's go find those roosters!"

Like a debutante, she takes my arm, and I lead her slowly outside. She's a tiny woman and spunky, despite her age and her lack of sight, with a bright, smiling face.

I guide her around a bunch of ankle-twisting walnuts scattered on the ground.

"I was so fond of walnut trees when I was a girl," she says. "I asked my mother once, I said, 'Mother, will there be walnut trees in heaven?' She said, 'No.' I told her, 'Then I don't want to go.'"

A fowl flutters past with a startled cluck.

"Is that a rooster?" Dot asks.

"I have to admit my ignorance," I say. "I can't tell the difference."

I'm only here because of what I call our "country cred," which is like street cred, only different. Because we are living off the land, people assume we know more than we do about country life. Not even Liz Cross cooks on a woodstove or drives a horse and buggy, and Liz can do anything—including strip down a car engine to a pile of nuts and bolts and parts and piece it back together (which I know, because Jack Cross told me so while wearing a look of pure husbandly pride on his face). But even though I've learned some 1900 skills, I still have a hole a mile wide in my country-living résumé. No matter. Liz still comes to *me* to kill the roosters for the blind woman.

"Oh, the roosters have bigger combs on their heads," she says, matter-of-factly. "And they're a lot more aggressive."

We enter the henhouse, where twenty birds of all sizes, shapes, and colors explode in a panicked cackling, beating up a toxic, lung-choking dust.

"Be careful," she says. "They can be mean."

Gloves on, I chase what looks like a rooster into a corner, yanking its legs out from under it before it can peck my eyeballs out. I carry it upside down, holding it well out of range of anything it might target below my waist. We walk back up the hill, where an axe leans against a stump.

"Just chop the neck," she says, holding the head. "And try not to cut off my hand." Gripping the legs in my left hand and the axe with my right, I try to concentrate, but Dot won't stop talking.

"Roosters flop around so much after you cut their heads off," she says. "Drop it quick. Otherwise, you'll get covered with blood."

I raise the axe, arm wavering under its weight.

"I hope people don't do that," she says.

"Do what?" I say, lowering the axe.

"Flop around when you kill them. It would be horrible—in a war or something. You'd see bodies flopping around."

"I'm pretty sure they don't," I say, raising the axe. I lower it again when I realize she's not finished.

"I hate war. The one we're in has me so angry," she says, referring to the U.S. invasion of Afghanistan, now about a month old, which we know because the neighbors have kept us informed. "I can't really say anything, though, since I don't vote."

"Why not?"

"I'm a Jehovah's Witness. We don't believe in it."

Determined to finish the job, I stop asking questions. Soon, the conversation peters out.

"Here goes," I say, raising the axe again. The bird, still stretched across the stump, wriggles pitifully. I let the heavy iron head fall. It bounces, as though I've just hit a rubber hose. The rooster's eyes bulge. I raise the axe again. *Thud.* The head tumbles.

Stepping back, I drop the rooster and the axe, the blade barely missing my foot. The rooster hops away, shaking out its wings in a gesture of freedom as blood spurts from its neck. But then, as if suddenly realizing that something is terribly, irrevocably wrong, the bird panics, flapping and flopping in a silent scream. Spraying blood, it somersaults down the hill, regains its feet, tries to fly. Blind—*worse* than blind—the bird smacks into a tree and pinballs off in another direction. It hops. It spins. *My God! Will it never end?*

But it does, and we go after more roosters. The second one flops, just like the first. I don't drop the third bird quickly enough and blood spatters my cheek and pants and boots. Dot is effusive in her thanks, and it's all I can do to convince her that I don't need a dead rooster for my services.

Pedaling home covered in blood, I spy a handsome brown-and-white hound dog guardedly trotting across a field. Picturing the dog's scar-faced owner, I think, *keep riding. Pretend you never saw him.* But I can't. It feels wrong. Maybe it was my visit to Dot's or my run-in with the sad-sack deer hunters, but I suddenly see this community in a new light. It's like family. You've got to take the bad with the good.

"Clipper!" I yell, and the dog stops and cocks its head. "Clipper! Come, boy." He sees me, but instead of coming, he darts in the opposite direction.

გ80

Election Day arrives, and Heather and I decide to vote, even though the women of 1900 were still twenty years away from suffrage. What Dot Makely said makes me more eager than ever to let my voice be heard. There's only one problem: Though we both have the right to vote, we lack an easy way to get to the polls, which are six miles away at a county high school. Belle might break a leg trying to cross the train tracks. So we pump up the bike tires—this time we take the other eBay bike, which David Weinraub kindly fixed when he was here—and pedal off after lunch, leaving Peggy to watch Luther.

This is the first time either of us has left our quiet pocket of Swoope since we began, and we're both excited and nervous. Huffing and puffing, we roll into the high school parking lot and drop the bikes on the grass near the auditorium door. We take turns pulling the lever behind the stained curtain—it's over in a matter of minutes—and return to the bikes. On the way home, we pass a filling station with a fiberglass buffalo perched on the roof and marvel that even though we have not stepped foot in a store for five months, there's nothing inside we really need. We follow a different route home, one that is slightly shorter but hillier and unpaved. My chain pops off, and I have to flip the bike and hammer the chain back onto the sprocket with a rock. I get off the bike and walk at least ten times before finally topping the last hill and coasting home, dusty and exhausted. For the first time in my life, the effort required to vote seems to fit the importance of the task.

CRED

After dinner, the blue pickup with the dog box pulls into the driveway and the 'coonhunter named Dale gets out of his truck. "Still looking?" I say, stepping out of the kitchen.

"Yessir," he says, with a new deference. I'm about to tell him I saw Clipper, when he says, "Listen!"

I hear yelping in the distance.

"He's treed!" Dale says. "I know he is." Happy, strung-out from lack of sleep, apologetic, with a couple more "sirs" thrown in for good measure, he asks if he can walk behind the barn to get his thousand-dollar dog. The goats are already penned up for the night. Belle's probably off in the pasture somewhere.

"Sure," I say, "but don't leave the gate open."

"Aw, hell no," he says, grinning widely, sticking his hand out again in thanks and then pulling on a fancy-looking headlamp and strapping a battery pack to his belt. "Folks around here, most of them, are pretty nice."

I smile, feeling more than ever like one of the folks around here.

An hour later, I hear barking and then the truck engine and then the rattle of the dog box as he leaves the driveway.

CHAPTER NINE

Home for the Holidays

*I*nstead of the traditional four seasons, the ancient Roman writer Varro suggested six seasons per year: Preparing Time, Planting Time, Cultivating Time, Harvest Time, Housing Time, and Consuming Time. Two-thousand years later, the pre-mechanized farmer of 1900 would have basically followed the same schedule. With the calendar year drawing to a close and our summer vegetables safely housed in the cellar, we're approaching Consuming Time, a period of rest and celebration, when—during Varro's day at least—no hard work was to be done outdoors.

At Trimbles Mill, the last of the cool-season greens we managed to grow have withered and what Washington Irving called the "golden pomp of autumn" has exited the stage, leaving the landscape mostly lifeless and gray. As relieved as we are to have had a successful harvest and canning period, we're anxious about the coming months. Have we put up enough food? Do we have enough fuel? Neighbors recall the winter of '93 and the odd sight of Swoope's fenceposts lost beneath deep snowbanks. Could we handle such harsh conditions? Summer was a challenge, but winter will be our true test. And the build-up is killing me. I worry that winter will reveal some unanticipated flaw in our system—a frozen well pump, conditions too cold for the animals—that will shut down the project halfway through. Or that we'll be plain miserable—cold and stuck indoors for three months with a two-year-old bouncing off the walls.

For now, our extra free time gets gobbled up by holiday preparations and out-of-town guests. Our friends all seem to have the same idea—a fall getaway in the Shenandoah Valley (fresh meals! wagon rides! scenic views! no cell-phone service!). Over the course of several back-to-back weekends, they arrive from all corners of the country—Chicago, New York, California, Alabama—like emissaries from the modern world. One couple brings their new Bernese Mountain Dog puppy, another their new baby. The husband of Heather's cousin *insists* I take a peek at his new van's GPS-based navigation system.

As happy as we are to see everyone, all this company raises questions: Do we enforce our 1900 rules with visitors who never signed up for our time trip? Is it cheating if they bring along gourmet cheese, California wine, or H & H bagels from Manhattan? Or does the generosity of a few groceries make up for the dent guests put in our larder? It's the same paradoxical choice we've faced here in Swoope: Stick by our rules and risk alienating our well-meaning neighbors, or bend the rules and enjoy the sense of community that has blossomed from the creation of those rules? At times, it's a bit too much—enough to make me want to say, *Pass the bagels.*

Funny how we once worried about getting lonely.

We're also gearing up for visitors of a completely different sort—our parents. Whereas our friends responded to our decision to drop out of the twenty-first century with bemusement and enthusiasm, my mother and Heather's father were shocked, disappointed, and afraid (not so much my father and Heather's mother, though they were more bemused than enthused). With my folks coming for Thanksgiving and Heather's for Christmas, this holiday season will be our chance to give them a glimpse of our life in 1900. We hope it's a reassuring one.

We face the same broad quandaries we did when our friends visited, of course, and yet as my parents' arrival date draws near, the questions grow more specific: Will my mother bathe in the livestock tank and use the outhouse? Can my father survive without his cell phone? And where will he plug in his breathing machine?

My seventy-year-old father, John, a retired pathologist, suffers from sleep apnea, a disorder that causes him to periodically stop breathing during sleep. To keep him breathing, every night without fail he switches on a small machine that pumps air to a clear rubber mask covering his mouth and nose. This machine has traveled with him to Europe and even to a remote bamboo-stilted river lodge in the Ecuadorian Amazon. In rural Virginia in 1900, thirty years before the arrival of power lines, his machine is worthless. So he checks into a motel fifteen miles away, where he can sleep without the fear of asphyxiation. My mother, Nini, gets the unheated spare room, where she puts a Tupperware chamber pot on newspaper in a corner.

I admire her for coming. She's a city girl, raised in Birmingham, Alabama, educated in Boston and Columbia, Missouri. For a long time, she has questioned my choices. Why did I stop going to church? Why did I want to run off to Africa after college? Didn't I want to get a real job, like a banker or an insurance salesman, with benefits and security, instead of struggling to be a writer? And *New York*? Why live so far away in such small apartments? Collapsed into so few sentences, her negativity sounds crabby and overbearing. It's not. It's just there, like the pink lipstick smears on the glasses she uses, which I notice as I scrub dishes by candlelight. My mother, slow to change, has learned to live with my decisions, and we maintain a fairly close relationship.

I distinctly remember her response on the day I called to tell her about our project. Granted, I must have caught her completely off guard. Hearing "big news," she probably thought Heather was pregnant again. I told her we were moving. Her voice brightened. *Finally*—I could almost hear her mind working—*they're leaving New York!* "It's not really *where* we're moving to, it's *when* we're moving to," I said, explaining the 1900 experiment. Her voice soured. "What do you want to do *that* for?"

My father, raised in a small South Carolina town, is excited about our project, not so much because it is a challenge we have taken on or for the window it opens onto an earlier way of life but rather as an excuse to tinker with some old-fashioned toys. A pack rat and inveterate browser of antique shops, he drove here with my mother in a pickup truck hauling a heap of his manic accumulations—a two-man cross-cut saw, a six-foot log (for trying out the saw), a wooden goat cart, and a box full of old kitchen implements, including a wooden lemon squeezer and a rusty open-hearth popcorn popper, even though we have neither lemons nor open hearth.

Their first morning here, Dad shows up for breakfast showered and shaved and looking far more rested than my mother. He drops an orange from the motel fruit basket on the table. My eyes light up at the treat, but before I can reach for it, Mom, bouncing Luther on her lap, grabs the orange and casually begins to peel it.

"Why don't you two take Luther for a walk," I say. "I'll come find you after my chores."

Heather has already begun cooking the Thanksgiving meal. She had to get a jump on things, since the oven is so small and we don't have enough pots and pans and casserole dishes to handle everything at once. This morning, she's making pumpkin pies and bread. While I finish my coffee, I join her before heading out to the barn.

After dropping a log on the breakfast coals, Heather slams the firebox door, adjusts the damper, and begins making the pie crust. She moves with purpose, her flower-print apron hugging her slim figure. I'm surprised by her confidence. Not so long ago, she was terrified by the woodstove. In her mind, I was the one who figured out the mechanics of the stove, and I was splitting the wood, so naturally, firebuilding fell to me. If I was off milking or pumping water, Heather would call to me from the screen porch to come add another log to the fire. One day, she was just about to put some biscuits in the oven, but the fire was dying. She poked her head outside. "Logaaan!" But I must have been out of earshot. She cautiously opened the firebox and stood back, tossing in kindling like tiny spears. The fire roared to life. Then she shoved in a bigger log. Soon, the flames wrapped themselves around the oven box. Her biscuits came out fine. She never called for wood again.

"Will you cut that pumpkin for me?" asks Heather, rolling dough, flour dusting her forearms.

I grab a wooden cutting board and work our largest knife through the middle of the pumpkin, a pre-1824 heirloom variety called Tan Cheese that I fetched from the cellar. I scoop the seeds and begin separating them from the slime.

"Did Peggy ever stop by?" I ask.

"I haven't seen her," says Heather, filling two pie pans with the soft dough. Heather had invited Peggy and Bill to join us for the Thanksgiving meal, since neither of their children will be home. "I'll have to check with Bill," Peggy had said. "He has cooked a turkey every Thanksgiving for twenty years, and just the other day he bought a twelve-pound bird." Bill's also in denial about his cancer, unwilling to admit that he'll probably need radiation treatment or that the surgery to remove the grapefruit-sized tumor in his abdomen was no small matter. As much as they would love to join us, she didn't think he'd feel up to it. If they do decide to come, we'll have plenty of food.

Next, Heather lays the pumpkin halves face down on a tray and slides the tray into the oven. She tosses the seeds in a bowl with oil and salt, spreads them on a pan, and puts them in the oven as well—a crunchy snack for later. Heather has always been a good cook, but in New York, with a career and later a baby, she never had the time or interest to bake breads and pies or experiment much in the kitchen. Maybe she would have if she had grown up in a household where everything was made from scratch. But her mother, like so many women of her generation, discovered alternatives to the drudgery of domestic chores: kitchen appliances, washer/dryers, frozen and packaged foods. Back then, quicker was better. For Heather—hustling home from work, picking up a baguette to serve with pasta—quicker was often the only way.

The typical farm wife 100 years ago couldn't choose convenience over made-from-scratch. Neither can Heather. At times, she'll stand outside the henhouse tapping her fingers, waiting for an egg to round out a recipe (once, while making brownies, she impatiently reached under a hen and was sharply pecked). Last June we had assumed we were embarking on a year-long involuntary diet. But using our limited ingredients, Heather has adapted to the challenge of cooking three meals a day, seven days a week, with energy and creativity. We have never eaten better in our lives. True, at first we consumed lots of cabbage (it got to the point where I couldn't squeeze another cabbage worm, not because squeezing worms is gross but because their guts reeked of, well, cabbage). And eggs still turn up at many meals, though these are so fresh and rich I don't mind. But Heather really mixes up the daily menu, serving soups (pumpkin, curried zucchini and lentil, corn chowder), salads (garden salad, tangy slaw, potato salad), quiches, bread pudding, tomato sauce over noodles, roasted root vegetables, squash fritters, corn pudding, and on and on. She bakes constantly—custards, pies, cookies, cakes, biscuits, and bread. Plus, she makes yogurt and cheese, including an herbed goat's cheese that could go head-to-head with any chèvre this side of the Pyrenees. She has even made a few oddballs—lentil pie with peanut butter crust, for instance—that she uncovered from nineteenth-century cookbooks.

Heather moves on to her rolls. Yeast bread is another new accomplishment for Heather, and from the way she patiently kneads the dough, I can tell it's a source of pride. With the help of Liz Cross, our homesteading/prison-counseling neighbor, Heather worked at it for weeks. Some batches of dough were too wet and stuck fast to her bread board. Others were too dry and never rose properly. Liz, who has been making bread for fifty years, would sit and watch Heather knead until her dough was just right. Liz is what Ishtar would call a "real *woman*," meaning she can do anything. "Baking bread's like a lot of things in life," Liz told Heather. "Easy once you know how."

By now, Heather knows. Once her dough has risen, she punches it down and plucks off little pieces, pressing each one into a patty and then folding the edges into the center. When she's done, twenty dough balls line a pair of trays, waiting to become fluffy, chewy rolls. Soon the smell of baking bread will mingle with the roasting pumpkin and a hint of woodsmoke, and the stovetop will be filled with simmering, bubbling pots. I swill my coffee, kiss Heather, and grab the water buckets. Off to work. Wiping the dough from her hands with a kitchen towel, Heather clanks open the firebox door and adds more wood. Her day of cooking has just begun.

Cঙ৪১

On Thanksgiving morning, Heather's still focused on the food, especially the eleven-pound turkey—her first ever—cooking in the woodstove oven.

So focused, in fact, that she hasn't given any thought to decorations.

"What are you going to do for a centerpiece?" asks my mother.

"Oh, Nini!" Heather says, "I completely forgot."

"Don't worry!" my mother says, jumping into action. "I'll take care of it." And she does, departing with a basket and returning with russet-colored leaves, a few pine boughs, and two small pumpkins from the cellar.

Bill Roberson may not feel up to socializing—it turns out he underwent a second surgery the day before—but he and Peggy show up anyway. And of course they don't arrive empty-handed. Bill has prepared a cranberry salad for the occasion, and Peggy has made candied yams. Quieter than usual, Bill wears a smile plastered to his face to mask the pain from the surgery. When no one else is looking, he pulls me aside and shows me a fluid-drainage bag strapped to his side.

Though we've known Bill and Peggy for only six months, they're like family. They serve us meals made from their own fresh and preserved garden vegetables, take care of Luther, share their gardening knowledge and nineteenth-century novels. Knowing how much we missed music, they even once invited a teacher friend of theirs over to play guitar and sing for us on their deck. Having them here for Thanksgiving is a chance to do for them. We're grateful they've come.

We're grateful for so much more as well—our health and safety, the bounty of our garden, our cellar full of food, having my family here with us. My brother, Bill, and his Ecuadorian wife Michelle have joined us from Brooklyn. As they visit with everyone in the living room, Heather and I sneak off to the kitchen. "It's overwhelming," she says to me, in the moments before we give the signal to line up with plates. She's eyeing the bowls and platters of food, cooking that has consumed her for days now. "I mean, last spring we didn't know how to plant a seed, and now look at this spread! I'm not sure I ever understood Thanksgiving before now."

The sight is enough to make everyone gasp. Food rests on every kitchen surface available: steaming bowls of corn pudding, roasted potatoes flecked with rosemary, green beans, and rice and gravy; pans of moist cornbread dressing seasoned with sage that Heather planted, harvested, and strung up to dry; pickles, deviled eggs, the Robersons' cranberry salad and candied yams; Heather's yeast rolls, including a couple of misshapen ones kneaded by Luther; her two pumpkin pies; and a platter of sliced turkey, which cooked to perfection in the intensely hot, slightly smoky box, the heat searing in the juices and Heather's seasoning.

As the nine of us hold hands around the table, stoic Bill Roberson, hiding any discomfort, blesses the food and our friendship. Awed by everything that went into creating the meal on my plate, I remember something Heather told me about her grandmother, Christine—that she shows her affection with food. Any time Heather and I visit her, she lays out a feast and sends us home with armloads of her fig preserves, sauerkraut, and famous homemade peanut brittle. I did the same thing, too, I realize, when I cooked for Heather on her birthday. And now, there's the meal before us—grown, prepared, and served with love.

I raise my glass in a toast. "To Heather."

CRBD

No, my mother doesn't brave a splash bath in the livestock tank, but her opinion of our 1900 project has clearly shifted. "I had no *idea* the food would be this good," she admits in the lazy aftermath of the Thanksgiving meal, as we rock on the front porch (there being no televised football game to keep us inside). But it's not just the food. It's the lack of hurry and distraction. We have lingered over meals, pressed apple cider, and visited with the neighbors. My mother has taken walks along the gravel road, pulling Luther in his wagon. An artist, she has been sketching the cows, barn, and mountains. Both of my parents have grown immediately attached to Bill and Peggy (I caught them whispering something about exchanging phone numbers, in case of emergency). I'm sure viewing our project through the post-9/11 lens has helped them appreciate the community we've found here in Swoope.

A couple of days later, my mother confirms my suspicions as we say our goodbyes in the driveway. After hugging Luther, she turns to me. "You and Heather have created a wonderful life for yourselves here."

CRBD

Not long after my family leaves, I wake to find Luther standing beside our bed. "Up! Mommy-Daddy's bed." The tiny hands that reach for me

168

are hot. I lay my palm on his forehead. Fever.

Back in New York, we might have given Luther some children's Tylenol and tucked him back into bed. We would have slept easily knowing that if he still felt bad in the morning, we could take him to the doctor up the street. Now, all I can think of is something my mother told me when she was here.

She had been reading a novel set in a poor, turn-of-the-century Appalachian mountain community. "I can't get over how similar their lives are to yours," she said. "The washroom, the well, the oil lamps." Then she described a scene involving a feverish child. His parents carried him down the mountain at night to the home of a doctor, but the doctor could do nothing but give him throat lozenges. They returned home, where the child died. I can't seem to shake the image of the family walking the dark, lonely mountain road carrying a child destined to die.

My mind flashes to our car in the pasture, now a mouse motel. Michael Godfrey discovered the infestation one day as he and I hiked up our hill to inspect our pasture grass. On the way past the weed-swallowed station wagon—almost invisible to my 1900-focused eyes—he peered inside and gave a little yell. "Good God, man!" he said. The mice had confettied a road atlas and littered the seats with droppings.

"Oh, no," I groaned, cracking the passenger door and recoiling from the reek of mouse piss. Bits of paper hung from the air-conditioner vents. Inside the glove box, the registration (expired) and insurance policy (canceled) were shredded, too. Outside, straw nests poked from the air vents beneath the windshield wipers. When we popped the hood, Michael shook his head and said, "I knew it." Half a dozen of the colorful little electrical wires that snake around the engine block were severed. Clumps of straw and paper nestled in the engine's dimples. "Oh, well," I said, slamming the hood. "Next summer's problem."

Now Heather stands over Luther's bed, stroking his hair by the soft glow of an oil lamp. We're both afraid, having been conditioned to rely on doctors and spoiled by easy access. At what point do we throw in the towel and violate our rules for the sake of our child's health? In Brooklyn as we planned our project, the same questions had come up. Do we bring along antibiotics for Luther, who suffered chronic ear infections and croup? We chose not to, gambling that the illnesses would clear up once he left germ-ridden daycare. And until now, Luther has been healthy.

A century ago, we would have faced grim prospects. Exposing a child to the cold and damp of night might have worsened his condition. You had to ride things out until you could summon a doctor to your child's bedside. And even then, you weren't much better off, since doctors were basically powerless against most illnesses, including viruses and bacteriological infections. In their little black bags, they kept morphine to alleviate pain, quinine for malaria, as well as a variety of tinctures, plasters, and poultices, much of which would be considered quackery today. Some also carried what might have been mistaken for a carpenter's kit, with saws for amputating arms and legs. In 1900, only 10 percent of all doctors had attended college.

The next day, Luther won't stay in bed. He's up and following us around the house, whining mostly but also playing some. At first we worry that he might wear himself down, but if he were really sick, his body would force him to rest. Luther's fever, we soon realize, is neither life-threatening nor rule-threatening. In two days, it's gone, allowing us to conveniently shelve the debate about breaking our rules to see a twenty-first-century doctor.

CR&O

Athletes dream of entering the zone, when their ability to focus is so great that mind and body become one. During these fleeting moments, they ski faster, drive golf balls farther, and jump higher than ever. The clock stops ticking. Miracles happen. One writer calls it the "sweet spot in time."

Now that the early days of fumbling over harness straps, blistering our hands on garden tools, and barking orders at each other are over, we've found our sweet spot in time. Gone, at least temporarily, is what Wendell Berry calls man's "strange, almost occult yearning for the future." We feel comfortable enough with our recreation of the past to focus our energy on the present. With Varro's Consuming Time in full swing, the outdoor chores have dwindled to a minimum. Heather fixes meals from mason jars of vegetables with the work—growing, picking,

170

snapping, slicing—already sealed in. I no longer fear silence. The bad pop songs in my head are gone. That, along with the lack of technological distractions, leaves me available both physically and mentally to witness nature's wonders: the nightly march of the stars, muskrats gliding for great stretches beneath the river's frozen surface, the misty-morning revelation of spiderwebs by the hundreds, glistening like spiral galaxies in the meadow grass.

With a fire in the big, iron heating stove in the dining room roaring around the clock, I've been burning through more wood than ever. But after months of sore shoulders, mishits, and busted axe handles, I have finally learned the secret of splitting: Don't think about it. Warm the muscles, focus the mind, find a rhythm, and then heave the maul almost blindly overhead, letting its blade divine the energy coiled within every round of oak, blasting the two halves apart with the hollow *chok-a-blok* of scattered bowling pins and the tannic-acid tang of bourbon.

I am amazed at my sturdy, competent hands and marvel at my patience and drive, a reversal from the run-down edginess that dominated my moods in New York. Especially around the holidays.

Back in New York, I was turning into a Scrooge. Each year, I grew more cranky and cynical as the powerful Holiday vortex bore down on us, spinning from Thanksgiving to New Year's Day, sucking into it everyone and everything. This year, we've traded the ghosts of Christmas past—the jostle of holiday shopping, credit-card hangovers, airport check-in lines coiled up on themselves and throbbing like irritated intestines—for the ghosts of Christmas *long* past. So far, things have been very different.

We actually started preparing for the holidays earlier than ever, back in September, when Ishtar brought us a piece of fruitcake. This was not the kind of fruitcake that comes packed in a round red tin, doorstop heavy and radioactive with Day-Glo candied fruit. This was a slab of moist, black fruitcake, made from a recipe passed down by a friend's great-grandmother. Sweet, dense, and earthy, the bite I took went down like a poem.

When wrapped in cloth and soaked in brandy, Ishtar said, the fruitcake lasts for months. In 1900, saving food from one growing season to the next sometimes meant the difference between life and death—certainly between survival and good living. To preserve a fruit-studded treat

171

from the summer into the depths of winter must have been almost magical. Like trapping a bit of sunshine in your cellar.

But today, who remembers the magic of fruitcake? Hardly anyone, because when refrigeration, chemical preservatives, and airtight plastic wraps began prolonging the shelf life of other sweets, an all-natural treat that could last for months was no longer needed. Then food factories started mass-producing fruitcake and packing it in red tins, sounding the death knell for this king of the confectionary world. Today, fruitcake is little more than a punchline.

Thanks to our history experiment, we need fruitcake once again. And that need, coupled with the boozy goodness of Great-Grandma McEndree's recipe, has awakened us to the pleasures and practicality— to the magic—of fruitcake. For us, fruitcake has come to symbolize all those small joys from the past that are corrupted, disparaged, or forgotten in the march of progress. Not long after Ishtar's September visit, we decided to stage our own fruitcake comeback.

Which explains the two dozen cheesecloth-swaddled fruitcake loaves lining the countertop like newborns in a maternity ward. For weeks, they have been in the cellar seasoning in a big oval tub. Now, as Heather drizzles brandy—a gift from David and Meryl—over each cake, a heady sweetness fills the warm kitchen. She gently flips them and soaks the other side, returning each to its wax-paper wrapping and restacking them in the tub. Back to the cellar they go, until they're ready to give away as gifts.

The fruitcakes are just one of the many things we have to make from scratch this Christmas. Heather has been stamping her own Christmas cards using green paint and a potato carved into the shape of a Christmas tree. For ornaments, we spread the dining table with the craft items we stocked up on last spring: wooden beads, spools, ribbon, rickrack, glue. We make toy soldiers by decorating old-fashioned clothes pins. Luther and I roll his red wagon into the yard and collect spruce cones and black-gum seed pods. Back inside, he helps me drip glue on the cones, and then we dust them with corn starch to look like snow. String them through the top with an upholstery needle for hanging on a tree, and voilá. Eat your heart out, Martha Stewart! The black-gum seed pods are nature's own readymade ornaments; their starburst balls come

172

with stiff curly stems shaped like an upside-down J—built-in hangers! We dropped our plan to string cranberry and popcorn garlands after imagining mice snacking on the strands at night while we slept.

Years ago, Bill Roberson planted an acre of white pine and spruce trees, thinking he'd supplement his teacher's income by one day selling them as Christmas trees. But Christmas-tree farming requires regular pruning and doesn't pay off until years later, so Bill let the stand go. Today, it's an impenetrable forest shielding the southern end of his twenty-five acres. Most of the trees are huge or impossible to reach. But I have been eyeing a few smaller ones growing around the periphery, and Bill says we're welcome to have one.

On the day we've arranged to fetch our Christmas tree, it's cold and gray. I turn my collar up against the wind as I stand in the barnyard, hitching Belle to the wagon. Having never cut down a Christmas tree before, I toss both an axe and a saw in the wagon bed, along with some sisal rope. We haven't been on a family drive since last July, when we traveled to the Wilsons' party. After that wild ride, we decided that drives were too risky for Luther. But we make an exception today. We're not headed far. Besides, we're excited about getting a tree. Christmas is coming, and our ornaments need a place to shine.

Luther is thrilled to be on a buggy ride, though we all feel the chill when Belle begins to trot. In no time, she's pulling us up the Robersons' short, steep driveway. Their vehicles block the way, so I swing right and cross through the garden plot, now dry and empty. Bill steps out the kitchen door and meets us at the fence, where I tie Belle to a post.

With Bill's help, we choose a seven-foot Norway spruce. The handsaw quickly slices through its green trunk, leaving a nice, flat mounting surface. Stamping against the cold, we don't stick around to chat. We lash the tree to the wagon bed, thank Bill, and head for home, with Luther snuggled warmly between Heather and me.

All Christmas trees seem tailor-made for the spaces they fill, giving a room a piney perfume and twinkle of expectancy. What's different this year is how deeply connected we feel to the place where our tree grew and the man who grew it, to the wintry season in which it was cut and to the work that went into getting it home. Standing in our living room, its branches throwing off their scent and sagging under the weight of homemade ornaments, our humble, slightly misshapen spruce brightens our home more than any perfectly pruned specimen ever could.

❧

We are not completely spared from Holiday Season anxiety. Instead of Christmas shopping, we're making all of our presents. Heather and I collaborate on a book—*A Day in 1900*—for my seven-year-old goddaughter, Hazel, who lives in Richmond. I write the text, and Heather brings it to life with beautiful watercolor scenes. Heather has also been making gift bags filled with fruitcake, pumpkin bread, and blackberry jelly. She delivers them by bicycle, pedaling up and down the hills of Swoope, bundled against the cold. She keeps ginger cookies and jars of pickles and apple cider handy for neighbors who drop by. She even packed up eight boxes of goodies—jelly, fruitcakes—to mail to out-of-towners. (Let's see anyone make fun of *Heather's* fruitcake!) Because of the cold, neither of us has felt like venturing as far away as the post office. We try to enlist the help of a UPS delivery man, who brings us a package one day. "You have to call 'em in," he says, standing at the kitchen door, eyeing our woodstove and the load of laundry drying on racks beside it.

"We don't have a phone," says Heather.

"Do you ever get to town?"

"No."

"Sorry, I can't help you," he mumbles, hurrying back to his truck.

Even though we're making our presents, families in 1900 certainly did shop for one another. General stores geared up for Christmas by hanging toys and ornaments from ceilings and arranging oranges, coconuts, nutmeg, and other exotic produce in geometric displays. Children often found china dolls and toy soldiers, jackknives, and comb-and-brush sets in their stockings. Though Christmas back then was far less commercialized than it is today, the new wish books of the late nineteenth century helped lead the Christian holiday further down the path of materialism. For fun one day, I flip through our 1897 Sears catalog, trying to imagine what I might have ordered for my family.

For Heather, I find pages of filigreed jewelry, toilet waters, and salves and, under Human Hair Goods, a bundle of curls called the Parisian

Bang. For Luther, the pickings in the 786-page book are slim, which says a lot about how our views of children have changed over the years. Under the index listing "Toys" are six dreary entries: toy brooms, toy carpet sweepers, toy safes, toy sad irons, toy trunks, and toy wagons—and even the wagons seem meant for chores, not fun.

And for the man of the house? There are bicycles, guns, sleek buggies. The DVD player of the day was the magic lantern projector, lit by kerosene lamp. Picture a dark, low-definition slide show cast against a wall. Shoppers could purchase Bible scenes or comic views, such as a man riding a pig. There was darker fare as well. One series, called *Ten Nights in a Bar Room*, featured the following scenes: 1. Arrival at the Sickle and Sheaf, 2. Joe Morgan with Delirium Tremens, 3. Willie Hammond induced to gamble, and 4. Frank Slade kills his father.

I personally don't care much for *stuff*. All the meaningless gift-giving that happens—and the waste and guilt that accompany it—helped bring out my inner Scrooge. It's ironic, then, when I receive a sample Gillette MACH3 razor in the mail and am consumed by material lust. Arriving in an unmarked box the size of a videotape, the sleek, glittering, triple-bladed "system" represents the latest and greatest in shaving technology. I want it, and I want it bad. But I'm tormented by the fact that I can't use it. Instead of tossing the razor, I hide it in a bureau drawer. Occasionally, when no one's looking, I'll ogle the silver device, lingering over descriptions of its "lubricating strip" and "comfort edge" that give a man "the closest shave ever in fewer strokes." The packaging's French translation is even more seductive. *Ainsi, MACH3 glisse sans effort et en douceur sur votre visage!*

My beef with modern life never included razors. Every five days or so, when I sit down with my chipped-enamel bowl and cutthroat blade, I can't help but feel a little ridiculous. *Just use the MACH3*, a voice in my head now says, *and end the bloodshed.* Why undergo torture when a perfectly good alternative has existed for nearly—but not quite—100 years? After King C. Gillette introduced the world's first stamped-steel-bladed safety razor in 1903, men clamored to own one, even at a retail price of five dollars, half the average workingman's weekly pay. What I wouldn't give today to join them! And yet I resist temptation, slipping the package back in the drawer and walking away.

See you in a Hundred Years

CR80

Heather's parents arrive a few days before Christmas in a black sedan straining its shocks under the weight of everything they've brought. In addition to hanging bags and duffels of clothing, shoes, and boots, they've brought Christmas gifts (including a set of plastic golf clubs for Luther), tree ornaments, bags of groceries, cardboard boxes of preserves from Mamaw, and two huge coolers full of wild game, all of it shot or caught by John on one of his hunting or fishing trips. He's got dead flesh in there from one end of the country to the other.

John Higginbotham—hunter, horseman, golfer, lawyer—has every reason to be skeptical of our project. As a boy, in Depression-era Alabama, he and his family *were* dirt farmers, and he has spent his entire adult life distancing himself from that hardscrabble existence. When Heather and I first explained our plan, I could almost hear the *whys* echoing in his mind: Why throw away that expensive education? Why grovel to grow your supper when you can easily afford to buy it? Why deprive yourselves? Why deprive your son?

During their first night with us, as John and Ginnie acclimate to our rustic abode, we sit in front of the cookstove drinking tea. John, a handsome man with wavy brown hair and a baritone drawl, shares his stories—how as an eleven-year-old he plowed fields with mules, how he milked his family's two cows (plus one for a neighbor, who paid him $1.50 a week), and how, when his own chores were done, he would moonlight (literally) for another farmer by turning his fields with a Farmall tractor. "He'd bring me fuel and something to eat and leave me 'til two in the morning," John says. That work earned John one dollar per day. He picked cotton, getting paid by the 100-weight, going out early in the morning before the dew dried, "because the cotton was heavier that way." The oldest of four children, John helped his mother run the family farm. Bad health kept his father laid-up. They raised a garden, stacked mason jars of food in a root cellar, hauled water from a dug well with a rope and bucket, did their business outside in a hole in the ground. John hated it. At age seventeen, he ran away to New Orleans and tried to join the Merchant Marines, but he was underage. At eighteen, he finally escaped the farm by joining the Air Force. That led to college and law

176

school and a successful practice as a small-town attorney, including a term as president of his state trial lawyers association.

Back in Alabama, John keeps a pair of horses. Their names are Black Bart and Diablo, and he rides them in field trials with his champion bird dogs, who flush coveys of quail to earn points. Those horses, I realize now, symbolize John's ascendancy from mule-farming into the leisure class. And now we've come full circle: the daughter, raised in privilege, educated at some of the country's finest schools, trading the sterile, high-stress world of the think tank for the backbreaking immediacy of small-farm life. Though he might not see it this way, maybe the greatest measure of John's success is that his daughter has the luxury to return to the dirt.

Because John is a horse person, he is fixated on Belle and is looking forward to a wagon ride. Though the idea makes me nervous, the next day I halter Belle and tie her to the post in the barn, preparing for the drive.

"You got a curry comb?" asks John, eyeing Belle. Mud clings to her belly hair, cakes the ridge of her back. Her mane is clumped into early-stage dreadlocks. I rummage around the shed until I find the stiff-haired brush I bought at the local farm co-op. It's not a curry comb—I'm not even sure what a curry comb is—but it will have to do.

Calmly and methodically, John brushes Belle's coat. She takes to him immediately. At home, after a trail ride, he hoses his horses down. After the drive, he says, we'll fill a bucket with soapy water and give Belle a bath.

Soon, we're off on what I hope will be a picturesque five-mile loop, out along the Middle River and back across a pretty ridgeline. Ginnie sits up front with me. John crouches on a makeshift bench in the wagon bed. When we reach a farm that straddles the road, house and outbuildings hugging both shoulders, Belle balks. *Oh no*, I think. Another shed.

"Come up, Belle," I say, trying to keep my cool.

She struggles against the harness, clearly not wanting to go any farther. I pop her with my switch, and she jerks forward. *Snap!* Something gives. The wagon shafts yaw to the left. One of the points drives into Belle's side.

"WHOA!"

Belle jerks forward again.

"HEY!" barks John, from in back, and then he leaps out, as if from a burning car, and helps Ginnie down. I stay in the wagon, holding the reins. Belle calms down. John's inspecting the damage—a pair of broken harness straps—when suddenly Belle bursts forward again.

"Get out of the way!" John yells, throwing a shoulder at Ginnie and knocking her roughly to the side, as Belle pulls the wagon into the ditch.

I pull out the bailer twine, and we get to work on a repair. The ride is over. We turn the wagon and head for home.

The drive is a big disappointment to me, but John and Ginnie quickly shrug it off. They both roll up their sleeves and dive in to 1900 life. Ginnie adds some old-fashioned ornaments she brought to our tree and helps Heather prepare for a Christmas dinner that promises to be every bit as impressive as our Thanksgiving meal. John works like he's sixteen again and trying to please his industrious mother. He splits wood and pumps water, tosses hay to the animals. In the barn, he helps me hammer up a cattle panel between the feed room and the goat stall. We fix latches on the barn doors. Though the broken harness prevents us from attempting another drive, we continue to work with Belle, John showing me how to bathe her and trim her mane. During a downpour, I even find John tugging at a section of leaky barn roof. "You got any gutter nails?" he asks.

While I had hoped to impress John with my driving skills, the prosaic side of our experience seems to have won him over, much as the peacefulness of our life here helped change my mother's opinion of our project. The chores, the smell of woodsmoke, the soft glow of the lamps at night must conjure up a nostalgia in him for a simpler, if more impoverished time in his life. As much as he may have disliked the toil of the family farm, that experience instilled values in John. It made him the man he is today. He knows it, too. You can tell by the way he respects his mother and from the hint of pride in his voice as he recounts the hard times. After all he and Ginnie have done for Heather, an only child, I can understand how the news of our 1900 project may have seemed like a slap in the face. But in many ways, it was exactly the opposite—a loving embrace—and I think John is beginning to understand that.

❧

It's Christmas Eve, and I haven't yet started making my gifts for Heather and Luther. I decided months ago that I wanted to carve something for them out of wood using a draw knife and shaving horse like the one I saw at Michael Godfrey's. That meant I'd first have to make the shaving horse. So for more than a month, under Michael's tutelage, I have ducked out between chores to split and hack away at an oak log with froe and hatchet. I've chiseled mortised joints, shaved tenons, whittled pegs, and cranked furiously on a bit and brace to drill holes. I've finally finished, and now only hours stand between me and Christmas morning.

Turning to my gifts, I carve and sand 'til dark and then by the light of an oil lamp, feeling like an outcast elf in this cold, cluttered, rodent-scampering shed. My wrists ache, and so does my back from all the bending. Wood shavings cling to my sweater like dirty snow. But I forge ahead, determined to put something under the tree for Luther on what is his first real Christmas—at least the first he's aware of.

When morning breaks, I'm up early as usual, stoking both wood-stoves. The thermometer reads eighteen degrees. John and Ginnie are asleep in the guest room, freezing cold probably, since the heat barely reaches it. The Christmas goose John bagged in South Dakota lays dressed in a big pot, naturally refrigerated and waiting to be cooked. I fetch water from a frozen water barrel. Setting the coffee pot, tinkling with ice, on the stovetop, I huddle close to the firebox, rubbing and blowing my chafed and blistered hands.

When Luther wakes, he rushes to the tree and finds a Huck Finn raft made from lightweight basswood "logs," each about two feet long and lashed together with sisal twine. The boat has a mast and boom, a linen sail, and taut blue-bandana decking. When he gleefully grabs the boat, I beam like a child myself.

Heather's present is smaller and not nearly so elaborate—a pair of black-walnut chopsticks. I've attached a note. "Now that we live in the sticks," it reads, "I thought you'd like a pair of your own."

CHAPTER TEN

Winter

Mother Nature sends an Arctic blast on New Year's Eve. We wake (in 1901?) to temperatures hovering around zero. Heather's parents are gone, having taken with them gifts of food grown and preserved on our farm, including a box for Mamaw—the first canned food *we've* ever given to *her*. Holiday time is over. Now the cold grabs and shakes us to get our attention.

Making the New Year's cold snap worse is the wind. Since the Wind-Chill Index was not created until 1939 by the Antarctic explorer Paul A. Siple, 1900 farmers would have acknowledged winter's turbo boost with grunts and curses, as we do, rather than numbers. Our old friend the summer breeze, which cooled us and kept away the bugs, has turned foe. It now slices through our little valley like an icy blade, stabbing at the gaps in the windows and doors, stinging exposed skin when we venture out. It's the same prevailing wind that Jefferson, who lived fifty miles away, described as laying on "a distressing chill . . . heavy and oppressive to the spirits." I tack wood over the holes and stuff newspaper under the washroom door at night. On the windward side of the barn, I hammer up sheets of tin over missing windows, but still the animals complain. The wind crumples crows in mid-flight and threatens to launch the chickens across the yard like tumbleweeds. I half expect to glance up at night and see the stars blowing around the heavens.

Now that it's getting cold, we've both been wearing long underwear and blanket-lined canvas coats made by a company established in 1889 and still making work clothes today. On my feet are a pair of wool socks, and when I wear them the itching reminds me of how difficult it was to find them. Last spring, at an outdoor-gear store, the kind of place that sells Gortex jackets and featherweight tents, I asked a young clerk for help:

"Do you have any wool socks?" I asked.

"Sure do," he chirped, leading me to a spinning sock kiosk. "Here you go, sir."

I looked them over and saw only wool-synthetic blends, a brand called Smart Wool. "Do you have any made of 100-percent wool?"

"These *are* wool," he says.

"These are Smart Wool," I say. "I need something a little dumber."

"Excuse me?"

"No synthetics," I say. "Just plain wool. The kind that makes you itch."

"Oh, no. They don't make those."

We eventually found them. Plain wool gloves, too. Lately, with even the south winds blowing cold, I've been wearing both—and itching—more frequently.

A century ago, a farmer would have woken on a cold morning, forced himself out of his warm mounds of blankets, leapt into an icy pair of overalls, cracked through the skim of ice on the washstand basin for water to wash his face, and headed outside to the outhouse. Winter mornings are not so different at our house.

I hurry into my clothes beside a frosty, moonlit window. With the fire in the downstairs heating stove either out by now or barely smoldering, the temperature in the house is probably below freezing. Lighting my way with a lantern, I venture outside to empty my bladder—teeth rattling, steam rising—and then smack through the ice in the water barrel. Even frozen to the bone, I experience a bracing joy in the morning. I'll pause, my breath crystallizing, and listen to the cows lowing in the distance as the sky begins to blush. On days when the clouds billow up in the east, they reflect the dawn light onto the river, turning it into a molten flume of orange and pink beneath the leaning sycamores.

Mornings have become my reading time. Once I've built fires in both the heating stove and the cookstove, I'll huddle close to the kitchen stove listening to the crackle, soaking up the heat, and reading a book. My new powers of concentration astound me: I've raced through Dickens, Hardy, Wilde, Hawthorne, Irving, William Dean Howells, the collected letters of Thomas Jefferson, and several novels published in 1900, including Charles Waddell's *The House Behind the Cedars*, Dreiser's *Sister Carrie* (which would have shocked the average rural reader), and a couple of bestselling romances long since forgotten.

On this particular morning my nose is literally (because of the dim lamplight) between the pages of George Eliot's *The Mill on the Floss*. Soon, I'm transported to the hearth in Maggie and Tom Tulliver's "left-hand parlour." I open my own firebox with a clank of iron. Light and heat leap out at my face. I toss in a log and shove it to the back with my poker. For a moment, the wavering, jewel-like marvel of the orange coals holds me fixed, until the smell of coffee and the pot's rattle jerks me away. I pour a cup, top it off with creamy goat's milk. Stomach grumbling, I scrape the crusty brown oil-soaked edges of yesterday's cornbread into a bowl and stir in a spoonful of honey—a rare treat I call cornbread cracklin'—settling again before the stove to rejoin the Tullivers. Soon Heather and Luther are up. Eggs are frying. I gather my pails and set out for the milking room. When I return, I'll join them at the kitchen table for breakfast and a second cup of coffee.

Later, we might write some letters, since along with reading, Heather and I are also catching up on our correspondence this season. We pen long, blotchy missives to family and out-of-town friends. We mail thank you's and other brief notes to neighbors, the letters traveling fifty miles to Charlottesville just to be sorted and driven back over the Blue Ridge Mountains to a house two miles down the road.

The writing and receiving of letters, like other activities this year, assumes its own pleasing rhythm. It's hard, messy work dipping and scribbling with the steel nib and holder—Heather and I each have callouses near the tips of our middle fingers—and when you're finished, you must blot the letter and leave it to dry. Same with the envelope. The whole process can take half a morning. But the writing is rewarding, and the thrill of peering into the mailbox is worth the effort. Who might have written? What news is waiting? We recognize handwriting instantly—our friend Kirk's small, blocky characters; my father's looping doctor's scrawl; Ishtar's measured script, so old-fashioned, like the wax paper she places over her gifts of food. I'll silently skim through a letter for news, and then read it again, savoring the words, sometimes reading it a third time aloud to Luther or Heather. You can drive or stir a soup pot with a phone to your ear, but penning a letter demands your attention, and that extra care shows in the finished product. At first, my father, who would be lost without his cell phone, could hardly imagine surviving a year without calling us. But he has come around. He writes often, and I get more substance and sincerity from one of his letters than a dozen distracted phone chats.

Winter forces us closer to home. As the temperatures drop, so do the number of neighbors who visit. It's as if everyone is hibernating following the summer gardening, fall canning, and bounty-sharing holiday season. We, too, follow the lead of the furry creatures. Home becomes our cave. The woodstoves radiate heat. Orange smudges light our rooms. I can barely hold my head up at dinnertime and sometimes fall asleep beside my plate.

As cozy as we feel in our home, we grapple mentally with the gloom. Life in 1900 was inextricably linked to the seasons, and ours this winter is no different. If last summer the teeming abundance of life—weeds and bugs and rodents, all competing for resources—disturbed us, now the stillness of death haunts us. Tree branches reach down like bony fingers. The birds' songs have been replaced by the hollow whistling of the wind. The plants in our once-verdant garden have withered and dried into rattling husks. One night I hear a horrific screeching and scrabbling outside the window and the next morning find a dead possum wedged beneath the porch lattice. Possums don't hibernate. They relocate to warmer dens, often human basements, which is where this one must have been headed until one of our cats killed it. Early in the season, Luther and I found a dead chickadee in the yard. Feeling the need for meaningful disposal, I grabbed a shovel, and we walked beyond the maple tree. As I laid the bird in a hole in the ground, Luther said, "That's where it sleeps." His words struck me as so innocent that I froze before filling the hole. James Agee describes his ancestors as "folded under the earth like babies in blankets." I could almost hear Luther's little mind working: *Why is Daddy putting dirt over a sleeping bird?*

Chores, however, manage to keep us preoccupied. I milk in the cold, fingers stinging but warmed by the goats' bags. At night, I milk by lamplight, rattling my buckets to stir the rats that feed on spilled grain beneath the milking stand. Though we moved our own water barrel inside the washroom, I am constantly hammering through the ice in the animals' water buckets, scooping out the big bergs and refilling often. I've stepped up the wood-splitting now that I'm fueling both house stoves.

Heather scrubs laundry inside, rinsing and wringing in the washroom, where it's still cold, with temperatures often barely hovering above freezing. She hangs clothes on wooden racks in the kitchen near the cookstove. On days when temperatures creep up, she moves the operation back outside. On one such day, she had just hung a set of sheets to dry when a north wind swirled in, shoving the mercury back down into the twenties. By the time we remembered the laundry, both sides of the sheets were frozen together and as stiff as cardboard. When I tried to remove one, it tore like construction paper. Another time, after forgetting to empty the diaper-soaking tub before a cold snap, we found ourselves with a big frozen block of dirty diapers—the diapersicle, we called it. Even in the washroom it took three days to thaw.

One morning, the cold air stinging my nose like a snort of cayenne pepper, I crunch to the well pump through frost-stiffened fescue that powders my overalls at the calves. But the pump won't work. The hose is frozen. I'll have to haul buckets.

Which I do, making seven sloshing, thigh-drenching trips back and forth from the pump to the house. The average single-family home in the United States at the turn of the twenty-first century consumes about 100 gallons of water per person per day. At 700 feet per round trip, one bucket per hand, I walk nearly a mile to add fourteen gallons to our water barrel.

Because of the ongoing drought, fourteen gallons is all we can pump. The rains we've had have not been enough to replenish the aquifer. If the water level drops ten more feet, we'll be dry. Talking to Swoope's farmers doesn't ease my worries. They've never seen a drought this bad. The river's so low, Joel and Edie Wilson are worried that it'll freeze solid, leaving nothing for their cows to drink. Our friends Deb and Walt, whose cattle ponds are icy mudpuddles, are really in trouble. "I can't get enough water out of our well to swallow aspirin," Walt told me. They're willing to spend the $10,000 or so it costs to drill a new one—*if* they can ever get off the well-driller's waiting list. Jeanne dropped by not long ago with some beers after feeding her cows and stayed for a bowl of chili. We were clowning around with Luther—"One sip," he said, beckoning toward my bottle—when I brought up the drought. Jeanne took a swig, and when she lowered her beer, her smile was gone. "We've got to get some rain or snow soon," she said. "It's at the point now where if we don't, things are going to change. You won't be able to graze cows. The hay fields won't grow. It won't make sense to raise cattle."

After two more pumping sessions—and two more miles of hauling water—I unscrew the hose and lug all 350 feet of it into the cellar. The next day, with all the ice melted, I reattach it. When it's cold, I'll have to empty the hose every time I pump to keep it from freezing again.

Even the cellar is not safe. It's partially above ground and has four windows. Ideally, jars of food should be stored at fifty to seventy degrees. One morning, during a cold front when temperatures fall into the single digits, the basement dips below freezing.

Freezing food could expand in a jar just enough to break the seal, leading to spoilage. Sometimes food spoils, and you notice. With *Clostridium botulinum*, the bacterium that causes botulism, you don't. It's tasteless, odorless, and invisible.

Clostridium botulinum, which produces the botulinum toxin—the most poisonous substance known to man—thrives in low-oxygen conditions. Most botulism comes from home-canned food. The illness, sometimes mistaken for stroke, paralyzes the muscles. It starts with your eyelids, which droop, and travels downward through the body, slurring speech and making swallowing difficult. Arms go limp. Chest muscles seize up, then the diaphragm. Literally unable to take your next breath, you die by asphyxiation. The toxin is so potent that some researcher somewhere figured out that a quarter teaspoon is enough to kill a million people. After the 1991 Persian Gulf War, Iraq admitted to the

United Nations inspection team to having produced enough of the crystalline nerve poison to kill the entire human race three times over.

Learning that botulism is rare is cold comfort when I think that so is a pair of city slickers pretending to live 100 years ago. Every new jar of food we open raises new doubts. Did we boil the jar long enough? Is the seal still good?

When I discover the freezing temperatures in the cellar, I act fast, covering the windows with crumpled newspaper and wood for insulation. The mercury climbs back to forty degrees.

CRBO

The risk of fire is another heightened winter threat. A century ago, in rural America, beyond the reach of city fire departments, when people relied on fire for cooking, heating, lighting, and warming laundry and bath water, the threat of house fire lurked in every home. During their Christmas visit, Heather's parents told their own tragic stories about winter house fires. When Ginnie was two years old, her house—her father's homeplace—burned to the ground late one night. Though her mother blacked out from smoke inhalation, her father was able to carry his wife and their three children to safety. When John's grandparents' farmhouse burned down in 1945, the family wasn't so lucky. John was nine years old at the time, living less than a mile away in a house without electricity.

"When we heard there was a fire, we all ran up the gravel road that night," John told us. "The neighbors had already carried Clyde to the hospital in their black Chevrolet Coupe." Clyde was John's eleven-year-old uncle, Mamaw's youngest brother. John and Clyde were inseparable, "the best of buddies," John said. That night, the coal grate had gone cold. Thinking it was out, Clyde splashed kerosene on it and *whoosh!* the fuel exploded, igniting the can and covering the boy in flames. "They said 75 percent of his body was burned," John remembered. "Clyde was crying and asking for me when he died."

Their stories come to mind some nights when I'm loading the big heating woodstove before bed. I swing open the heavy iron doors and pile on as many logs as I can. I close the door and let the pile burn slowly, fed by air pouring through gaps in the door gasket. This is called banking the stove. If I'm lucky, the fire will burn all night, and there will be enough orange coals left in the morning to spark a fresh blaze. If not, I have to start from scratch, rebuilding a new fire and waiting for the house to warm. To avoid the latter, I cram that sucker so full that sometimes I have to kick at the wood and lean against the door to latch it. Often, it rages awhile before burning itself down to a smolder. I go to bed still hearing the fire's roar and feeling uneasy about leaving an iron box full of flames unattended for all those hours.

One blustery night, the smell of smoke wakes me. The house is full of it. My eyes are stinging as I light a lamp and walk downstairs to investigate. When I open the dining room door, a cloud chokes me. Covering my mouth and nose with my shirttail, I dive in, expecting to see flames licking at the walls. Instead, I find only smoke pouring from the vents and seeping through cracks.

Heather has awakened, too. She stands at the door, holding Luther and rubbing her eyes. Then she looks at the stove. "Is that the Forbidden Log?" she asks accusingly.

"Yeah."

"I knew it," she says, coughing. "You were just looking for revenge."

The Forbidden Log is the name I've given to a hulking round of locust that preys on wooden axe handles. I learned my lesson trying to split the Forbidden Log months ago. Now, every time we get a male visitor, I find him pounding on the hard-as-iron wood, despite my warnings. Each time, I toss the log to the rear of the woodpile, but it always winds up back on the splitting block. *Prove your manhood by swinging the mallet and ringing the carnival bell!*

Thinking about how much energy must be stored in such a dense log—and, yes, maybe also seeking revenge—I had used the Forbidden Log to bank the stove. Once again, the log has gotten the better of me. It's burning so slowly that there isn't enough heat to carry the smoke out of the chimney. And now, the wind's shoving smoke back into the house. If we don't do something fast, we'll be forced out on a cold and windy night.

"Who cares why I did it," I yell, jerking up the window sash. "We've got to air out this house!"

I open the front door. The wind is so strong that the screen door bucks and stamps to get loose from its hinges. Heather puts Luther down and opens the door to the backyard. The wind barrels through like a freight train, whipping past her nightgown, tearing calendar and post-cards off the wall, rattling pots, shoving an empty jar off the washstand, glass shattering. In the dark, the lamps flicker. Luther screams. The scene is straight out of a horror movie.

"Close it! Close it!" I shout. She does, and hurries to pick up Luther.

"I don't know what to do," I yell. We could pour water on it, but that might crack the stove. *Focus. Focus.* It's hard, with the wind pummeling the house and the smoke billowing. This is not the stuff that bothers you around a campfire. It's thick and foul, like toxic exhaust, lying on my tongue, turning my stomach. I stick my head out the window and gulp fresh air.

Then I remember the livestock tank outside the door, with three inches of soapy water from our bath. "We can get the log out!" I say.

"WHAT?"

"Put Luther in the high chair, and when I'm ready, open the wash-room door."

Luther is silent now, groggy, but wide-eyed. Strapped into the wooden high chair in his little red union suit, he looks confused. *Why is it dark? What are Mommy and Daddy doing? Where's breakfast?*

Pulling on my leather fire gloves, I open the stove door and grab the smoldering log. It's heavy, and my grip is poor, and I worry that I might drop it on the pine floor. Revenge? This bastard is fighting back. It would just love to burn the house down.

"Go!" I shout, and Heather flings open the door. The wind hits the log and lights it up, like it's been doused with gasoline. With sparks shooting in my wake, I scuttle out and heave it into the tub. When it hits, embers scatter across the dry, brittle grass. I grab a bucket of water and skitter around barefooted and in my underwear, snuffing each would-be fire. I spin around and see the log in the tub, still spitting its fiery seeds. I rock the tub back and forth, sloshing water over it with a hiss of steam. Shivering, I head back inside, where Heather is scooping sparks off the floor with the stove shovel. The stove is no longer smoking.

We decide to sleep in the guest bedroom, the farthest from the fire and smoke. Heather and Luther head up, while I ventilate the dining room.

By the time I crawl into bed, feet dusty, clothes smelling like a smoke-jumper's, it's nearly time to get up and build the cooking fire. This room, on the side of the house we keep shut off to conserve heat, is frigid, and with windows on either side, it feels like the prow of a ship beating into a gale. Still coughing and too wired to sleep, I read by lamplight while the wind rattles the house and buckles the roof. I keep waiting for a window to shatter.

"Is the wind playing rough with the roof?" Luther asks. Cuddling close to Heather, he's still frightened and confused.

"It sure is," I say. I rub my eyes.

"What's wrong, Daddy?"

"My eyes are burning."

"Is there fire in them?"

"No, they're just stinging from the smoke."

"Like a bee sting?" he says.

"No, sweetie," I whisper. "Daddy's alright. Go to sleep." I blow the light out and pull the covers up to my chin. "Everything's all better now."

The next morning, I step outside and peer into the bathtub at the charred, half-submerged corpse. I carry the Forbidden Log to the driveway. "So long," I say, and with a heave send it tumbling over the edge and into the river below.

○३♡

We grow more accustomed to the short winter days and our shrinking circle of activities. The snug quarters and our first windfall of free time in six months begin to lift our spirits. We pause for tea breaks in front of the cookstove, singing whatever children's ditties we can muster. Heather fills the house with the smells of baking cookies and bread. She and I catch up on our correspondence and continue reading nineteenth-century novels aloud to one another.

New rituals draw us together. Our favorite is a winter bath in front of the cookstove. Bath night comes around every third day. I slide the live-stock tank into the kitchen after dinner, stoke up both stoves, and heat both big canning pots of water until twin columns of steam rise toward the ceiling. Luther goes first, laughing and splashing as we scrub behind

his ears. We put him down to bed, and then we bathe, cauldrons bubbling, lamps and candles aglow. Hot water warms our skin, soothes our
tired muscles. The scent of lavender bath soap envelopes the room. By
now, the bare windows have fogged up, concealing us from the darkness
outside. We dry ourselves in front of the big stove, cupping the heat
around our naked bodies with outstretched cloths like birds drying their
wings. Afterward we dive beneath the quilts, our bodies clean, our skin
flushed, sniggering at the squeaking antique bed frame, hoping Luther
doesn't wake up and wander in.

As much as we enjoy the warmth of our home, we don't let the cold
imprison us. I hoist Luther to my shoulders and we hike into the woods,
looking for deer. We toss pebbles onto the frozen river. Pick and Banjo
skate onto the ice, batting the stones with their paws like hockey play-
ers. The first snow is magic.

Even here, with no jobs or school to be canceled, with no snowbound
car forcing us to stay home, with nothing much at all changed except the
blanket of white stuff on the ground, it still feels like a snow day. I pull
Luther around on an old junior-sized maplewood toboggan, his stubby
legs tucked under the curled nose. My slick-soled leather boots give me
no traction at all, so after spinning my wheels all morning trying to
reach the barn and the well pump and ending up on my butt at least
three times, I wrap the boots in burlap and tie them off at the ankles,
looking, with my wild hair and seven-day beard, like some rag picker
from a Dickens tale. All three of us zip down the far side of the pasture,
snow flying up and smacking us in the face, Luther screaming, "Again!"
after each run. And then, Luther suddenly realizes that snow is cold, and
the fun is over. A minute ago he was diving and digging in the powder,
and now he's holding his arms stiffly in front of his body, screaming at
them as if they were alien creatures attacking.

The snow lingers for a while before it melts. We get another snow, and
while it's fresh, Heather gathers a bowl of powder and mixes it with custard to make snow cream. We love watching the bright red of the cardi-
nals set against the snow's whiteness as the birds pick around the sunflower garden. Though we harvested the sunflower seeds for ourselves,
plenty fell for the birds to scavenge. And like some kind of code-deci-
phering overlay, the layer of snow reveals the tracks of all the different

animals—skunks, raccoons, coyotes—that crisscross the yard at night, from the riverbank to the cats' milk bowls, from pasture to compost bin, across the barnyard to the henhouse. It's just one more reminder of how even in winter, nature is alive and constantly in motion.

CB€O

I haven't been driving Belle as much lately. It's not so much the cold as my growing anxiety over shoddy equipment. Since the belly strap broke less than an hour after I bought the harness last spring—an ominous sign—at least three other harness straps have torn, and one of the metal rings that hold the reins has snapped off.

More alarming is the wagon. At first I marveled at its engineering, at how wooden parts so thin and spindly—spokes, shafts, axles—could be so durable. Then I realized they weren't. In more experienced hands, our wagon might serve for Sunday drives and such, but through overuse and bungling, I've abused it—shattered the wheel, cracked a shaft tip, gouged the sides of the wooden bed with the steel treads. Any time I take it on the road, I expect something to crack or snap.

As I do the morning we all pile in and drive to the Robersons'. Heather and I are dropping Luther off so we can go to the post office.

"We'll be back in an hour," I tell Peggy. "If we're not, that means we're probably having mechanical problems."

Off we go, Heather and I nervous about leaving the woodstoves burning but excited for the chance to get out of the house. For early February, the day could hardly be nicer—sunny, forty-five degrees—and that helps take the edge off my equipment worries. We pass Ishtar on the road, stopping to say hello. Michael Godfrey drives up behind us, waving as he turns his pickup into a pasture. When we roll into the post-office parking lot, Heather steps inside. Cowboy Joel Wilson drives up and rolls his window down.

"Howdy, neighbor," he says.

I'm feeling good chatting here at the P.O., me in my royal-blue wagon and Joel in his brand-new champagne-colored Dodge Ram pickup truck. But out of the corner of my eye, I catch at least half a dozen unfamiliar vehicles whizzing by on Hewitt Road. Close calls with cars is another reason I've been reluctant to drive. Once, a Scout-filled BMW hurtled over Jeanne's hill, straddling the middle of the single paved lane, swerving to miss Belle and me as we trotted uphill from the opposite direction. Another time, a tricked-out compact car with a whining, high-revving engine was playing Mario Andretti through the curves of Spitlers Woods. The driver caught sight of the wagon just in time to veer onto the gravel shoulder and pass.

With Joel gone and Heather on board again, I pause at the edge of the parking lot, letting three cars go before pulling out onto the busy road. Belle is acting tired, distracted, and unfamiliar with the route. She's weaving, one minute dragging the right wheels onto the grassy shoulder and the next tugging the left ones into the path of the oncoming traffic. As a result, we're not getting anywhere fast. An overloaded hay truck rumbles up behind, nearly nudging our wagon bed.

"You want to pull over?" Heather says.

"There's no shoulder," I say. "He'll just have to be patient."

Then I see a driveway leading into a tight gravel lot beside a railway berm. I pull in and the truck roars around us. "Asshole," I say under my breath.

Belle's still fidgeting, and I'm focused on how I'm going to turn us when—WHOOOOOOSH!—something sucks the air from where we sit. It's a train, a gleaming silver Amtrak train rocketing by nearly overhead.

Belle rears up, eyes wide, head twisting. Heather screams. As the horse backpedals, I turn and see a car approaching. "Come up, Belle!" I yell, and she moves forward just in time for the car to pass. But she has nowhere to go but into the berm. *Chuka, chuka, chuka, chuka.* I'm trying to keep her steady when an ear-splitting whistle pierces the wall of sound.

Belle spooks. We hold on for dear life, Belle jerking and pulling, wheels scraping and unseen parts popping and groaning. Our earlier plan to jump to safety seems impossible. When Belle backs far enough into the road, I tug the left rein and bellow, "Ya! Come up!" She leaps into the road and begins galloping alongside the train, racing it. Beside me, Heather is wide-eyed with fear. I'm yanking on the reins, hoping nothing splinters. But no matter what I say or how hard I pull, I can't seem to slow Belle. Suddenly Belle is ten years younger, every muscle in her body flexed, dragging the wagon around like a toy. We weave back and forth, and she nearly drags the wagon down an embankment where a barbed-wire fence waits below. I catch myself panicking, jerking on the reins. Then I remember the words of Clyde Tillman: "Make 'em walk, make 'em work."

I draw the reins in tight, keeping my arms low and steady. I try to soothe the horse with my words. The train continues clacking past—will it never stop?—but Belle straightens and slows a bit. Our turn lies ahead. I aim Belle toward the gravel incline. She takes it and slows even more. Soon, the last train car is past, leaving us trotting in heart-pounding silence.

CRED

The scare sends me back to Tillman's late one afternoon. I throw on a couple extra layers and bundle Luther up and take him with me. Ellen is sitting at the kitchen table. "He's in there," she says, pointing into the dark den. Luther clings to my thigh. Tillman is dozing in his fully reclined La-Z-Boy, boots off, television on. He comes to and gazes at us for a minute, scratching the tuft of gray chest hair poking from the collar of his flannel shirt. Luther leaves my leg and wanders in front of the TV, the images and sounds strangely crisp amid the home's clutter and decrepitude. He stands two feet away and watches, mesmerized, as a couple of cocky snowboarders clown on the slopes.

"You like that, don't you, son?" the old man says, cackling. "*Where's ours, Daddy?* Heh-heh." But I wonder what Tillman really thinks about the fact that we've given up the television. He once told me that his grandson had lost interest in buggy driving, saying, "TV done rurnt that boy."

I explain why I've come. I plan to build a pulling sled and need to borrow a working harness—a rig with a stout whiffletree, collar, and hames to use in place of my slender Dutch harness.

"I have to load some hay tomorrow," he says. "Come by after dinner. And bring your horse."

"I'll do that," I say. I turn to the TV. "Come on, Luther. Time to head home."

He doesn't hear a word. "Luther. Let's go." He's glued. I carry him kicking and screaming out of the house and perch him on my shoulders for the walk home.

Late the next afternoon I show up driving the buggy.

"You want something like that?" Tillman says, holding a Dr. Pepper and pointing at a sled like his own, only much smaller, with no bus seat and made from rough-sawn pine, not steel beams.

I pause and say, "Well, yeah, but bigger. I plan to build something for hauling rocks and fence posts."

"Oh, I just thought you wanted sump'n to haul that boy around on."

Suddenly, I understand. "You mean you made that for me?" I say. "Today?"

"Yeah, well," responds Tillman, uncomfortably, "when you never showed up, I didn't have anything else to do." I realize that for him dinner means lunch. He was expecting me hours ago.

"That'll work out just perfect," I say, deeply touched.

He walks into his barn and returns with a heavy harness. With its crossed chains and thick leather, it looks like something that might have pulled a Civil War caisson. "This harness," he says, "is my granddaddy's. Be careful you don't take it off and lay it in a pile. You'll have a hell of a time untangling it."

As he crouches beneath Belle's neck to buckle the ancient hames, Belle nudges him with her head, and he butts her back with his.

With Belle harnessed, Tillman gives me the lines and says to walk her down to the sled. Once again, I find myself behind her, gripping the reins, just like on that eventful day she arrived. Belle turns in on me, but I tug on the right rein and hold my ground. "Whoa," I say, with a quiet authority that surprises even me. She obeys, straightening, and waits for my next command.

Tillman hitches the trace chains to the sled.

"Get on and ride it," he says.

"Come up," I say, and she walks. I hop on, and as the runners scrape the ground, a smile breaks out on my face.

When I was younger, I fancied myself a skateboarder. Though at my peak I could grind an axle on the broomstick coping of our neighborhood plywood halfpipe, I was never all that good, which was fine. What mattered was the feeling I got from skateboarding, a solo pursuit that was more about soulful cruising and carving turns than competition. All I needed was my board, some pavement, and a hill. To a twelve-year-old, it felt like flying.

Now, crouching for balance as a horse pulls me across the gravel barn-yard, I am swept back to my board-riding days. I may be traveling only slightly faster than a brisk walk, but I'm in the flow. The cold wind nips at my cheeks. I tug on the left rein and cut a tight turn—no fear of wheel scraping or wagon tipping—and return to Tillman feeling triumphant.

∞

I call my new sport slurfing—part sledding, part surfing. Turf slurfing. Back in our pasture, wearing gloves and a wool cap, I stand on the sled and slice through the dead, brittle grass. I snap the reins against Belle's flank—"Trot, Belle!"—carving a turn across the face of a hill. I tug on the left rein and Belle turns tighter, sending me skidding off in the other direction like a wakeboarder, adjusting my weight as the sled tips onto one rail. "Whoa," I say and skid to a stop.

Turf slurfing helps me finally connect with Belle. Instead of feeling apprehensive, now when I heave the harness over my shoulder, feel its weight, and hear the jangle of chains, I pick up my step in anticipation. It's just plain fun. And I don't have to worry about crazy drivers, busted wagon wheels, or loud passing trains. Belle perks up, too, even though she still grumbles when I push her uphill. So she's fat, huh? Just wait.

I'm reluctant to slurf Swoope's roads, so it's not like my new rig offers improved transportation. But it does come in handy around the farm. Lately, a few days have warmed up enough for me to work outside, and I have been using the sled like a pickup truck. Farmers 100 years ago would have used a similar contraption called a stone boat. I haul off the piles of debris junking up the barnyard—chunks of cinderblock wall left by the well driller and posts heaped up by the fencing contractor. Belle looks better than ever.

When Tillman drops by to ask for some of the old lumber and tin I've got stacked behind the barn (he needs it for another shed, no doubt), I seize the opportunity to show Belle off. She and I may not be ready to compete in the county fair's horse pull, but I'm proud of how hard she has worked. And it's all thanks to Clyde Tillman's neighborliness.

He's out of sorts this afternoon—no clacking dentures signaling sprightly spirits. The ongoing dry weather has him agitated. "I'll tell you the problem," he grumbles. "Too many goddamn people working on Sundays."

I'm about to ask what he means—what's the connection to the drought?—when he adds, "I'll tell you what else they gotta stop doing. They gotta quit going to the moon. If we was meant to go to the moon, they'd be a road up there."

"How is that affecting the weather?" I ask.

"Taking them big rockets up through the atmosphere. They ain't no need for that. It used to be if you saw a dark cloud over that mountain," he says, pointing, "you'd get wet if you didn't head straight for Mr. Trimble's old shed up there. Now the clouds just won't cut loose. And these big jet airplanes you see streaking across the sky. They're fucking with the clouds, too. It ain't right."

I'm not sure how to respond, so I say, "Come take a look at Belle." She's standing beside the milking room door, soaking up the sun. "She's looking pretty fit, eh?"

"Huh?" Tillman grunts.

"Belle. She's looking pretty trim, right? I've been working her with that sled you gave me. I've got her on a diet."

He slaps her side. "Boy," he says, "that ain't *nothin'* but fat."

I don't let Tillman's criticism discourage me. Belle and I keep slurfing. We start exploring the fields behind our property, searching for boulders for a retaining wall I'd like to build. One day after dropping off some stones, I'm riding the empty sled back for another load. I cut a turn too quickly. The sled digs into a rut and tips up on one edge. My feet slip, and I fall, crashing into the thick boards, the reins flying from my hands. "Whoa!" I yell, grunting from the pain. Belle stops before the sled can run me over. I ease myself up, shaken. Belle is stamping with fright. "Easy, girl," I say, reaching for the reins and rubbing my shoulder.

It's not my first close call during the project. I've suffered small mishaps: barking my shin on a wheelbarrow full of wood, cracking the bridge of my nose with a wooden clamp, working my hands and feet to bloody blisters. And I still have an angry red wound where I nearly sliced off my finger sharpening a drawknife. The winter cold is letting up and—so far, at least—none of us has gotten food poisoning or frost-bite. Thankfully, I have not been kicked by Belle or tossed from the wagon. Though the sled's safer than the wagon, I'll have to keep my guard up. We're no closer to medical care than when we began.

CHAPTER ELEVEN

Breeding Season

*S*pring is coming. I sense it in the warm currents riffling my collar, in the rising sun's slight shift north of east along Jeanne's hill, in the way the first buds reach from the tips of the maple tree like bathers toeing the water. Robins swoop from the woods in twos and threes to poke warily among the pasture grass. Even the flies clinging to the sunny side of the barn stir my soul, though I know soon enough their incessant buzzing will drive me crazy.

I survey our supplies. A good six dozen jars of our tomatoes, beans, corn, and pickles remain on the cellar shelves. The few potatoes left in the bin have sprouted long, glowing, alien-looking appendages, but we still have a couple of pumpkins and some winter squash, only just now beginning to bruise, as well as most of the beans and peas we dried. We're okay on our dry goods—rice, oatmeal, coffee, tea, sugar. It would have been nice to have some cabbages (by now, I'm over my squeamishness), but our attempt at cabbage storage failed. Old timers sometimes buried cabbages in the earth between layers of pine straw, retrieving them as soon as they could get a shovel in the thawing ground. Instead, we tried another method we read about—cellaring. We pulled a dozen plants up by the roots and strung them upside down from the basement rafters, where they draped like headless chickens. But I guess our cellar didn't stay cool enough, because after a few weeks, the cabbages were a stinking, oozing mess.

Eyeballing the firewood pile, I'm not quite as confident. Even though it has been a relatively mild winter, we've burned cords and cords of wood cooking and heating the house. If we run out, I'm not quite sure what we'll do. Scavenge the neighboring woods for dead limbs, maybe. Despite our concern over our fuel source and our constant worries about having enough rain, we feel good. For the first time since we started, it looks like we're going to make it.

Our confidence suffers a setback one morning when Heather returns from the outhouse ashen-faced and braces herself against the kitchen door jamb.

"What's wrong?" I ask, Melville's *Typee* opened on my lap, a half-eaten bowl of oatmeal on the table beside me.

"It happened again," she said.

"What did?"

"The pain. It was so bad I almost fainted."

It's not a new pain. This is the third time since January. We've been trying to ignore it, but I'm not sure we can anymore.

"Well," I say, "you could ride to the clinic."

"Seven miles?" she asks. "On one of *those* bikes?"

Besides, it's a country clinic with one general practitioner. If they *could* fit her in, he'd only send her to a specialist, one of the realities of the modern-day medical system. Heather bites the nail of her index finger.

I pause. "Bill and Peggy could take you to a doctor."

"I know," she says, looking away uncomfortably. She's probably been dreading this discussion for weeks.

"Let's see what happens," I say. Our friends Kirk and Michael from New York are coming in two weeks. They could take her when they arrive. The pain could be nothing. Something related to going off the pill last spring. She said so herself. Or it could be an ovarian cyst or endometriosis. We just don't know. That's the hard part—no answers. Nothing is certain. Neither of us has mentioned the C word. It seems silly and paranoid to bring it up, but it's on my mind, and hers, too, probably. Seven years ago, doctors removed a malignant tumor the size of a walnut from her mother's ovary. Still, we can't assume the worst right off the bat. It's probably nothing.

For a while, the pain goes away, and other things occupy our minds. For the first time since fall, for instance, Heather, Luther, and I find ourselves back in the garden on a warm day. I'm so used to bundling myself against the cold that I feel almost naked in my T-shirt and overalls. We're planting peas, and I'm determined to get it right this time, given our embarrassing failure last spring.

Dramatically clearing my throat, I make a public vow: "We will eat peas before this project ends!" Looking up from her hoeing, Heather nods her head.

Thanks to a long, dry winter, the garden plot is a dusty expanse littered with straw and weeds. I pull brittle cornstalks and head-high ragweed, beating the topsoil from the roots. I unearth six missed carrots, the final holdouts from last summer's bounty, but they're too shriveled to eat. It's hard to believe that half a year ago, this barren soil was a jungle of green. You could enter with an empty basket and walk out again five minutes later with it brimming like a cornucopia. It's a miracle. And indeed, as recently as the mid-nineteenth century, many a learned man believed that plants sprang from earth spontaneously, the act of some divine force, since seeds can lie dormant for years beneath the soil, producing plants without appearing to be sown. But when you stop to think about it, the reality of the seed is no less incredible: all the potential of fully matured plants—volume, shape, color, nourishment—contained in a tiny speck of matter.

Scratching at the dirt with a hoe, finding life-giving moisture below, stirs hope and awe. I pause, wanting the sensation to fix itself in my being. I want my bones to remember.

"Funny," says Heather, one row over, watering newly planted pea seeds. "I did this so many times last summer that now my body just takes over. It's like dance. They say the mind forgets but the body doesn't."

It feels good to be planting again together. So much potential.

In defiance of the drought, spring is beginning to explode all around. Creatures big and small have been flirting and coupling and having

201

babies. I am surprised to find that most prominent among them are literally *the birds and the bees*—the birds chasing, shrieking, wing-beating to pick a mate, and the bees buzzing the lilac spray like singles beneath a disco ball.

Something must be stirring in Heather, too. She gives me a sideways glance and says, seductively, "You know what tonight is, don't you? Bath night."

Back in New York, as we debated what sacrifices we'd be willing to make to recreate 1900 life, Heather made one thing absolutely clear: "I'm not giving birth in 1900." A century ago, childbirth was a leading cause of death for women, one factor contributing to a life expectancy of just forty-eight years for white women and thirty-three years for black women. In 1900, 90 percent of births took place at home, and the maternal mortality rate was a shocking 1,000 women per 100,000 births.

Heather is living proof of a century of medical progress. During Luther's birth, after seven hours of agonizing pushing, she was wheeled into a bright, sterile operating room. I stroked her hair and whispered to her as a team of strangers in blue masks worked behind a screen that went up at her waist. The emergency C-section saved her life.

Though we both want a second child, we decided we'd simply have to wait until after our project was over. Heather gave up birth control pills for the sake of our experiment, but instead of jeopardizing our project with an unplanned pregnancy—or our marriage with a year of abstinence—we brought along condoms, which would have been available in 1900, only made out of sheep gut or thick, reusable vulcanized rubber.

Last week, we put away the condoms to join the birds and the bees. We're trying to have another baby, which is another reason Heather's pain worries us. Could it affect her fertility?

CRED

For a couple days now, Star has been complaining non-stop, bleating like she is about to die. I see no signs of mastitis, but a bloody, stringy fluid oozes beneath her tail, and she runs along the fence, shaking her backside and rubbing it against the posts. Clearly she is in agony. Could it be some kind of vaginal infection? Is it life-threatening? If we could summon a vet, would we bend our rules to administer antibiotics, which weren't available until the 1930s? After nearly letting Mudflap die in that tree, I am not going to fail Star. No dying. Not on my watch.

The next morning, I return from milking. With Star's cries echoing in my ears, I plunk down my pails and turn to Heather, who is feeding Luther toast. "We've got to do something about Star," I say.

"Why don't you see what Carla suggests?" Heather says, referring to Carla Emery, author of the *Encyclopedia of Country Living*.

I page through the book's goat section. My eyes light up. "Hey! Listen to this," I say, and then read aloud from page 710: "You can tell when a nanny is in heat because she bleats all day long, runs up and down the fence looking longingly out, and wiggles her tail provocatively and constantly. She is spotting blood if you look closely, and the labia of the vagina are swelled up and red."

"Star's not dying," Heather says. "She's looking for love!"

Calving season has just begun for our cattle-farming neighbors. For Jeanne and Jean, this is the busiest time of year. They spend their days driving the fenceline with binoculars, counting newborns, and watching pregnant cows for signs of trouble. One day Heather, Luther, and I walk over the hill to Jeanne's with a basket of pumpkin bread and eggs. Jeanne has just delivered an oversized calf. She is exhausted, her jeans caked with dust and blood, her long black hair matted to her face. The cow and its calf are in a separate pen beside the house. But as the calf struggles to get up, the mother ignores it, even kicks at it.

"What's wrong with it?" Luther asks.

"What's wrong with it is that the mama is a bitch," Jeanne says, and then catches herself. Her tone softens. "She doesn't know what to do with the poor thing, bless his heart."

Jeanne says that earlier Michael Godfrey called her for help removing the afterbirth from a cow. This is only his second or third year raising heifers (cows that have not yet calved), his first breeding them, and he's sticking to a strict organic regimen.

"The cow needs to be cleaned," Jeanne told him over the phone. "Then she'll need penicillin."

"Penicillin's not in my program," Michael replied.

"Where's the dead cow in your program?" Jeanne shot back.

At Wheatlands, after the deed had been done, she tossed the foul, bloody lump on the ground. "Look at it!" she said. "It's almost rotten." Jeanne is not afraid to speak her mind. She'll do anything for you, but she's not going to cut Michael any slack for being charming or wealthy.

The calving season makes her tense, she admits. And despite what one might assume from her sometimes gruff demeanor, Jeanne cares deeply about her animals. Just yesterday, she walked up to our house. Dressed in dirty Carhartt overalls, she asked me to keep an eye on the brush pile she was burning across the road. "I found a dead calf. Just a little guy," she said, wearily, holding her hands apart to show me how big. "We don't know whose it was or what happened. If I seem a little out of sorts, that's why."

⁂

The first snake of the season catches me completely off guard, the way snakes will do, insinuating themselves neatly into their surroundings. I nearly step on it while chasing a hen that Luther let loose. Suddenly, there it is, stretched out on the barnyard gravel. I'm surprised but otherwise not afraid. It's a black snake, and I've learned to live with black snakes. They help control the mice, which attack our food supply. Someone even said black snakes fend off rattlers and copperheads. So I turn and walk away. Black snakes, I now know, are our allies.

I can't say the same for the Boy Scouts.

Though the camp has mostly been quiet during the off-season, periodic weekend events descend like low-pressure systems to roil the tranquility of Swoope. Once, during a University of Virginia student retreat at the camp, car after car sped past the house (each one loudly bottoming out on the bridge). One car crashed in a ditch a few hundred yards up the road. We could see it through the window. The driver was fine. We kept waiting for him to ask to use our phone.

On a Sunday following one of these weekend events, as the cars are leaving camp, we are standing in the front yard when we see Jeanne, her black hair pulled into a ponytail, riding up on her horse. Her Australian shepherd, Dexter, races around her, barking, sniffing for mice. Speeding toward her from the opposite direction is a maroon van trailed by a rooster tail of dust. Separating them is a blind curve with a steep embankment. She can't see the van, and the driver can't see her.

I motion for the driver to slow down. Then Heather and I start yelling, "Slow down!" At the curve, he hits the brakes and skids. His tail end swings around toward Jeanne and her animals. A few feet from impact, the van stops. The dust keeps coming, bathing us all in a choking film. Lips clamped tight, eyes glaring, Jeanne wheels her horse around.

"Sir!" she says. His window is down, but he ignores her. The tires spin, and he's off, blowing through the stop sign.

"Can you believe that asshole?" she says. "Another one almost hit me over by the Tillmans' house."

Not long after, Luther and I are in the front yard when a car parks along the road. A man gets out, adjusts his wire-rimmed glasses, and approaches. It's the regional Scout director who dropped by months ago, the one who wants our nine acres so he can turn the land into a conference facility, parking lots, and "mom-friendly" campsites. He thrusts out his hand—it appears to lead him forward—and booms, "Eugene Gibson."

"Yes, I remember. How are you?" I say warily, self-conscious of my dirty cutoff jeans, dirty T-shirt, and stubbly face.

"How's your . . . endeavor?" he asks, looking around.

"We're fine. How are things at the camp?"

"Good," he blusters. "Busy! We've got a little construction project going."

"We've seen the trucks," I say. Luckily, it's only a dining hall remodeling project and not the major expansion. That's still on hold.

"I'm here to ask you a favor," Gibson adds. He proceeds to explain how the camp is hosting a statewide jamboree in a couple weeks—600 Scouting enthusiasts of all ages converging in our backyard! Because the crowd includes some cardio cases and asthmatics, he wants permission to land a life-flight helicopter on our back field. "Only in case of emergency," he promises. My first thought is: *What? Help these people who shuttle to and from camp with no regard for this community, treating Swoope like nothing more than a big speed bump?* But even though the image of SUV-choked roads and retirees in khaki shorts and neckerchiefs makes my gut sink, I can't think of a valid reason to say no. It just wouldn't be right.

"Sure," I tell him. "Feel free to use the property—in case of emergency. Let's hope you won't need to."

"Thank you for your support," Gibson says, sticking out his hand. He sounds like a politician who has repeated his line so many times it has lost all meaning, and yet he also manages to make it sound like I should be thanking him for allowing me to help with his worthy cause. My permission is not support, but simple neighborliness, I want to say. But I don't. Let him figure it out for himself.

⊂₃₂⊃

Spring cleaning the house is one thing. This year, I get the itch to clean the barn and barnyard. I move nine months' worth of manure shovel by shovel from the barnyard to a garden pile, so that it will compost. I used to think nature's fertilizer was free, until I had to work to make it useable. Once the barnyard is clean, I spend a week forking up many years' worth of spilled hay from the hayloft floor, pushing it out the second-story hayloft door and into the barnyard below.

When the pile is ten-feet high and nearly touching the hayloft floor, I yell down to Heather and Luther, who are in the garden, "Wanna watch me jump?"

"Are you sure that's safe, Logan?"

"Yeah. It'll be great," I say, imagining a soft, springy landing. When will I ever get the chance to leap into a pile of hay again?

The landing is soft enough, but instead of bouncing, I sink into a cloud of hay dust so thick that for a minute I fear suffocation. I have to fight my way out for a breath, spitting, coughing, sputtering hay and dust. The itching starts almost immediately. I strip down to my underwear, rubbing and scratching my whole body. Heather, by now, is rolling on the ground with noiseless laughter.

"Do it again!" screams Luther.

Still wheezing, I pick hay out of my socks for an hour.

ଔୠ

It's the middle of the night, and Heather is moaning with pain. She lights a lantern and sits up.

"Your stomach?"

"Yes," she whimpers. "It hurts *so* much."

"I'm sorry, honey," I say, feeling helpless.

She squats to pee into the chamber pot. Back in bed, she blows out the light, groaning occasionally as we both try to fall asleep.

The next morning, sun streaming through the windows, she lies in bed, blinking thoughtfully. "I need to see somebody."

It's clear from Heather's tone that she means to settle this issue once and for all. She's in pain. We're both scared. And we're both worried about breaking one of our most sacred project rules, the one that says we can't get in a car and drive.

As exhaustively as we tried to map out our 1900 year before it began, we never really planned for a major health crisis. All along, we've been winging it. Lately, there have been times, I'm ashamed to admit, when I've questioned the seriousness of Heather's situation. Our year's almost over. Can't she just wait until then to see a doctor? But then I think, *What has gotten into me?* As important as our project is to us, Heather's health is still what matters most.

We've proven we can thrive using 1900 technology. And we've grown so much—as individuals and as a couple. We've also proven that no matter how hard you try, you can't perfectly recreate the past. Modern life is stamped into our being. Even if we put up a wall to keep out cars and plastic and out-of-season fruit, twenty-first-century technology would still be there for us, like a safety net.

We've done a good job sticking by our rules, but at some point it becomes foolish. I think we've just reached that point.

At breakfast, with clarity and determination, Heather says, "Here's what I'll do: I'll call and ask the nurse at the practice for the name of an OB/GYN and then call for an appointment."

"Okay," I say. "When?"

"Today. I'll try to get an appointment for next week. If Kirk and Michael can't take me, I'll ask Deb."

When we decided to leave the phone line active, we had Luther and some dire emergency in mind. Now Heather needs to make a doctor's appointment. She could walk to Bill and Peggy's house to use the phone, or she could simply plug in our phone. She makes the call from our house.

"Well?" I say, when she's done.

"I've got an appointment Monday at 10 A.M. She asked if I'm pregnant. I told her I'm not sure, which she thought was odd. I told her when my last period was, and she said, 'Well, then, you're twelve weeks pregnant.'"

Maybe Heather *is* pregnant. Could that explain the pain? She begins searching for signs—swelling breasts, heartburn, stomach ache. She's just not sure, though her belly does show a noticeable bulge.

"I bet that's it," I say, trying to be positive. "You're pregnant. That's what we've been hoping for."

❧

Kirk Walsh and her husband, Michael Dolan, drive down from Manhattan in a borrowed Saab convertible looking like they've materialized from the future—hipster clothes, colorful drawstring sneakers, sunglasses that are mere slivers. I feel a tinge of jealousy, less over their stylishness—I've never been a fashion plate—than how crisp and clean their clothes are.

After we all exchange hugs, Kirk leans over to greet Luther, who is clinging to my leg in a rare moment of shyness. "*Does Luther like a pie?*" she says, remembering the line that had us in stitches during their last visit, a year ago, when they helped us turn the garden before our launch. Neither of them can get over how much our little farm boy has grown.

Kirk was my first roommate in New York. Raised in the wealthy Detroit suburbs, she answered for most of her life to Sheila, a name that fit the preppy schoolgirl in the stories she told me. By the time I moved in with her more than a decade ago, she had begun a transformation from social butterfly to sincere friend, struggling dyslexic to confident writer. She even gave herself a new name: Kirk, the maiden name of her charming, imperious paternal grandmother, whose long, full life spanned the entire twentieth century.

While Kirk and Michael carry their luggage to the guest room, Heather pulls me aside and says, "When should we tell them our news — our *possible* news?"

"Any time," I say, remembering the excitement when we finally told friends and family that Heather was pregnant with Luther.

The topic comes up when Heather and Kirk take a walk. Kirk is surprised — and concerned about the trip to the doctor — and will be happy to drive Heather.

In the meantime, we try to forget about the appointment and have fun with our friends. We hike the woods behind our property, pausing on the ridge-encircled meadow we call Echo Hill to scream out "COWPIE!" and "LU-THER!" and listen as the words bounce back to us. We go slurfing. We stuff ourselves on Heather's cooking — squash casserole, green beans, Swiss chard, rice peas, homemade bread and cheese, a cherry pie made from the cherries the Wilsons gave us last summer — the food even more special knowing Kirk and Michael helped plant some of it.

We pair up and write shadow-puppet plays. That night after dinner, we perform the plays for Luther using construction-paper cutouts glued to tongue-depressors and an oil lamp that casts shadows against a broad white wall. Michael, an actor, and I present the tale of a boy named Luther, swept away by a twister. In search of the Wizard of the Outback ("Goodaye, mate"), who he hopes can lead him home, Luther meets up with a fearful chicken, conniving pig, and brainless goat on the yellow brick road. In Heather and Kirk's play, Mudflap the cat, raised on *foie gras* Tender Vittles in an upscale New Jersey suburb, reluctantly joins Pick the cat in a search for Pick's sun-loving playboy brother, Banjo, after he goes missing. ("Do I have to?" purrs Mudflap, who'd rather have a paw-dicure than brave the scary forest.) Luther munches popcorn and squeals with glee, repeating his favorite lines. Who needs television?

All this time, sitting in the driveway is Kirk and Michael's borrowed convertible — a dual-edged artifact from the future. We've seen plenty of cars these past ten months, but since they were off-limits, we easily ignored them. The Saab, however, represents both Heather's salvation and a serious breach in our commitment to give up post-1900 technology. Every time I pass, I eye it warily.

Before bed, Heather bustles around, preparing for the morning's trip. She gathers up her purse, checkbook, and insurance information and lays them on the floor beside the door. In the morning, nervous energy drives her. She straightens the rooms and double-checks Luther's cloth-diaper supply.

As Kirk waits by the car, Heather and I stand on the screen porch.

"I'm scared," she says. "I feel like someone might see me, like I'm hiding a secret." We kiss and look into each other's eyes. Before her pooling tears can spill, she busies herself by wiping the mud off her black clogs with a rag. Her jeans are clean, and she's wearing a white shirt she's been saving for a special occasion. Some special occasion.

"Don't worry," I say. "I'm glad you're going. We'll at least know."

"Yeah," she says. "Maybe it will be good news." She turns to leave. Halfway out the screen door, she turns back. "Logan, don't worry if I'm not back in a couple of hours. If I'm pregnant, they might have to send me to the hospital for a sonogram." I hear hope in her voice.

To anyone else, this would be a routine afternoon. Schedule a doctor's appointment, jump in the car. For us, it's traumatic.

CR80

When the Saab pulls into the driveway three hours later, I'm outside before Kirk cuts the engine.

"Well?" I say, greeting Heather at the passenger-side door.

She wears a dour expression. "They couldn't tell me."

"What?" I ask. "Couldn't you do a pee-on-a-stick test?"

"Just give me some space."

"I'm going inside," I huff.

"Logan, don't do that."

Later, when our emotions have simmered down, we talk. "The pregnancy test was inconclusive," Heather says. "They think my urine may have been watery. I went to the hospital and they took blood. They'll know for sure at 4:00 P.M. I have to call them."

She walks with Kirk and Michael while Luther naps, and I read and doze on the front lawn. At 4:25, Heather calls. I'm waiting in the hall when I hear crying. The test was negative.

After a long, tearful hug, Heather says, "I'm going back at 3:30 next Wednesday afternoon to find out what is in there."

⋘⋙

After four days, Kirk and Michael leave for New York. Watching their car cross the Middle River bridge, I think how it's beginning to feel strange every time someone drives away and leaves us. It's like we're stuck in purgatory—a purgatory of our own creation—but allowed visitors.

"Where are Kirk and Michael?" Luther says, when he wakes up from his nap.

"They had to leave," I say, feeling sad for him. "Remember earlier, when we said goodbye?" With a child's ability to forget, he's soon digging into his galvanized bucket of wooden blocks, a big smile on his face.

With Heather and me, it's not so easy. "How are you doing?" I ask, hugging her.

"Not so good. How about you?"

"Me neither."

CHAPTER TWELVE

Back to the Future

B y now, spring is in full bloom. The flank of North Mountain is greening up. The birds wing overhead and flit between branches, so numerous and vocal that it feels like they're the ones watching us, as if we—stuck here on this hillside—were living in the human equivalent of an aviary, a homo*sapiary* you might call it. The deer have been traipsing down from the hills to nibble the leaves and tender limbs of our fruit trees. We fend them off with raw eggs, not by pelting the deer but by shaking the eggs up in a quart of water and dousing the branches. The wild asparagus is back, shooting up among the thistles along the fenceline. Every few days we walk the roads and pick a dozen or so spears for steaming, relishing their foraged freshness.

While the new season is firmly in place, Heather and I find ourselves in transition. Stirring within us is a mixture of excitement and trepidation over the end of our project one month from now. In many ways, staring into an unknown future, with its endless possibilities, is more frightening than facing a year of living without modern conveniences. A year ago, we were intensely focused on 1900. Now, it's hard to keep our minds from wandering back into our own century and the uncertainty of the years to come.

Heather's unresolved abdomen pain is one distraction. It's also a source of tension between us. One morning after breakfast, I start to put away the placemats, and Heather barks at me to stop. "They don't go there," she says. "I take them outside and shake them out first."

"I already shook them out."

"Where are the crumbs?"

"On the floor."

She huffs and shakes her head. "Then they get all ground into the floor."

"I'm going to sweep," I say. "What's bugging you?"

Instead of answering, Heather disappears into the washroom to scrub the dishes. I hear clanging pots, glass near the shattering point. A little later, she pokes her head back in the door. "I think we should try to start the car."

"Why?"

"We've already compromised our rules for me to go to the doctor. Taking our car wouldn't really be any different."

"No!" I say, shaking my head. "We're not even supposed to have the car. Besides, it's not going anywhere. The engine's a mess. The mice chewed through the wires, remember?"

"What am I supposed to do then?" Heather asks. "Deb can't take me. She and Walt are hauling cattle to West Virginia."

"Let's wait and see. Something will work out."

This whole car thing feels like a slippery slope, and I'm trying my best to stay firmly planted in 1900. But how meaningful is the no-car rule when we've already broken it?

In the end something does work out. Deb and Walt postpone their West Virginia trip. On the afternoon of Heather's appointment, Deb zooms up the driveway in her gray Volvo. Before she climbs into the seat, Heather, her hair wet from a kitchen bath, says, "I'm leaving the phone connected, in case I need to reach you."

I pause, thinking as much about why she might have to call as plugging in the phone. "Okay," I say.

Later, when I'm searching for pen and ink, the sight of the silent phone, its cord coiled on the pine floor, startles me. Knowing it might ring makes me jumpy. Changing Luther's diaper, I hear a car and quickly look out the window.

"What is it?" he says, sensing my anxiety.

"Nothing."

Later, Luther blasts some high notes from his harmonica, and I bolt for the phone. I'm a wreck.

Heather returns around dinnertime. The air is cool. I hug my chest to keep warm. Fighting my instinct to pounce, I hang back, waiting for details.

"Everything's okay," she says. "As far as they know." She thanks Deb and says goodbye, and we walk inside.

"Mommy!" Luther shouts and runs to her for a hug.

"Hi, sweetie," she says, and I can tell from her easy smile that a burden has been lifted. "Did you and Daddy have fun this afternoon?"

She puts him down and hugs me. Her shoulders are soft, and she's in no hurry to let me go. "The doctor thinks it's a cyst," she explains. A common, harmless cyst that will probably disappear on its own. That's the good news. The bad news is that the pain caused by the cyst coincides with her monthly ovulation. "So we have to try to conceive when it hurts the most."

⋘⋙

As if our fortunes and the forces of nature are intertwined—and who's to say they're not—shortly after Heather gets the doctor's good news, the rain returns. Which is a good news/bad news proposition as well. The bad news is that the dry, hard dirt channels water straight into the privy hole. Up rise the contents—toilet paper, a broken beer bottle, shit—to the top of the hole. Whereas before the view through the wooden seat was mercifully black, now the contents are plainly visible, like a port-o-potty that the honey wagon forgot to empty. It rains for three days and two nights. In the middle of the torrent, I slog out and trench the uphill side of the outhouse, diverting the runoff around it. When the storms blow over, the low-lying pasture is flooded, and the river is bloated and muddy. The rushing water sounds like cars on a freeway.

215

But the good news is that the rain raises the water level in the well and quenches the thirsty sprigs in our garden. When the river subsides, Luther and I launch his toy raft, using long sticks to dislodge it from log-jams and tree roots.

The rain stops in time for Luther's third birthday. We invite every small child we know—about six—and hold a Farm Fun Day, with hay-bale benches and a chicken race, during which each child urges a be-ribboned chicken toward a finish line. Luther may be the only American child in the past century to request fruitcake for his birthday. Figuring parents don't want their preschoolers gobbling down a 40-proof confection, Heather makes an iced lemon cake instead.

It's hard to believe how much Luther has changed since his days as a daycare kid in Brooklyn. Dressed in his little overalls and a plaid button-up shirt, his brown hair in a Beatles mop, Luther collects chicken eggs, learning to count as he places them one by one in the wire basket. He climbs the fences and calls for Belle, and when she comes, he leaps down and hides behind my legs. I marvel at how he absorbs the natural world around him. Already he can identify the calls of half a dozen birds, including the *pretty-pretty-pretty* of the cardinal and the screech owl's trill.

One day, we walk up Boy Scout Lane picking wild asparagus. It's warm and peaceful. "Shhh," I say. "Listen." It's a cricket calling from the grassy ditch. And then, reaching over to snap a green sprig from a branch, I say, "Know what kind of tree this is?" I hold it under his nose. "It's a cedar tree."

He sniffs and says, "Then where are the seeds?"

Up ahead, we spy a pair of bluebirds on a fencepost. The male puffs up, the female flicks her tail into the air, and the male mounts. He lingers for an instant and then flutters left and right a few inches above her, repeating this ritual several times. For some reason Luther can't stop giggling. "What are they doing?" he asks.

"They're mating."

"They are marketing?" he asks.

"Mating," I say, chuckling.

As we walk, he keeps giggling and saying, "Those bluebirds were marketing."

I once said I wanted him to know what a cow looked like—a real cow, not a cow in a picture book—and to recognize the sounds of real animals, not the electronic moos, oinks, and chirps of microchips in children's toys. The other day, he was doing his business in the outhouse. "Is this what poopy looks like?" he asked, making a fist.

"Well, yeah, sort of," I said.

He held two fists side by side and said, "This is horse poopy."

"Yes, it is," I said, following his logic.

"And this is cow poopy." He laid his hand flat on the wooden outhouse bench.

"Yes!"

CR80

On Mother's Day, Heather says she's feeling "sort of blah."

"Depressed?"

"More like dirty, greasy, and hairy."

"You don't seem greasy to me," I say, hugging her. "And I like your hair long."

"Even when it's on my legs?"

"Hey, you're beautiful, leg hair and all."

"I'm just ready for a hot shower," she says.

I'm ready for a hot shower, too—and ice cream and listening to music—but I'm also nervous about what's to come. Last summer, I assumed we'd be bursting with joy here in the home stretch. Instead, we're anxious about yet another major change. Reverse culture shock. I've experienced it twice, after living in Kenya and Ecuador. It's harder to return to what you've always known, because the newness wears off more quickly. And then you're left facing the future.

More than treats, I've been missing small things, like Scotch tape and Tupperware. I'm wearing holes in everything—clothes, coat, work gloves. The stitching on my boots disintegrated. I replaced it with wire, which was kind of cool—I sparked at night crossing the gravel barnyard with my milking pails—until the wire loops wore through and what was left got filed into points. The points scratched the floors and punctured my foot. I had to pull them with pliers and start over.

Heather misses the bathroom scale, her razor, contact lenses, shampoo and hair conditioner, body lotion, Lycra stretchy pants for exercising, vitamins, protein bars. I miss my double-bladed razor, dental floss, trash bags, bossa nova CDs, Graham Greene novels. We both miss the kitchen sink and those carefree days when water poured from a tap and ran by force of gravity down a drain. I also miss traveling. Lately, I've booked passage on the memory train, returning to the dappled courtyard of our honeymoon house in Cartagena, Colombia; to the beach in Mexico, where we drank beer after breakfast and spent all day watching the surfers; to the road trip we took along South Africa's dramatic coast.

Even Luther's feeling pent-up. One day he holds a wooden block to the side of his head and says, "Hello?" and then carries on an imaginary conversation with one of his grandparents. Another time, he wakes from a nap and whines, "I want to *goooo* somewhere."

"I know how you feel, honey," Heather says, remembering that in his brief existence Luther has already flown to Paris, Ecuador, California, and Maine. "Where would you like to go?"

"Bill and Peggy's."

⁣⊶⊷⁣

It's an old narrative rule of thumb: If a gun will fire in Act 3, show it hanging over the mantel in Act 1. (Being a wise-ass, I gently rebelled against a college writing teacher who preached this Chekhovian principle by beginning a story with a swordfish over the mantel; you can imagine the murder by impalement that happened by the end.) Earlier in this story, I referred to a rusty shotgun in kraft paper hidden on a high shelf. That same gun now lies in two pieces on the workbench in the shed, amid draw knives and wood shavings and tobacco tins filled with brads.

Last fall, when Michael Godfrey discovered the rodent infestation in the Taurus, I began setting snap traps on the floorboard and engine block. Every week or so, I check the traps, tossing any dead mice I find into the tall grass. Last week, I tugged at the hood-release latch to inspect the engine traps. But when I lifted the hood, something big, brown, and furry popped up beside the battery. It bared its teeth, hissed, and then dove back into the engine. "YAAAA!" I screamed, slamming the hood and high-stepping away from the car. "What the HELL was that?"

I grabbed a stick and walked back to the car, warily eyeing the under-carriage for signs of movement. I popped the hood latch. Easing the hood open, I raised my stick to defend myself against slashing claws and gnashing, feral teeth. All was quiet. And there it lay, buried amid the hoses—furry back, strange gray foot with long toes. Possum? Too big. Raccoon? Whatever it was, it had to go.

I jabbed the animal with my stick, and the creature burrowed deeper into the engine. Nothing ran out from beneath the car, so I gave up and walked back to the house, puzzling over this latest critter problem. Though I was trying to stay focused on the here-and-now, with only a few weeks until we returned to the twenty-first century, I couldn't help but worry about how we would get around.

Convinced the animal was a raccoon, I borrowed a trap from Bill Roberson, hoping to catch it and release it as far into the woods as pos-sible. Corn season is over. Let it go pester someone else.

But it's not a raccoon, it's a groundhog. And now it waits, frightened and bloody, in Bill's wire trap, while I stand in the shed, eyeing the gun.

My head swirls with conflict as I revisit the debate Heather and I had months ago after a groundhog hole turned up in our front yard. I want to set the groundhog free, but I don't want it to return to the car engine. I don't want to shoot it, but I don't want it to endanger a neighbor or their cattle by digging a new hole somewhere else. Turf-slurfing with Belle recently, I found a groundhog hole in the middle of our pasture. If she breaks a leg, we might have to shoot *her*. David Fleig's words—*you've got to learn when to kill*—echo in my head. I wonder if a 1900 farmer would shrink from life's messier responsibilities the way I am. Then again, is taking out a groundhog really my responsibility?

The farmers around here would say yes. As we have well learned, killing groundhogs is as natural to them as trapping the mice that scurry around the larder gnawing cheese. Just a few days ago, while Heather and I were in the front yard, Jeanne roared up on her all-terrain vehicle, Dexter racing alongside. She jumped off and tossed a mink carcass on the ground.

Mud caked the mink's fur, and blood stained its sharp teeth. Its left eyeball hung by a mucousy thread. But Jeanne was pumped, because

Dex, the same big puppy who six months ago nipped playfully at Luther's penis, giving us a fright (and later a good laugh), had killed it. "Good boy, Dex," Jeanne said as he shook the dead mink like a rag doll. "If Dex had been older, I'd have called him off. But because he's got to learn to kill groundhogs, I can't let him be afraid."

She continued: "I was talking to mom on the phone yesterday, and a groundhog lumbered across the yard. Dex went after it, and it climbed a tree!"

"What did you do?" Heather asked.

"I threw a broom at it," Jeanne said, demonstrating how she held the phone to her ear with her shoulder, keeping up the conversation while trying to javelin the groundhog. "That didn't work, so I got off the phone, grabbed my shotgun, and blasted it out of the tree. Dex chased it down and killed it." Pause. "Then I burned it."

In the shed, I pick up the gun parts and slide the barrel into the stock, fiddling for five minutes trying to connect them. As a boy, after bird-hunting trips, it was second nature to break down, swab out, and reassemble this very same 16-gauge pump. In those days, I enjoyed an uncomplicated relationship with guns. We owned more than half a dozen, including shotguns, pistols, and a .22 rifle purchased after I came home from summer camp proudly bearing a stack of bullet-riddled paper targets and a Pro-Marksman patch. Handling guns seemed perfectly normal.

In the years since, I have mostly forgotten about hunting and guns. I was never passionate about either and eventually lost interest in killing for sport. I all but officially renounced hunting, which is fine if you're living in the city. Moving to the country and adopting 1900 farming practices has complicated matters. During our preparation period, I was torn: Stick by my no-hunting ethic or strive for authenticity by arming myself and bagging dinner every so often? On a trip to my parents' house, practicality won out. I would not hunt, but I'd pack my old pump gun and a single box of shells—just in case.

Opening that box now, my fingers tremble. I'm out of practice. I haven't heard the blast or felt the kick of a shotgun in years. I slip two shells into the magazine and pump one in the chamber. I leave the shed and march past the barn to the pasture.

When I reach the trap, I stare for a few minutes at the bristly beast. It's big, with sharper claws and teeth than I had imagined. I carry the trap thirty yards into the pasture. When I lift the gate, the animal bolts down a hill toward the fence before I can raise my gun. I fire from the hip, hitting nothing, the thundering crack and smell of powder sweeping me back twenty years. Then I run, pumping another shell into the chamber and pointing the barrel in the groundhog's direction, nearly blasting the fence point blank. *Slow down*, I think. *You're about to do something stupid.* Short legs pumping, the groundhog scurries under the fence and down the leafy hill. I poke the barrel through the wire, aim, and fire. The animal rolls. It lies there, jerking. Standing now and leaning over the fence, I pump the last shell into the chamber and peer down the barrel at the helpless creature. *Gotta make this one count.* BOOM! Direct hit. I stick around long enough to make sure the groundhog is dead, and then walk back to the shed. My adrenaline rush is gone. Halfway there, Belle stares at me, ears pricked, nostrils blown.

I dismantle the gun, hide the parts in the shed, and walk to the house. Heather has laid out dinner on the picnic table. Luther's got a cloth napkin tucked in his collar. "Hi, Luther," I say, forcing a cheerful voice. "What are you doing?"

"Eating," he says, fist stuffed with cornbread.

My face must betray my emotions, because Heather flashes me a sympathetic smile.

"Well," I say, shoulder throbbing, blasts ringing my ears, "that's done." Inside, though, I'm lacking any sense of finality. Killing is a brutal business, no matter how justified. I can't shake the images—the trapped groundhog's bloody claws and terror-stricken eyes, its panicked scrabbling to flee the minute I raised the door, the body's final convulsions rustling the leaves. Part of my sadness, I'll admit, is the realization that my boyhood self, the one who could blast a duck from the sky with excitement and pride but no guilt, is long gone. *You've got to know when to kill*, I think. But that doesn't mean it will be easy.

As dinner proceeds, however, my spirits lift. Watching Luther, with those innocent blue eyes and his unadulterated passion for anything buttery and baked, how could they not?

One day Heather says to me, "Why don't we switch places for a day?"

"What do you mean?"

"We've got our routines down, but I'm bored. I'll do your chores, and you do mine. It'll be good for us. Shake things up."

I'm finally comfortable with my routine and, frankly, I'm feeling too lazy to break from it. "I don't feel like it," I say.

"Come on!" she says. "What? Are you chicken? Scared of a little laundry?"

"No. It's just that we're almost finished."

"That doesn't matter."

I eventually give in. "So when do you want to do this?" I ask. "Next week?"

"*Nooo*," she groans. "Let's do it tomorrow!"

Once I'm on board, the advantages leap out at me—sleeping late, no goats, a day's rest from all that backbreaking physical work. But the next morning, I try to sleep in and can't. Not knowing what comes next makes me feel out of sorts and cranky. I dress Luther and make the beds, empty the chamber pot, and drop Luther's dirty diaper in the soaking bucket, while Heather stokes the cook fire, brews coffee—and reads a book!

Breakfast is my responsibility. Oatmeal. No sooner have I collected the dirty bowls than it's time to cook lunch and dinner.

Meanwhile, Heather takes Luther on the mid-morning chore rounds of pumping water and watering and feeding the animals. When she returns, she huffs, "What do you do about those goats?"

"About them doing what?" I say, stifling a grin.

"They were all over us! I had to put Luther on my shoulders. They wouldn't leave us alone at the pump, no matter what I said—shoo, get, go away.'" She sighs, exasperated. "How do you get anything done with those pests?"

"I guess they know not to mess with me."

"Luther, what does Daddy do to keep the goats away?" Heather asks.

"He throws a bucket at them."

Soon I start to get frustrated. After sweating over the meal preparation and picking and washing lettuce, I start on the laundry. Heather has mercifully included only socks on her list. I toss the socks in the wash tub, add soap, and carefully pour boiling water over the pile. A purple bloom spreads through the clear water. "Oh, no!" I scream. I nearly scald my fingers trying to pluck out the dark socks.

"What, Daddy?" Luther yells down from the garden.

Heather says, "What happened?"

"The socks are bleeding."

"You didn't put dark socks in with the white ones?"

"Yeah," I say, continuing to fish around, which is difficult, since the water is now the dark gray of a thunderhead. *What a dumb-ass*, I think. Have I already forgotten the most basic of all laundry rules?

Starting over, I pile all the colored socks in the left-side tub and all the whites (now grayish) in the right side. More soap. Once again, I pour boiling water over the dark pile. "Ahhh!" I yell, as the color seeps out of them. I've also forgotten the second-most basic of laundry rules: cool water for dark colors.

Normally, I'm not much of a cook, but today it has all come together: a fresh salad and Swiss-chard-stuffed enchiladas made with hand-rolled tortillas, goat's-milk feta, and a tomato-cumin sauce.

"I have so much more energy being outside," chirps Heather as we sit for lunch on the screen porch.

"We'll see about that at the end of the day," I grumble, picturing manure shoveling, hay forking, water pumping, and wood splitting.

At the end of the day, Heather *is* exhausted, but so am I, in a restless way that feels less than satisfying. I'm thankful when she doesn't insist we switch chores another day. That night, with Luther tucked in bed, we sip bourbon on the side porch, reading to one another. Then, because Heather thinks she's ovulating, we head upstairs for one chore we absolutely must do together.

Two weeks later, when Heather's period comes, we are crushed. We have not been trying long, but since we're already feeling behind schedule after postponing our second child for the 1900 Project, every delay stabs at us. Is the cause of her abdominal pain also making her infertile? Conceiving Luther was so easy. Now we find ourselves in unknown territory, feeling hamstrung not being able to type "infertility" or "ovarian cyst" into a Web browser.

CR80

My thirty-sixth birthday is a daylong procession of treats from Heather—pancake breakfast, a lemon cake with buttercream icing—along with champagne from Ishtar. Luther makes me a card, orange scribbles on white paper. In her card, Heather has tucked a list: Thirty-Six Things You Learned to Do This Year. I am deeply touched and already feeling nostalgic as I read entries like "drive a wagon," "make a shaving horse," "run 'coons out of the corn patch," and "tell hay from straw." She gives me a pencil sketch of the barn, and I mentally add "make a pencil sketch" to the list of things Heather has learned.

I also get a day off.

I decide to go for a walk—a just-for-fun walk, which is a rare pleasure for either of us. I set out after breakfast the next day, carrying a bandana, my wide-brimmed hat, a pen knife, and a coil of wire in case my boot soles separate. I'm exhilarated to be traveling, if only by foot, and to be literally walking away from my chore routine, but I also sense a nagging vulnerability leaving the family. Heather, Luther, and I have been side-by-side for so long that even being out of earshot for the day seems strange.

But soon, I'm caught up in the beauty and peacefulness of the Swoope countryside. Though I've been to the post office and to vote, to the Salatin farm, to Ishtar's, I haven't struck out in this direction—toward town—in almost a year. Everything looks new to me, the sprouting corn, the stubbly hay fields dotted with fresh bales, the old brick-and-frame farmhouses. At the top of Swoope hill, the smell of honeysuckle battles the stench of manure. I take in the broad sweep of mountains, spotting the V-shaped Buffalo Gap. Except for the occasional faraway tractor etching a dusty path and a radio tower rising in the distance, I could be walking through a 1900 landscape. A rumbling interrupts my daydream, and I turn to see a truck barreling down on me. Springing into a ditch, I narrowly miss being flattened by a shoulder-hugging Farm Bureau chemical tanker.

"Son of a bitch!" I yell, turning and glaring after the truck. I'm carrying no wallet, no ID. Two feet closer, and they would have been scooping up dental samples.

Around the next bend, a pair of orange highway department trucks roar past, blowing my hat off. Now I know how squirrels feel.

The next vehicle to approach is a beat-up pickup. It creeps up beside me and stops. The white-haired, leathery-skinned driver, straw hat cocked on his head, leans out his window and says, "You just walkin', or you want a ride?"

"Just walking, thanks."

I'm headed to the home of a friend—John Foster. I met John shortly after we turned back the clock, but since he lives on the other side of Swoope, I have never visited him. He stops by our place occasionally. Last time he was by, I told him to expect me.

Soon, I've left the main road for a gravel tributary, traffic no longer an issue. I pass a ramshackle farmhouse that I recognize from John's directions. It's the home of his elderly neighbor Kathleen, a farmer's widow who, I was surprised to learn, still lives without running water. Several times a week, John hauls milk jugs of water in his pickup truck and takes her warm, foil-covered plates of food.

I turn into a driveway beside a towering white oak, ascend a hill, and find John, dressed in faded jeans and a black T-shirt, sitting on the porch of his log cabin. Sunglasses perch atop his spiky black hair. He is hand-polishing an old iron tool.

"How was it?" he says.

"Dangerous. I was almost roadkill."

"Some birthday present *that* would have been."

I had heard from others about John's spread (he's not the type to boast). Now, sitting on his porch, sipping ice water (the ice a simple birthday treat), I take it all in—the expansive views of North Mountain, the house's hand-dressed limestone foundation, the ancient chestnut logs, rescued from the brambles before the earth could reclaim them.

John, in his late forties, built this place with his own two hands. Twenty years ago, while running a plant nursery in the booming suburbs of Northern Virginia, he bought these eleven acres and a caved-in log cabin on the property. Camping here on weekends, he painstakingly rebuilt the cabin. After retiring early and moving here full-time with his wife Sarah, John built another story-and-a-half cabin using salvaged logs and connected the two with an wood-and-glass hyphen. One hundred yards north, at the edge of a walnut wood, he added a small log guest cabin with a fireplace and sleeping loft. Across a meadow in the opposite direction, you can just make out a log barn. John has spent more than two decades creating this place. It's his *magnum opus*, and he's not about to rush it. The proportions are perfect. Everything has its rightful place. Unless you knew the truth, you might think his compound has been here for 200 years.

If Clyde Tillman inherited his rural skills and values as a matter of course, John—a suburban Washington D.C. Baby Boomer (he saw the Rolling Stones at RFK stadium for six bucks in 1972)—willfully chose this life. As a young man, not long after hitchhiking cross-country with $195 in his pocket, John started coming to the Valley to visit his grandfather, who managed a cattle farm. He would fight the Friday Interstate exodus and drive three hours to sit and listen to stories about the old ways. History is John's religion. He finds truth and beauty—possibly even transcendence—in a hand-turned chair or a forged strap hinge. He can read the materials and markings of old buildings like Egyptologists read hieroglyphics. Once, he identified the chunk of stone I was using for a henhouse step as a millstone fragment from the grist mill that used to stand in our front yard. "Sometimes," he says, as we follow a meadow path to his log barn, "I think I was born a couple centuries too late."

After the tour, we head back to the porch for a sandwich with Sarah and the Fosters' two-year-old daughter, Katie. Hanging out with John dredges up a question that has long puzzled me: Why should we care about the past? Strange as it sounds, I've never been a history buff. In fact, when I got to college, I vowed not to take a single history class if I could help it. The past had already happened. It was dead. Loading up on studio art and English and philosophy courses, I would have succeeded, too, had it not been for a university policy requiring me to take one American history course, my only history class during my entire four years. I got a D. Since then, my take on history has softened, of course, or I wouldn't be here today, attempting to walk in the shoes of a 1900 dirt farmer. But I still struggle with the past in other ways.

I rattle the ice in my glass and turn to John. "Why bother about the past?"

He is silent for a minute. "When you think about it, the past is all we have. It's where we've been," he says. "And we sure as hell don't know where we're going."

"Then it's a guide for how to live?" I ask.

"I don't think the past should dictate the future, but it's a good foundation. Passing down culture from generation to generation is one of the things that separates man from other creatures. Personally, I want that link to the past. We find ourselves through the long trail of those who've come before us."

Those who don't care about the past are disoriented, he says, showing no regard for the land, for humanity, for themselves. John's words bring into focus my own realization—that the skills Heather and I have learned, the hardships and joys we've experienced, the people we have met during this year in forgotten America, have awakened me to the power of the past. I think of Clyde Tillman and his intuitive grasp of draft horses, Michael Godfrey and his shaving horse, Bill Roberson and his heirloom tomatoes, Liz Cross and her homesteading ways, and David Fleig, whose quest for meaning blends old wisdom and entrepreneurism. I think about the magic of fruitcake and the relentless march of progress. The past may be easy to forget, but it is not dead. It lives in us all. The point is not to return to another time but to enrich the experience of our own time. By respecting the past, we can live a more meaningful present—and future. All my doubts about why we left New York? The fear that I was fleeing adult responsibility, putting my family at risk because I could not cope with reality? Those worries were unfounded. This project isn't about escape. It's about exploring those inalienable realities facing humanity since the dawn of time—food, water, nature, community. It's about finding our place in the continuum of history.

The sun is marching west—time for me to leave. In *Typee*, Melville writes with youthful flourish that "a rightabout retrograde movement . . . appears indescribably repulsive" to anyone with a love of adventure. I can't stand backtracking either, so rather than return on the main road and risk getting pancaked, I strike out for unknown territory, even if it does add five miles to what was already a ten-mile round-trip walk. Before I go, John tells me about a pre–Civil War mill along the route, one of the few not torched by Union troops. "Take a good look at that mill," he says. "It's one of the most beautiful things you'll see."

CR80

Even though our project is not driven by nostalgia, we find ourselves growing nostalgic for our 1900 experience even before it comes to an end. Heather sees a daylily and is reminded of our first day, when Jeanne delivered a handful of the orange flowers on horseback. One day, after we put Luther down for his nap and finish our chores, we tiptoe up to the guest room and sneak under the covers. Afterward, we are silent, and I sense an unspoken understanding between us that soon this, too, will change. I'll get busy again with work, the phone will ring, we'll spend too much time in the car driving to and from town.

And then there's the nagging reality of how we'll support ourselves. Simmering on the back burner all this time was our idea of starting an artisanal goat-cheese farm. Talking to David Fleig last summer about his ex-con dairy only fueled our inspiration. We have the land and the barn. With some training—perhaps a few sabbaticals to France—we could build on Heather's already considerable cheese-making skills. It would be perfect: We'd use what we learned in 1900 to build a new life once we returned to the twenty-first century.

But there are two problems.

They come to light one evening at dinner, when I offer Heather the last slice of an olive-oil-drizzled *chevre* that I have pretty much devoured.

"You can *have* the cheese," she says, an odd smile on her face.

"What's that supposed to mean?" I say.

"I can't eat it."

"You can't *eat* it? It's delicious."

"I can't *stand* it anymore. I stopped eating goat cheese a couple months ago. I stopped drinking the milk, too."

I'm dumbfounded. "I never noticed."

"I kept making it for your sake," she confesses. "I didn't want you to find out. I thought you'd be disappointed."

"About our farm idea?"

228

"Yeah."

I burst out laughing.

"What's so funny?" she says.

"I've got a confession, too," I say. "You don't like the cheese. I can't *stand* the goats!"

CR80

A few days before our 1900 project is to end, I tromp past the barn and beyond the leaning shed to the car, keys jangling in my pocket, and peer through the windows at the shredded paper and turds, shaking my head. When I open the door, I hear a loud buzzing and see a paper nest, undulating with wasps, attached to the car's frame near the door hinges. Two wasps spiral up from the nest to sniff me out. I leave the door open and move away carefully. I open another door and find another nest glued in the corner. Other two doors, same thing.

Jack Cross, husband of Liz, comes by that day to give us some extra cabbage seedlings. "Wasps?" he says loudly, when I mention our problem. "You know the old-fashioned way of getting wasps out of a nest, don't you? Hang a fish over a bucket of water. They'll suck so much liquid out of the fish that they can't fly. They drop in the bucket and drown."

"Sounds like a good idea, but we don't have a fish," I say.

Instead, I return that night with a tin of gasoline. By moonlight, I carefully knock each small nest into the can and cap it until the wasps are dead.

The next day, Heather and I bang on the sides and drum the seats to scare off any other critters. I peek under the hood and am relieved to find no groundhogs. I reattach the battery terminals and hope against hope that the car will turn over. No chance. It's completely dead.

We're both quiet for a while.

"I've got it," I say, brightening. "Belle can pull it!"

"What?"

"All she has to do is pull the car to the barnyard. It's downhill from there. We can roll it to the driveway and work on it—clean out the mouse shit, splice wires, call a tow truck if we have to. But we've got to

229

get it out of this field."

How perfect. One live horse towing a dead 150-horsepower car.

When we return that afternoon, the air is hot and still. Flies swarm Belle as I walk her up past the shed. The car faces downhill. Belle will have to pull it backward up the hill to reach a point where we can let gravity do the rest. Heather straps Luther in the back seat of the Taurus and climbs into the driver's seat.

"It stinks in here," Heather says. "I can't get the windows down." They're automatic and won't work without the battery. So much for modern conveniences.

"Just twenty-five feet straight back," I say. "That's all we need." Hitching Belle's trace chains to the two hooks below the rear bumper, I realize how huge a jump this is from turf slurfing, like leapfrogging from Little League straight to the Majors. I whisper to Belle, "You're pulling two tons, girl. Make Mr. Tillman proud."

"Ready!" Heather says.

"Come up!" Belle churns her legs and then jerks to a stop, startled by the immovable object.

"Come UP!" Again she pulls and stops.

"Come up, Belle!" The Taurus rocks slightly. "Ya!" I say, popping her with the line. She works, ears pricked, her big, beefy body swaying left and right, looking pinned by the harness. But the car won't budge.

"Whoa, Belle."

I lay the lines across her back and stoop to take a closer look at the wheels. Each one rests in its own earthen wheel well, formed during the rains but now hard again. She'll never pull the car uphill *and* out of these wells.

I unhitch Belle and walk her around to the front as Heather and Luther get out of the stifling car for a breather. Grass and thistles choke the gap beneath the front bumper. I kick at the mass of vegetation with my foot, and then kneel to poke my nose under the car, looking for something to hitch to. As I reach blindly into the hollow space behind the front bumper, envisioning a family of rattlers nesting there—the abundance of mice *would* lure them—I pray my good snake karma will serve me well.

It does, though I don't find a tow hook. For lack of anything better, I

230

hang the J-shaped hooks over the bumper's lip. With Heather and Luther back in position, once again I address Belle. "Come up."

This time, thanks to the downhill tilt of the pasture, the car leaps out of its resting place and rolls, carried by gravity now, only in the wrong direction. Five feet. Ten feet. Feeling the slack, Belle stops. The car keeps rolling.

"Whoa," I scream. "Whoa! WHOA!"

Finally Heather brakes.

I glare at her through the windshield.

"What?" she says.

"You stopped this far from her legs," I yell, thrusting my thumb and forefinger at her, an inch of space between the two.

"We were *going*, Logan. You were the one who told her *whoa*."

"No, I didn't. I was telling you *whoa*." At that moment, Belle lifts her tail and drops a steaming, pea-green pile of shit right in the middle of the hood.

As soon as we stop laughing, we try again, but the chain falls off the bumper. The same thing happens over and over, each time Belle swatting me with her tail as I bend to make the connection. "Stop it, Belle!" When she knocks my hat off, I say, "Enough! Let's try the rear tow hooks again."

But the hill is too steep to climb. Instead of twenty-five feet straight back, we'll have to travel down-pasture, make a U-turn, and loop back up to a more gently sloped shoulder, a total of at least 150 feet. And we have to do it all backward, with Heather steering through the rearview mirror and holding the door open so she can hear me.

"Ready?" I say. "Come up!"

By now, Belle is completely confused. We've been at this for nearly an hour, and she hasn't pulled more than a few feet. I've been working her for a few months on the sled, asking her to run with me around the pasture as I play out my skateboarding fantasies. She's in good shape, regardless of what Tillman says, and she likes to run.

Now, she's fed up with jerking this big silver bubble. At least that's how it appears, because this time, when I urge her forward by snapping the rein, she leaps into action. Using the slope to her advantage, Belle starts running, two legs at a time, like a big black jackrabbit. Heather squeals. Luther screams. Still holding the reins, I sprint alongside to keep up. The car whomps over the uneven ground. My hat flies off. Up ahead, I see a ditch. "Whoa!" I scream, pulling hard on the lines. And then, "Brake! BRAKE!"

Belle stops. The car stops. Heather spills out, doubled-up with laughter. I'm laughing, too. Luther is screaming with glee. "You were hauling ass!" I say to Heather. "Again! Again!" screams Luther.

Again it is, though not at the same out-of-control pace. Tugging hard on the lines, I make Belle walk. She struggles up the hill—*don't stop now*—and then she's on top, and we're cheering and celebrating and patting Belle. Good girl!

⊂℥⊃

What do we do on our last day? Sleep late, take the day off, celebrate? No. We milk, pump, cook, clean, whack weeds, shovel manure, and mulch the garden paths.

We also prepare for re-entry. John Foster drops by and helps me remove the animal nests from the Taurus and splice the chewed wires. We pull enough straw out of the engine to stuff a mattress. He takes the battery and brings it back fully charged. Even though we're not going anywhere—until tomorrow—I can't resist sitting in the driver's seat and giving the key a try. She sputters and starts up. I let the engine run for a while, and then I shut it off and pocket the key.

At the end of the afternoon, Heather throws her arms up in a gesture of triumph. "Wooohoo!" she yells, "I did everything on my to-do list today. I think that's a first."

That evening at dinner, in addition to rice and beans, we fulfill my vow to eat fresh English peas before the project's end. We only share a few forkfuls between us, a meager harvest, I know. But at least we've done it! We planted, cultivated, and picked these peas—the first yield in this year's long growing season—so that they may now nurture us. If I take away anything from our 1900 experience, it is a newfound appreciation for the miracle of the seed. Heather and I have proven that a rubber-band-bound clump of seed-filled envelopes can feed a family of three for a year. And also that an idea—no matter how quixotic—when tucked into the fertile folds of imagination can grow into a complex and miraculous thing.

Later, both of us are on hand to kiss Luther goodnight. We smile down at him and hint at the excitement that awaits us the next morning. Though he doesn't understand the significance, to us this night feels magical, like Christmas Eve.

"I had the craziest dream last night," Heather says, as we brush our teeth out back, beneath the maple tree. "I dreamed it was our last day. I decided to plug in the phone early. What's a day? I thought. I'll just make sure it works. But then it rang, and I panicked."

"Did you answer it?" I ask.

"Yeah. The voice on the other end said, 'Gotcha!'"

We climb into bed, dreaming of all we'll do. Basking in our accomplishment, feeling secure at having found a home, we're not worried right now about the future. We have money in the bank for renovations, though less than we had hoped. More important, we have each other. The future will fall into place.

Heather turns to me. "See you in a hundred years," she says, and blows out the lamp.

Epilogue

I have great faith in a seed. Convince me that you have
a seed there, and I am prepared to expect wonders.
—HENRY DAVID THOREAU

Two weeks after returning to our own century, we throw a party and
invite all the neighbors who helped us get through our 1900 year. Fifty
people show up.

We have hauled hay-bale benches from the barn and iced-down bottles of beer and soda in our laundry tubs. With a bluegrass CD playing
in the background and the sun sinking over North Mountain, we all
mingle in the front yard eating barbecue sandwiches and coleslaw.

I break free from a conversation to collect my thoughts. I want to say
a few words of thanks to all who have come. But I'm distracted by
Luther, all smiles, leaping off hay bales with a friend. How much does he
understand about what we've done? Is he happier now? On our way to
town our first morning back in the modern world, he had screamed with
delight, "Daddy, the fence posts are moving!" We took him to a coffee
house for bagels and later for fries and ice-cream cups at Wright's Dairy-
Rite, a fifty-year-old drive-in that we joked was our mid-twentieth-cen-
tury transition. At one point Luther asked what the thick red sauce was
that I squeezed onto my fries. I self-consciously explained that it was
called *ketchup*, drawing stares from the family in the next booth. I could
almost hear the whispers: *What kind of freak kid has never seen ketchup?*

I mount the front porch and tap my beer bottle with my wedding ring
to get everyone's attention. I'm wearing a crisp, clean shirt, and my face
is baby-smooth for the first time in a year, thanks to the MACH3 I pulled
out of the drawer.

"Thank you all for coming," I begin nervously, my lip wavering, as if
at any minute I might choke up. "We ordered take-out because we wanted to serve food that Heather didn't have to cook on our woodstove.
After three meals a day for a year, she deserves a break."

235

The laughter and the familiar, smiling faces—the Godfreys, Jeanne and Jean, the Wilsons, three generations of Salatins—put me at ease. I see the Crosses. I see Peggy and Bill—Bill, whose cancer is in remission, looking healthier than ever. The only people missing are Clyde Tillman—I'm really sorry he didn't come—and Ishtar, our guardian angel, who's traveling with her daughter Leasha. But then, maybe a guardian angel is never really that far away.

"When we moved here," I continue, "we were pretty sure we could learn how to feed ourselves, heat our house with wood, and scrub our clothes with a washboard. But there was one aspect of life in 1900 we weren't sure we could recreate, and that was community spirit."

I talk about how in 1900, before the invention of social security, 401(k)s, and Medicare, family and friends were the social safety net. I explain how when we moved to Swoope from New York City, we had no idea if neighborliness was still alive and well in rural America. Hell, we didn't even know if people would speak to us. For that reason, we came prepared to live a year in isolation. Luckily, we didn't have to.

"We could not have failed this year," I say. "Our neighbors—all of you—would never have let us. Thank you for making us part of this community."

Afterward, paper plate in hand, Peggy says, "Because of you all, I know neighbors I haven't met in the twenty-five years we've been here." Liz Cross, with characteristic abruptness, echoes the thought: "I gotta thank you people. You connected us to the community."

C3❧80

Later, after everyone has gone, and we're cleaning up, Heather wraps an arm around my waist. "I liked what you said at the party."

"I thought I was going to get emotional up there."

"No one would have cared."

"I know," I say, turning to Heather, hugging her deeply.

She puts her lips to my ear. "I never want to forget what we learned here," she whispers. "I mean about us."

"Never," I say.

And how can we, with a living reminder of our love for one another due to arrive this winter? A few days after the bagels and drive-in french fries, when Heather had finished washing a couple of Hefty bags full of grimy clothes at the laundromat, she stopped at a pharmacy to buy a home-pregnancy kit. The test was positive. By our reckoning, our baby may be the first child ever conceived in 1900 and born a century later.

Great-Grandma McEndree's Black Fruitcake

This recipe comes from Genie Elder of Maryland, who milks a Jersey cow and makes her own butter—even in the twenty-first century! Her dear friend Ishtar Abell passed it on to us, sparking a fruitcake revival in our household. I altered it slightly to suit our needs. Enjoy!

Heather

10 eggs
1 pound butter
1 pound flour
1 pound sugar
2 pounds washed, seeded raisins (can't really buy these anymore)
1 pound seedless raisins
2 pounds currants
1 pound citron
2 teaspoon cinnamon
1 teaspoon nutmeg
½ teaspoon mace
½ teaspoon cloves
1 tumbler currant or grape jelly
1 small glass of brandy, rum, or whiskey

The recipe contains 6 pounds total of currants, raisins, and citron, for which I substituted:

1 pound currants
1 pound dried apricots, chopped
1 pound dried cherries
1 pound raisins
2 pounds nuts (pecans, walnuts, or both)

I added the following:

3–4 tablespoons lemon juice
3 tablespoons vanilla
9-ounce jar blackberry jelly instead of currant or grape

Mix with hands, line pans with brown paper (I used wax paper), and cover loosely with a piece of paper through most of cooking (this is to prevent top from browning). Cook at 250° F for a long time, about 2–3 hours or until top looks crackly. One batch makes 6 medium loaves.

To cure the cakes, I soaked cheesecloth in brandy, wrapped it around each loaf, and stored the loaves in a critter-proof container for about one month. This can be done for up to twelve months. Check every month or so to see if the liquor has dried up, and if it has, re-soak the cheesecloth (the liquor is the preservative).

Acknowledgments

You don't go back in time without a lot of help.

First, the people we met in Swoope: Not only did they welcome us, but they pitched in, giving us tomato plants, loaning us wash basins and walnut crackers, and teaching us how to bake bread, mend leather, and build a shaving horse. The list goes on and on. For these things, as well as for their friendship, Heather and I are grateful to Peggy and Bill Roberson and their children Sarah and William, Ishtar Abell and Leasha Fulton, Victoria and Michael Godfrey, Sarah and John Foster and their daughter Katie, Frances and Bill Shuey, Anne and John Sills, Jeanne and Jean Hoffman, Mary Alice and Carl Cox, the whole Salatin clan (Theresa, Joel, Rachel, Daniel, and grandmother Lucille), Edie and Joel Wilson and their children Tina and Tommy, Crystal and Wesley Truxell, Deb McConnell and Walt Hylton, Liz and Jack Cross, Carla and Frank Perrenot, Chris Miller and family, and Shani and Bill Willett and their daughter Addison. No matter what twists and turns our lives take, a part of our hearts will always remain in Swoope.

A broader community in the Shenandoah Valley befriended us as well. For their visits, our deep gratitude goes out to the following people and their children (whose names I include in parentheses): Kathy and Will Moore (Anna and Katharine), Mia and Jimmy Kivlighan (Isa, Hannah, and Jimmy), Joelle and Peter Aaslestad (Juliette and Claire), Billie Jean Banks, Kim and Fred Powell (Josh), and Kyle Johnson. Thanks to Salatin apprentices Chris Gowen and David Fleig, and to Genie Elder for her great-grandmother's fruitcake recipe. Long live fruitcake!

We are grateful to all those friends who traveled from afar to brave the outhouse: Meryl Schwartz and David Weinraub (and Elias and Lily), SanSan Kwan and Kenny Speirs and the inimitable Joan Speirs, Laura and Tony Davis (Michael), Katherine Pew and Troy Hollar, Sally and Walker McKay, Sara Lyon and her friend Bobby, Beatrice and George King (George, Charlie, and William), Bobby Houck, Suzanne Hoffman (Emmet), Margaret Wrinkle, Megan Golden and Peter Neiman (Eliza and Anna), Donna Avedisian and Craig Chanti, and Andrea and Bill Geissler (Mary Karlin and Rachel).

Heather and I are both blessed to have understanding and supportive families. A heartfelt thanks goes out to my parents, Nini and John, for all they have done for me, and to my brother, Bill, who sacrificed a thumbnail so that the hens might have a roof over their heads, and his adventurous wife, Michelle. Thanks to my uncle Tommy Ward and his wife Kaye for their company and home-canned goodies. Thanks to Heather's parents, Ginnie and John Higginbotham, and to Lavelle "Granny" Reid, for making the trip back in time to see us, and to Christine "Mamaw" Higginbotham, who did not visit but was with us in spirit every step of the way. And to our children, Luther, too young to say no to 1900, and Eliot, who just missed it, I am grateful for the joy they bring me every day. I hope they grow to appreciate their place in the continuum of family and history.

How can I begin to express my gratitude to friend and mentor Dean King? After giving me my start as a writer, Dean has guided me ever since, including helping to shape this book with his astute observations. For his talent as a writer, his perseverance, his goodness, and so much else, he is a beacon. Thanks also to Jessica King, Dean's wife (and the rock upon which the beacon stands!), for reading my manuscript in the late stages, and to the rest of the family—Hazel, Grace, Willa, and Nora—for the joy they brought during their surprise visits to Trimbles Mill.

I owe a debt of thanks to friend and writer Charlie Slack, who generously read and commented on my first draft, taking time not only to point out the rough patches but to help me iron them out with his excellent suggestions. I am in awe of his skills. Writer Kirk Walsh, a dear friend, gave me invaluable feedback on the manuscript. Even more important, long before the pages existed, she and her husband, Michael, rolled up their sleeves and helped us turn the soil that became our garden. For that we are grateful.

Thanks also to Alice Leonhardt and the members of the Blue Ridge Community College Writer's Group, as well as to Katherine Pew and Jerry Beilinson, who helped me fine-tune the manuscript. I am grateful to the Virginia Center for the Creative Arts, for giving me a quiet space to work, and to writer and friend Jim Campbell, who has generously shared his publishing insights, including one key piece of advice: It's a long road to the bookstore shelf; don't forget to enjoy the ride. Thanks to Eiley and John for the flowers.

I am grateful to Glenn Yeffeth, publisher of BenBella Books, and to my editor at BenBella, Leah Wilson, whose careful reading and thoughtful comments brought out the best in my writing. At BenBella, I would also like to thank editorial assistant Erica Lovett for copywriting, Jennifer Thomason for her proofreading and marketing work, and production manager Yara Abuata for shepherding the manuscript through the steps necessary to create a fine-looking book.

Jody Rein is all a writer could ever hope for in an agent. Not only is she sharp, insightful, and loyal to the bone, but she's delightful company. My deepest thanks go to her for believing in this book.

For believing in me, I thank my wife, Heather, with all my heart. I may have written this book, but we both shared equally in the 1900 experience. How lucky I am to have found a partner who is beautiful, smart, caring, *and* willing to cook with wood for a year. You can chalk it up to the Perseid meteor shower, but I'm still convinced the stars aligned that fateful night in Alabama. And once their work was done and our match was made, the heavens exploded in joyful fanfare. As long as we have each other, we'll always have fireworks.

About the Author

Logan Ward has written for many magazines, including *National Geographic Adventure*, *Men's Journal*, *Popular Mechanics*, *Southern Accents*, and *Cottage Living*. He lives with his wife, Heather, and their children, Luther and Eliot, in Virginia's Shenandoah Valley.